THE MAKING OF AN AMERICAN

THE MACMILLAN COMPANY
NEW YORK · BOSTON · CHICAGO · DALLAS
ATLANTA · SAN FRANCISCO

MACMILLAN & CO., Limited
LONDON · BOMBAY · CALCUTTA
MELBOURNE

THE MACMILLAN CO. OF CANADA, Ltd.
TORONTO

Jacob A. Riis

THE MAKING OF
AN AMERICAN
BY JACOB A. RIIS

THE MACMILLAN COMPANY
PUBLISHERS   NEW YORK   MCMXXIV

COPYRIGHT, 1901,

BY THE OUTLOOK COMPANY.

COPYRIGHT, 1901,

BY THE MACMILLAN COMPANY.

————

Set up and electrotyped November, 1901.

————

New Edition
Published October, 1924.

Norwood Press
J. S. Cushing Co. — Berwick & Smith Co.
Norwood, Mass., U.S.A.

To

LAMMET

TO THE READER

THE papers which form this autobiography were originally published in *The Outlook*, the chapter telling of my going "home to mother" in *The Churchman*, and parts of one or two others in *The Century Magazine*. To those who have been asking if they are made-up stories, let me say here that they are not. And I am mighty glad they are not. I would not have missed being in it all for anything.

J. A. R.

RICHMOND HILL, N.Y.,
    October, 1901.

CONTENTS

LIST OF ILLUSTRATIONS

INTRODUCTION BY THEODORE ROOSEVELT

It is difficult for me to write of Jacob Riis only from the public standpoint. He was one of my truest and closest friends. I have ever prized the fact that once, in speaking of me, he said, "Since I met him he has been my brother." I have not only admired and respected him beyond measure, but I have loved him dearly, and I mourn him as if he were one of my own family.

But this has little to do with what I wish to say. Jacob Riis was one of those men who by his writings contributed most to raising the standard of unselfishness, of disinterestedness, of sane and kindly good citizenship, in this country. But in addition to this he was one of the few great writers for clean and decent living and for upright conduct who was also a great doer. He never wrote sentences which he did not in good faith try to act whenever he could find the opportunity for action. He was emphatically a "doer of the word," and not either a mere hearer or a mere preacher. Moreover, he was one of those good men whose goodness was free from the least taint of priggishness or self-righteousness. He had a white soul; but he had the keenest sympathy for his brethren who stumbled and fell. He had the most flaming intensity of passion for righteousness, but he also had kindliness and a most humorously human way of looking at life and a sense of companionship with his fellows. He did not come to this country until he was almost a young man; but if I were asked to name a fellowman who came nearest to being the ideal American citizen, I should name Jacob Riis.

— From *The Outlook*, June 6, 1914.

THE MAKING OF AN AMERICAN

THE MAKING OF AN AMERICAN

CHAPTER I

THE MEETING ON THE LONG BRIDGE

Our Stork.

ON the outskirts of the ancient town of Ribe, on the Danish north seacoast, a wooden bridge spanned the Nibs River when I was a boy — a frail structure, with twin arches like the humps of a dromedary, for boats to go under. Upon it my story begins. The bridge is long since gone. The grass-grown lane that knew our romping feet leads nowhere now. But in my memory it is all as it was that day nearly forty years ago, and it is always summer there. The bees are droning among the forget-me-nots that grow along shore, and the swans arch their necks in the limpid stream. The clatter of the mill-wheel down at the dam comes up with drowsy hum; the

B   1

sweet smells of meadow and field are in the air.
On the bridge a boy and a girl have met.

He whistles a tune, boy-fashion, with worsted
jacket slung across his arm, on his way home
from the carpenter shop to his midday meal.
When she has passed he stands looking after her,
all the music gone out of him. At the other end
of the bridge she turns with the feeling that he
is looking, and, when she sees that he is, goes on
with a little toss of her pretty head. As she stands
one brief moment there with the roguish look, she
is to stand in his heart forever — a sweet girlish
figure, in jacket of gray, black-embroidered, with
schoolbooks and pretty bronzed boots —

" With tassels!" says my wife, maliciously — she
has been looking over my shoulder. Well, with
tassels! What then? Did I not worship a pair
of boots with tassels which I passed in a shop
window in Copenhagen every day for a whole
year, because they were the only other pair I ever
saw? I don't know — there may have been more;
perhaps others wore them. I know she did. Curls
she had, too — curls of yellow gold. Why do girls
not have curls these days? It is such a rare thing
to see them, that when you do you feel like walking
behind them miles and miles just to feast your eyes.
Too much bother, says my daughter. Bother?
Why, I have carried one of your mother's, miss!

The Meeting on the Long Bridge.

all these — there, I shall not say how long — and carry it still. Bother? Great Scott!

And is this going to be a love story, then? Well, I have turned it over and over, and looked at it from every angle, but if I am to tell the truth, as I promised, I don't see how it can be helped. If I am to do that, I must begin at the Long Bridge. I stepped on it that day a boy, and came off it with the fixed purpose of a man. How I stuck to it is part of the story — the best part, to my thinking; and I ought to know, seeing that our silver wedding comes this March. Silver wedding, humph! She isn't a week older than the day I married her — not a week. It was all in the way of her that I came here; though at the time I am speaking of I rather guessed than knew it was Elizabeth. She lived over there beyond the bridge. We had been children together. I suppose I had seen her a thousand times before without noticing. In school I had heard the boys trading in her for marbles and brass buttons as a partner at dances and games — generally trading off the other girls for her. She was such a pretty dancer! I was not. "Soldiers and robbers" was more to my taste. That any girl, with curls or without, should be worth a good marble, or a regimental button with a sound eye, that could be strung, was rank foolishness to me until that day on the bridge.

And now I shall have to recross it after all, to tell who and what we were, that we may start fair. I shall have to go slow, too, for back of that day everything seems very indistinct and strange. A few things stand out more clearly than the rest. The day, for instance, when I was first dragged off to school by an avenging housemaid and thrust howling into an empty hogshead by the ogre of a schoolmarm, who, when she had put the lid on, gnashed her yellow teeth at the bunghole and told me that so bad boys were dealt with in school. At recess she had me up to the pig-pen in the yard as a further warning. The pig had a slit in the ear. It was for being lazy, she explained, and showed me the shears. Boys were no better than pigs. Some were worse; then --- a jab at the air with the scissors told the rest. Poor father! He was a schoolmaster, too; how much sorrow it might have spared him had he known of this! But we were too scared to tell, I suppose. He had set his heart upon my taking up his calling, and I hated the school from the day I first saw it. Small wonder. The only study he succeeded in interesting me in was English, because Charles Dickens's paper, *All the Year Round*, came to the house with stories ever so much more alluring than the tedious grammar. He was of the old dispensation, wedded to the old ways. But the short cut I took to knowledge in that branch I think opened his eyes to some things ahead of his time. Their day had not yet come. He lived to see it dawn and was glad. I know how he felt about it. I myself have lived down the day of the hogshead in the child-life of New York. Some of the schools our women made an end of a few years ago weren't much better. To help clean them out was like getting square with the ogre that plagued my childhood.

I mind, too, my first collision with the tenement. There was just one, and it stood over against the castle hill, separated from it only by the dry moat. We called it Rag Hall, and I guess it deserved the name. Ribe was a very old town. Five hundred years ago or so it had been the seat of the fighting kings, when Denmark was a power to be reckoned with. There they were handy when trouble broke out with the German barons to the south. But the times changed, and of all its greatness there remained to Ribe only its famed cathedral, with eight centuries upon its hoary head, and its Latin School. Of the castle of the Valdemars there was left only this green hill with solemn sheep browsing upon it and ba-a-a-ing into the sunset. In the moats, where once ships sailed in from the sea, great billowy masses of reeds ever bent and swayed under the west wind that swept over the meadows. They grew much taller than our heads, and we boys loved to play in them, to track the tiger or the grizzly to its lair, not without creeping shudders at the peril that might lie in ambush at the next turn; or, hidden deep down among them, we lay and watched the white clouds go overhead and listened to the reeds whispering of the great days and deeds that were.

The castle hill was the only high ground about the town. It was said in some book of travel that

Ribe, from the Castle Hill.

one might see twenty-four miles in any direction from Ribe, lying flat on one's back; but that was drawing the long bow. Flat the landscape was, undeniably. From the top of the castle hill we could see the sun setting upon the sea, and the islands lying high in fine weather, as if floating in the air, the Nibs winding its silvery way through

the green fields. Not a tree, hardly a house, hindered the view. It was grass, all grass, for miles,
to the sand dunes and the beach. Strangers went
into ecstasy over the little woodland patch down by
the Long Bridge, and very sweet and pretty it was;
but to me, who was born there, the wide view to the
sea, the green meadows, with the lonesome flight
of the shore-birds and the curlew's call in the
night-watches, were dearer far, with all their melancholy. More than mountains in their majesty;
more, infinitely more, than the city of teeming
millions with all its wealth and might, they seem
to me to typify human freedom and the struggle
for it. Thence came the vikings that roved the
seas, serving no man as master; and through the
dark ages of feudalism no lord long bent the neck
of those stout yeomen to the yoke. Germany, forgetting honor, treaties, and history, is trying to do
it now in Slesvig, south of the Nibs, and she will as
surely fail. The day of long-delayed justice, when
dynasties by the grace of God shall have been re-
placed by government by right of the people, will
find them unconquered still.

Alas! I am afraid that thirty years in the land of
my children's birth have left me as much of a Dane
as ever. I no sooner climb the castle hill than I am
fighting tooth and nail the hereditary foes of my
people whom it was built high to bar. Yet, would

you have it otherwise? What sort of a husband is the man going to make who begins by pitching his old mother out of the door to make room for his wife? And what sort of a wife would she be te ask or to stand it?

But I was speaking of the tenement by the moat. It was a ramshackle, two-story affair with shiftless tenants and ragged children. Looking back now, I think likely it was the contrast of its desolation with the green hill and the fields I loved, of its darkness and human misery and inefficiency with the valiant fighting men of my boyish dreams, that so impressed me. I believe it because it is so now. Over against the tenement that we fight in our cities ever rises in my mind the fields, the woods, God's open sky, as accuser and witness that His temple is being so defiled, man so dwarfed in body and soul.

I know that Rag Hall displeased me very much. I presume there must have been something of an inquiring Yankee twist to my make-up, for the boys called me " Jacob the delver," mainly because of my constant bothering with the sewerage of our house, which was of the most primitive kind. An open gutter that was full of rats led under the house to the likewise open gutter of the street. That was all there was of it, and very bad it was; but it had always been so, and as, consequently, it could not

The View the Stork got of the Old Town.

be otherwise, my energies spent themselves in unending warfare with those rats, whose nests choked
the gutter. I could hardly have been over twelve
or thirteen when Rag Hall challenged my resentment. My methods in dealing with it had at least
the merit of directness, if they added nothing to the
sum of human knowledge or happiness. I had received a "mark," which was a coin like our silver
quarter, on Christmas Eve, and I hied myself to
Rag Hall at once to divide it with the poorest
family there, on the express condition that they
should tidy up things, especially those children, and
generally change their way of living. The man
took the money — I have a vague recollection of

seeing a stunned look on his face — and, I believe, brought it back to our house to see if it was all right, thereby giving me great offence.   But he did the best for himself that way, for so Rag Hall came under the notice of my mother too.   And there really was some whitewashing done, and the chil-

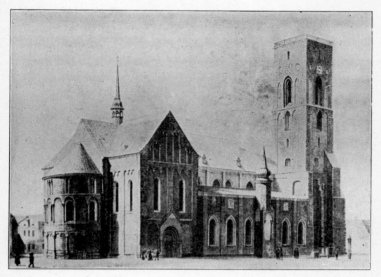

The Domkirke.

dren were cleaned up for a season.   So that the eight skilling were, if not wisely, yet well invested, after all.

No doubt Christmas had something to do with it.   Poverty and misery always seem to jar more at the time when the whole world makes merry.   We took an entire week off to keep Christmas in.   Till after New Year's Day no one thought of anything else. The "Holy Eve" was the greatest of the year. Then the Domkirke shone with a thousand wax candles that made the gloom in the deep recesses behind the granite pillars seem deeper still, and brought out the picture of the Virgin Mary and her child, long hidden under the whitewash of

Within the Domkirke.

the Reformation, and so preserved to our day by the very means taken to destroy it. The people sang the dear old hymns about the child cradled in the manger, and mother's tears fell in her hymn-book. Dear old mother! She had a house full, and little enough to manage with; but never one went hungry or unhelped from her door. I am a believer in organized, systematic charity upon the evidence of my senses; but — I am glad we have that one season in which we can forget our principles and err on the side of mercy, that little corner in the days of the dying year for sentiment and no questions asked. No need to be afraid. It is safe. Christmas charity never corrupts. Love keeps it sweet and good — the love He brought into the world at Christmas to temper the hard reason of man. Let it loose for that little spell. January comes soon enough with its long cold. Always it seems to me the longest month in the year. It is so far to another Christmas!

To say that Ribe was an old town hardly describes it to readers at this day. A town might be old and yet have kept step with time. In my day Ribe had not. It had never changed its step or its ways since whale-oil lanterns first hung in iron chains across its cobblestone-paved streets to light them at night. There they hung yet, every rusty link squeaking dolefully in the wind that never ceased blowing from the sea. Coal-oil, just come from America, was regarded as a dangerous innovation. I remember buying a bottle of " Pennsylvania oil " at the grocer's for eight skilling, as a doubtful domestic experiment. Steel pens had not crowded out the old-fashioned goose-quill, and pen-knives meant just what their name implies. Matches were yet of the future. We carried tinder-boxes to strike fire with. People shook their heads

at the telegraph. The day of the stage-coach was
not yet past. Steamboat and railroad had not come
within forty miles of the town, and only one steam
factory — a cotton mill that was owned by Elizabeth's father. At the time of the beginning of
my story, he, having
made much money
during the early years
of the American war
through foresight in
having supplied him-
self with cotton, was
building another and
larger, and I helped
to put it up. Of
progress and enter-
prise he held an ab-
solute monopoly in
Ribe, and though he
employed more than
half of its working

Mother.

force, it is not far from the truth that he was
unpopular on that account. It could not be well
otherwise in a town whose militia company yet
drilled with flint-lock muskets. Those we had in
the school for the use of the big boys — dreadful
old blunderbusses of the pre-Napoleonic era — were
of the same pattern. I remember the fright that

seized our worthy rector when the German army was approaching in the winter of 1863, and the haste they made to pack them all up in a box and send them out to be sunk in the deep, lest they fall into the hands of the enemy; and the consternation that sat upon their faces when they saw the Prussian needle-guns.

The watchmen still cried the hour at night. They do, for that matter, yet. The railroad came to town and the march of improvement struck it, after I had gone away. Century-old institutions were ruthlessly upset. The police force, which in my boyhood consisted of a man and a half — that is, one with a wooden leg — was increased and uniformed, and the night watchmen's chant was stopped. But there are limits to everything. The town that had been waked every hour of the night since the early Middle Ages to be told that it slept soundly, could not possibly take a night's rest without it. It lay awake dreading all sorts of unknown disasters. Universal insomnia threatened it; and within a month, on petition of the entire community, the council restored the songsters, and they squeak to this day. This may sound like exaggeration; but it is not. It is a faithful record of what took place and stands so upon the official minutes of the municipality.

When I was in Denmark last year, I looked over

some of those old reports, and had more than one
melancholy laugh at the account of measures taken
for the defence of Ribe at the first assault of the
Germans in 1849. That was the year I was born
Ribe, being a border town on the line of the
coveted territory, set about arming itself to resist
invasion. The citizens built barricades in the

The Deserted Quay.

streets — one of them, with wise forethought, in
front of the drug store, "in case any one were to
faint" and stand in need of Hoffman's drops or
smelling-salts. The women filled kettles with hot
water in the houses flanking an eventual advance.
"Two hundred pounds of powder" were ordered
from the next town by foot-post, and a cannon that
had stood half buried a hundred years, serving for a
hitching-post, was dug up and put into commission.

There being a scarcity of guns, the curate of the next village reported arming his host with spears and battle-axes as the next best thing. A rumor of a sudden advance of the enemy sent the mothers with babes in arms scurrying north for safety. My mother was among them. I was a month old at the time. Thirty years later I battled for the mastery in the police office in Mulberry Street with a reporter for the *Staats-Zeitung* whom I discovered to be one of those invaders, and I took it out of him in revenge. Old Cohen carried a Danish bullet in his arm to remind him of his early ill-doings. But it was not fired in defence of Ribe. That collapsed when a staff officer of the government, who had been sent out to report upon the zeal of the Ribe men, declared that the town could be defended only by damming the river and flooding the meadows, which would cost two hundred daler. The minutes of the council represent that that was held to be too great a price to pay for the privilege of being sacked, perhaps, as a captured town; and the citizen army disbanded.

If the coming of the invading army could have been timed to suit, the sea, which from old was the bulwark of the nation, might have completed the defences of Ribe without other expense to it than that of repairing damages. Two or three times a year, usually in the fall, when it blew long and

hard from the northwest, it broke in over the low
meadows and flooded the country as far as the eye
could reach. Then the high causeways were the
refuge of everything that lived in the fields; hares,
mice, foxes, and partridges huddled there, shivering
in the shower of spray that shot over the road, and
making such stand as they could against the fierce

Downstream, where Ships sailed once.

blast. If the "storm flood" came early in the season, before the cattle had been housed, there was a
worse story to tell. Then the town butcher went
upon the causeway at daybreak with the implements
of his trade to save if possible, by letting the blood,
at least the meat of drowned cattle and sheep that
were cast up by the sea. When it rose higher and
washed over the road, the mail-coach picked its way

c

warily between white posts set on both sides to guide it safe. We boys caught fish in the streets of the town, while red tiles flew from the roofs all about us, and we enjoyed ourselves hugely. It was part of the duty of the watchmen who cried the hours to give warning if the sea came in suddenly during the night. And when we heard it we shivered in our beds with gruesome delight.

The people of Ribe were of three classes: the officials, the tradesmen, and the working people. The bishop, the burgomaster, and the rector of the Latin School headed the first class, to which my father belonged as the senior master in the school. Elizabeth's father easily led the second class. For the third, it had no leaders and nothing to say at that time. On state occasions lines were quite sharply drawn between the classes, but the general kindliness of the people caused them at ordinary times to be so relaxed that the difference was hardly to be noticed. Theirs was a real neighborliness that roamed unrestrained and without prejudice until brought up with a round turn at the barrier of traditional orthodoxy. I remember well one instance of that kind. There lived in our town a single family of Jews, well-to-do tradespeople, gentle and good, and socially popular. There lived also a Gentile woman of wealth, a mother in the strictly Lutheran Israel, who fed and clothed the poor and did no end of good. She was a very pious woman. It so happened that the Jewess and the Christian were old friends. But one day they strayed upon dangerous ground. The Jewess saw it and tried to turn the conversation from the forbidden topic.

"Well, dear friend," she said, soothingly, "some day, when we meet in heaven, we shall all know better."

The barrier was reached. Her friend fairly bristled as she made reply:

"What! *Our* heaven? No, indeed! We may be good friends here, Mrs ——, but there –- really, you will have to excuse me."

Narrow streams are apt to run deep. An incident which I set down in justice to the uncompromising orthodoxy of that day, made a strong impression on me. The two concerned in it were my uncle, a generous, bright, even a brilliant man, but with no great bump of reverence, and the deacon in the village church where they lived. He was the exact opposite of my uncle: hard, unlovely, but deeply religious. The two were neighbors and quarrelled about their fence-line. For months they did not speak. On Sunday the deacon strode by on his way to church, and my uncle, who stayed home, improved the opportunity to point out of what stuff those Pharisees were made, much to

A Cobblestone-paved Alley.

his own edification. Easter week came. In Denmark it is, or was, custom to go to communion once a year, on Holy Thursday, if at no other season, and, I might add, rarely at any other. On Wednesday night, the deacon appeared, unbidden, at my uncle's door, craving an interview. If a spectre had suddenly walked in, I do not suppose he could have lost his wits more completely. He recovered them with an effort, and bidding his guest welcome, led him courteously to his office.

From that interview he came forth a changed man. Long years after I heard the full story of it from my uncle's own lips. It was simple enough. The deacon said that duty called him to the communion table on the morrow, and that he could not reconcile it with his conscience to go with hate toward his neighbor in his heart. Hence he had come to tell him that he might have the line as he claimed it. The spark struck fire. Then and there they made up and were warm friends, though agreeing in nothing, till they died. " The faith," said my uncle in telling of it, " that could work in that way upon such a nature, is not to be made light of." And he never did after that. He died a believing man.

It may be that it contributed something to the ordinarily democratic relations of the upper-class men and the tradespeople that the latter were generally well-to-do, while the officials mostly had a running fight of it with their incomes. My father's salary had to reach around to a family of fourteen, nay, fifteen, for he took his dead sister's child when a baby and brought her up with us, who

were boys all but one.   Father had charge of
the Latin form, and this, with a sense of grim
humor, caused him, I suppose, to check his children
off with the Latin numerals, as it were.   The sixth
was baptized Sextus, the ninth Nonus, though they
were not called so, and he was dissuaded from
calling the twelfth Duodecimus only by the certainty that the other boys would miscall him "Dozen."
How I escaped Tertius I don't know.   Probably
the scheme had not been thought of then.   Poor
father! Of the whole fourteen but one lived to
realize his hopes of a professional career, only to
die when he had just graduated from the medical
school.   My oldest brother went to sea; Sophus,
the doctor, was the next; and I, when it came my
time to study in earnest, refused flatly and declared
my wish to learn the carpenter's trade.   Not till
thirty years after did I know how deep the wound
was I struck my father then.   He had set his heart
upon my making a literary career, and though he
was very far from lacking sympathy with the work-
ingman — I rather think that he was the one link
between the upper and lower strata in our town in
that way, enjoying the most hearty respect of both
— yet it was a sad disappointment to him.   It was
in 1893, when I saw him for the last time, that I
found it out, by a chance remark he dropped when
sitting with my first book, " How the Other Half

Lives," in his hand, and also the sacrifice he had
made of his own literary ambitions to eke out by
hack editorial work on the local newspaper a living
for his large family.   As for me, I would have been
repaid for the labor of writing a thousand books by
witnessing the pride
he took in mine.
There was at last a
man of letters in the
family, though he
came by a road not
down on the official
map.

Father.

Crying over spilt
milk was not my
father's fashion, how-
ever. If I was to be a
carpenter, there was
a good one in town,
to whom I was forth-
with apprenticed for
a year.   During that time, incidentally, I might
make up my mind, upon the evidence of my re-
duced standing, that school was, after all, to be
preferred.   And thus it was that I came to be a
working boy helping build her proud father's factory
at the time I fell head over heels in love with sweet
Elizabeth.   Certainly I had taken no easy road to

the winning of my way and my bride; so reasoned
the town, which presently took note of my infatua-
tion. But, then, it laughed, there was time enough.
I was fifteen and she was not thirteen. There was
time enough, oh, yes! Only I did not think so.
My courtship proceeded at a tumultuous pace,
which first made the town laugh, then put it out of
patience and made some staid matrons express the
desire to box my ears soundly. It must be owned
that if courting were generally done on the plan I
adopted, there would be little peace and less safety
all around. When she came playing among the
lumber where we were working, as she naturally
would, danger dogged my steps. I carry a scar on
the shin-bone made with an adze I should have been
minding when I was looking after her. The forefinger on my left hand has a stiff joint. I cut that
off with an axe when she was dancing on a beam
close by. Though it was put on again by a clever
surgeon and kept on, I have never had the use of it
since. But what did a finger matter, or ten, when
she was only there! Once I fell off the roof when
I must crane my neck to see her go around the
corner. But I hardly took note of those things,
except to enlist her sympathy by posing as a
wounded hero with my arm in a sling at the
dancing-school which I had joined on purpose to
dance with her. I was the biggest boy there, and

therefore first to choose a partner, and I remember
even now the snickering of the school when I went
right over and took Elizabeth. She flushed angrily,
but I didn't care. That was what I was there for,
and I had her now. I didn't let her go again,
either, though the teacher delicately hinted that
we were not a good match. She was the best
dancer in the school, and I was the worst. Not a
good match, hey! That was as much as she knew
about it.

It was at the ball that closed the dancing-school
that I excited the strong desire of the matrons to
box my ears by ordering Elizabeth's father off the
floor when he tried to join in before midnight, the
time set for the elders to take charge. I was floor
committee, but how I could do such a thing passes
my understanding, except on the principle laid down
by Mr. Dooley that when a man is in love he is
looking for fight all around. I must have been, for
they had to hold me back by main strength from
running away to the army that was fighting a losing
fight with two Great Powers that winter. Though
I was far under age, I was a big boy, and might
have passed; but the hasty retreat of our brave little
band before overwhelming odds settled it. With
the echoes of the scandal caused by the ball episode
still ringing, I went off to Copenhagen to serve out
my apprenticeship there with a great builder whose

name I saw among the dead in the paper only the other day.   He was ever a good friend to me.

The third day after I reached the capital, which happened to be my birthday, I had appointed a meeting with my student brother at the art exhibition in the palace of Charlottenborg.   I found two

My Childhood's Home.

stairways running up from the main entrance, and was debating in my mind which to take, when a handsome gentleman in a blue overcoat asked, with a slight foreign accent, if he could help me.   I told him my trouble, and we went up together.

We walked slowly and carried on quite an animated conversation; that is to say, I did.   His part of it was confined mostly to questions, which I was no way loth to answer. I told him about myself and my plans; about the old school, and about my father, whom I took it for granted he knew; for was he not the oldest teacher in the school, and the wisest, as all Ribe could testify? He listened to it all with a curious little smile, and nodded in a very pleasant and sympathetic way which I liked to see. I told him so, and that I liked the people of Copenhagen well; they seemed so kind to a stranger, and he put his hand on my arm and patted it in a friendly manner that was altogether nice. So we arrived together at the door where the red lackey stood.

He bowed very deep as we entered, and I bowed back, and told my friend that there was an example of it; for I had never seen the man before. At which he laughed outright, and, pointing to a door, said I would find my brother in there, and bade me good-by. He was gone before I could shake hands with him; but just then my brother came up, and I forgot about him in my admiration of the pictures.

We were resting in one of the rooms an hour later, and I was going over the events of the day, telling all about the kind stranger, when in he came, and nodded, smiling at me.

"There he is," I cried, and nodded too. To my surprise, Sophus got up with a start and salaamed in haste.

"Good gracious!" he said, when the stranger was gone. "You don't mean to say he was your guide? Why, that was the King, boy!"

I was never so astonished in my life and expect never to be again. I had only known kings from Hans Christian Andersen's story books, where they always went in coronation robes, with long train and pages, and with gold crowns on their heads. That a king could go around in a blue overcoat, like any other man, was a real shock to me that I didn't get over for a while. But when I got to know more of King Christian, I liked him all the better for it. You couldn't help that anyhow. His people call him "the good king" with cause. He is that.

Speaking of Hans Christian Andersen, we boys loved him as a matter of course; for had he not told us all the beautiful stories that made the whole background of our lives? They do that yet with me, more than you would think. The little Christmas tree and the hare that made it weep by jumping over it because it was so small, belong to the things that come to stay with you always. I hear of people nowadays who think it is not proper to tell children fairy-stories. I am sorry for those children. I wonder what they will give them instead. Algebra, perhaps. Nice lot of counting machines we shall have running the century that is to come! But though we loved Andersen, we were not above playing our pranks

upon him when occasion offered. In those days
Copenhagen was girt about with great earthen
walls, and there were beautiful walks up there
under the old lindens. On moonlight nights when
the smell of violets was in the air, we would sometimes meet the poet there, walking alone. Then
we would string out irreverently in Indian file
and walk up, cap in hand, one after another, to salute him with a deeply respectful " Good evening,
Herr Professor!" That was his title. His kind
face would beam with delight, and our proffered
fists would be buried in the very biggest hand, it
seemed to us, that mortal ever owned, — Andersen
had very large hands and feet, — and we would go
away gleefully chuckling and withal secretly ashamed
of ourselves. He was in such evident delight at
our homage.

They used to tell a story of Andersen at the time
that made the whole town laugh in its sleeve, though
there was not a bit of malice in it. No one had
anything but the sincerest affection for the poet in
my day; his storm and stress period was then long
past. He was, it was said, greatly afraid of being
buried alive. So that it might not happen, he carefully pinned a paper to his blanket every night
before he went to sleep, on which was written: " I
guess I am only in a trance." [1] Needless to say,

[1] In Danish : " Jeg er vist skindód."

he was in no danger. When he fell into his long sleep, the whole country, for that matter the whole world, stood weeping at his bier.

Four years I dreamt away in Copenhagen while I learned my trade. The intervals when I was awake were when she came to the town on a visit with her father, or, later, to finish her education at a fashionable school. I mind the first time she came. I was at the depot, and I rode with her on the back of their coach, unknown to them. So I found out what hotel they were to stay at. I called the next day, and purposely forgot my gloves. Heaven knows where I got them from — probably borrowed them. Those were not days for gloves. Her father sent them to my address the next day with a broad hint that, having been neighborly, I needn't call again. He was getting square for the ball. But my wife says that I was never good at taking a hint, except in the way of business, as a reporter. I kept the run of her all the time she was in the city. She did not always see me, but I saw her, and that was enough. I watched her home from school in the evening, and was content, though she was escorted by a cadet with a pig-sticker at his side. He was her cousin, and had given me his word that he cared nothing about her. He is a commodore and King Christian's Secretary of Navy now. When she was sick, I

Down by her Garden, on the River Nibs.

pledged my Sunday trousers for a dollar and bought
her a bouquet of flowers which they teased her about
until she cried and threw it away. And all the time
she was getting more beautiful and more lovable.
She was certainly the handsomest girl in Copenhagen, which is full of charming women.

There were long spells when she was away, and
when I dreamt on undisturbed. It was during one
of these that I went to the theatre with my brother
to see a famous play in which an assassin tried to
murder the heroine, who was asleep in an armchair. Now, this heroine was a well-known actress
who looked singularly like Elizabeth. As she sat
there with the long curls sweeping her graceful
neck, in imminent danger of being killed, I forgot
where I was, what it was, all and everything except
that danger threatened Elizabeth, and sprang to my
feet with a loud cry of murder, trying to make for
the stage. My brother struggled to hold me back.
There was a sensation in the theatre, and the play
was held up while they put me out. I remember
King George of Greece eying me from his box as I
was being transported to the door, and the rascal
murderer on the stage looking as if he had done
something deserving of praise. Outside, in the
cold, my brother shook me up and took me home,
a sobered and somewhat crestfallen lad. But, anyhow, I don't like that kind of play. I don't see why

the villain on the stage is any better than the villain on the street. There are enough of them and to spare. And think if he *had* killed her!

The years passed, and the day came at last when, having proved my fitness, I received my certificate as a duly enrolled carpenter of the guild of Copenhagen, and, dropping my tools joyfully and in haste, made a bee-line for Ribe, where she was. I thought that I had moved with very stealthy steps toward my goal, having grown four years older than at the time I set the whole community by the ears. But it could not have been so, for I had not been twenty-four hours in town before it was all over that I had come home to propose to Elizabeth ; which was annoying but true. By the same sort of sorcery the town knew in another day that she had refused me, and all the wise heads wagged and bore witness that they could have told me so. What did I, a common carpenter, want at the "castle"? That was what they called her father's house. He had other plans for his pretty daughter.

As for Elizabeth, poor child! she was not yet seventeen, and was easily persuaded that it was all wrong; she wept, and in the goodness of her gentle heart was truly sorry; and I kissed her hands and went out, my eyes brimming over with tears, feeling that there was nothing in all the wide world for me any more, and that the farther I went from her the better. So it was settled that I should go to America. Her mother gave me a picture of her and a lock of her hair, and thereby roused the wrath of the dowagers once more; for why should I be breaking my heart over Elizabeth in foreign parts, since she was not for me? Ah, but mothers know better! I lived on that picture and that curl six long years.

The Picture her Mother gave me.

One May morning my own mother went to the stage-coach with me to see me off on my long journey. Father stayed home. He was ever a man who, with the tenderest of hearts, put on an appearance of great sternness lest he betray it. God rest his soul! That nothing that I have done caused him greater grief in his life than the separation that day is sweet comfort to me now. He lived to take Elizabeth to his heart, a beloved daughter. For me, I had been that morning, long before the sun rose, under her window to bid her good-by, but she did not know it. The servants did, though, and told her of it when she got up. And she, girl-like, said, " Well, I didn't ask him to come ; " but in her secret soul I think there was a small regret that she did not see me go.

So I went out in the world to seek my fortune, the richer for some $40 which Ribe friends had presented to me, knowing that I had barely enough to pay my passage over in the steerage. Though I had aggravated them in a hundred ways and wholly disturbed the peace of the old town, I think they liked me a little, anyway. They were always good, kind neighbors, honest and lovable folk. I looked back with my mother's blessing yet in my ears, to where the gilt weather-vanes glistened on her father's house, and the tears brimmed over again. And yet, such is life, presently I felt my heart bound with a new courage. All was not lost yet. The world was before me. But yesterday the chance befell that, in going to communion in the old Domkirke, I knelt beside her at the altar rail. I thought of that and dried my eyes. God is good. He did not lay it up against me. When next we met there, we knelt to be made man and wife, for better or worse ; blessedly, gloriously for better, forever and aye, and all our troubles were over. For had we not one another?

CHAPTER II

THE steamer *Iowa*, from Glasgow, made port, after a long and stormy voyage, on Whitsunday, 1870. She had come up during the night, and cast anchor off Castle Garden. It was a beautiful spring morning, and as I looked over the rail at the miles of straight streets, the green heights of Brooklyn, and the stir of ferryboats and pleasure craft on the river, my hopes rose high that somewhere in this teeming hive there would be a place for me. What kind of a place I had myself no clear notion of. I would let that work out as it could. Of course I had my trade to fall back on. but I am afraid that is all the use I thought of putting it to. The love of change belongs to youth, and I meant to take a hand in things as they came along. I had a pair of strong hands, and stubbornness enough to do for two ; also a strong belief that in a free country, free from the dominion of custom, of caste, as well as of men, things would somehow come right in the end, and a man get shaken into the corner where he

35

belonged if he took a hand in the game. I think I was right in that. If it took a lot of shaking to get me where I belonged, that was just what I needed. Even my mother admits that now. To tell the truth, I was tired of hammer and saw. They were indissolubly bound up with my dreams of Elizabeth that were now gone to smash. Therefore I hated them. And straightway, remembering that the day was her birthday, and accepting the fact as a good omen, I rebuilt my air-castles and resolved to try on a new tack. So irrational is human nature at twenty-one, when in love. And isn't it good that it is?

In all of which I have made no account of a factor which is at the bottom of half our troubles with our immigrant population, so far as they are not of our own making: the loss of reckoning that follows uprooting; the cutting loose from all sense of responsibility, with the old standards gone, that makes the politician's job so profitable in our large cities, and that of the patriot and the housekeeper so wearisome. We all know the process. The immigrant has no patent on it. It afflicts the native, too, when he goes to a town where he is not known. In the slum it reaches its climax in the second generation, and makes of the Irishman's and the Italian's boys the " toughs " who fight the battles of Hell's Kitchen and Frog Hollow. It simply means that we are creatures of environment, that a man everywhere is largely what his neighbors and his children think him to be, and that government makes for our moral good too, dreamers and anarchists to the contrary notwithstanding.   But, simple as it is, it has been too long neglected for the safety of the man and of the State.   I am not going to discuss here plans for mending this neglect, but I can think of three that would work; one of them does work, if not up to the top notch — the public school.   In its ultimate development as the neighborhood centre of things, I would have that the first care of city government, always and everywhere, at whatever expense.   An efficient parish districting is another.   I think we are coming to that.   The last is a rigid annual enrolment — the school census is good, but not good enough — for vaccination purposes, jury duty, for military purposes if you please.   I do not mean for conscription, but for the ascertainment of the fighting strength of the State in case of need — for anything that would serve as an excuse.   It is the enrolment itself that I think would have a good effect in making the man feel that he is counted on for something; that he belongs as it were, instead of standing idle and watching a procession go by, in which there is no place for him; which is only another way of saying that it is his right to harass

it and levy tribute as he can. The enrolment for
voting comes too late. By that time he may have
joined the looters' army.

So as properly to take my own place in the procession, if not in the army referred to, as I con-
ceived the custom of the country to be, I made it
my first business to buy a navy revolver of the
largest size, investing in the purchase exactly one-
half of my capital. I strapped the weapon on the
outside of my coat and strode up Broadway, conscious that I was following the fashion of the
country. I knew it upon the authority of a man
who had been there before me and had returned, a
gold digger in the early days of California; but
America was America to us. We knew no distinction of West and East. By rights there ought
to have been buffaloes and red Indians charging
up and down Broadway. I am sorry to say that
it is easier even to-day to make lots of people over
there believe that, than that New York is paved,
and lighted with electric lights, and quite as civil-
ized as Copenhagen. They will have it that it is
in the wilds. I saw none of the signs of this, but
I encountered a friendly policeman, who, sizing
me and my pistol up, tapped it gently with his club
and advised me to leave it home, or I might get
robbed of it. This, at first blush, seemed to confirm my apprehensions; but he was a very nice

policeman, and took time to explain, seeing that
I was very green. And I took his advice and put
the revolver away, secretly relieved to get rid of it.
It was quite heavy to carry around.

I had letters to the Danish Consul and to the
President of the American Banknote Company,
Mr. Goodall. I think perhaps he was not then the
president, but became so afterward. Mr. Goodall
had once been wrecked on the Danish coast and
rescued by the captain of the lifesaving crew, a
friend of my family. But they were both in
Europe, and in just four days I realized that there
was no special public clamor for my services in
New York, and decided to go West. A missionary in Castle Garden was getting up a gang
of men for the Brady's Bend Iron Works on the
Allegheny River, and I went along. We started
a full score, with tickets paid, but only two of us
reached the Bend. The rest calmly deserted in
Pittsburg and went their own way. Now here was an
instance of what I have just been saying. Not one
of them, probably, would have thought of doing it
on the other side. They would have carried out
their contract as a matter of course. Here they
broke it as a matter of course, the minute it didn't
suit them to go on. Two of them had been on
our steamer, and the thought of them makes me
laugh even now. One was a Dane who carried

an immense knapsack that was filled with sausages, cheese, and grub of all kinds when he came aboard. He never let go of it for a moment on the voyage. In storm and sunshine he was there, shouldering his knapsack. I think he slept with it. When I last saw him hobbling down a side street in Pittsburg, he carried it still, but one end of it hung limp and hungry, and the other was as lean as a bad year. The other voyager was a jovial Swede whose sole baggage consisted of an old musket, a blackthorn stick, and a barometer glass, tied up together. The glass, he explained, was worth keeping; it might some day make an elegant ruler. The fellow was a blacksmith, and I mistrust that he could not write.

Adler and I went on to Brady's Bend. Adler was a big, explosive German who had been a reserve officer, I think, in the Prussian army. Fate had linked us together when on the steamer the meat served in the steerage became so bad as to offend not only our palates, but our sense of smell. We got up a demonstration, marching to see the captain in a body, Adler and I carrying a tray of the objectionable meat between us. As the spokesman, I presented the case briefly and respectfully, and all would have gone well had not the hot blood of Adler risen at the wrong moment, when the captain was cautiously exploring the scent of the rejected food. With a sudden upward jerk he caused that official's nose to disappear momentarily in the dish, while he exploded in voluble German. The result was an instant rupture of diplomatic relations. Adler was put in the lock-up, but set free again immediately. He spent the rest of the voyage in his bunk shouting dire threats of disaster impending from the "Norddeutsche Consul," once he

Brady's Bend as I knew it.

reached New York. But we were all too glad to get ashore to think of vengeance then.

Adler found work at the blast-furnace, while I was set to building huts for the miners on the east bank of the river where a clearing had been made and called East Brady. On the other side of the Allegheny the furnaces and rolling mills were hidden away in a narrow, winding valley that set back into the forest-clad hills, growing deeper and narrower with every mile. It was to me, who had been used to seeing the sun rise and set over a level plain where the winds of heaven blew as they listed, from the first like a prison. I climbed the hills only to find that there were bigger hills beyond — an endless sea of swelling billows of green without a clearing in it. I spent all Sunday roaming through it, miles and miles, to find an outlook from which I might see the end; but there was none. A horrible fit of homesickness came upon me. The days I managed to get through by working hard and making observations on the American language. In this I had a volunteer assistant in Julia, the pretty, barefooted daughter of a coal-miner, who hung around and took an interest in what was going on. But she disappeared after I had asked her to explain what setting one's cap for any one meant. I was curious because I had heard her mother say to a neighbor that Julia was doing that to me. But the evenings were very lonesome. The girl in our boarding-house washed dishes always to one tune, " The Letter that Never Came." It was not a cheerful tune and not a cheerful subject, for I had had no news from home since I left. I can hear her yet, shrieking and clattering her dishes, with the frogs yelling accompaniment in the creek that mumbled in the valley. I never could abide American frogs since. There is rest in the ko-ax, ko-ax! of its European brother, but the breathless yi! yi! of our American frogs makes me feel always as if I wanted to die — which I don't.

In making the clearing, I first saw an American wood-cutter swing an axe, and the sight filled me with admiration for the man and the axe both. It was a "double-bitter," and he a typical long-armed and long-limbed backwoodsman. I also had learned to use the axe, but anything like the way he swung it, first over one, then over the other shoulder, making it tell in long, clean cuts at every blow, I had never dreamt of. It was splendid. I wished myself back in Copenhagen just long enough to tell the numskulls there, who were distrustful of American tools, which were just beginning to come into the market, that they didn't know what they were talking about. Of course it was reasonable that the good tools should come from the country where they had good use for them.

There was a settlement of honest Welshmen in the back hills, and the rumor that a Dane had come into the valley reached it in due course. It brought down a company of four sturdy miners, who trudged five miles over bad land of a Sunday to see what I was like. The Danes who live in Welsh song and story must have been grievous giants, for they were greatly disgusted at sight of me, and spoke their minds about it without reserve, even with some severity, as if I were guilty of some sort of an imposition on the valley.

It could hardly have been this introduction that tempted me to try coal-mining. I have forgotten how it came about — probably through some temporary slackness in the building trade; but I did try, and one day was enough for me. The company mined its own coal. Such as it was, it cropped out of the hills right and left in narrow veins, sometimes too shallow to work, seldom affording more space to the digger than barely enough to permit him to stand upright. You did not go down through a shaft, but straight in through the side of a hill to the bowels of the mountain, following a track on which a little donkey drew the coal to the mouth of the mine and sent it down the incline to run up and down a hill a mile or more by its own gravity before it reached the place of unloading. Through one of these we marched in, Adler and I, one summer morning with new pickaxes on our shoulders and nasty little oil lamps fixed in our hats to light us through the darkness where every second we stumbled over chunks of slate rock, or into pools of water that oozed through from above. An old miner whose way lay past the fork in the tunnel where our lead began showed us how to use our picks and the timbers to brace the slate that roofed over the vein, and left us to ourselves in a chamber perhaps ten feet wide and the height of a man.

We were to be paid by the ton, I forget how much, but it was very little, and we lost no time getting to work. We had to dig away the coal at the floor with our picks, lying on our knees to do it, and afterward drive wedges under the roof to loosen the mass. It was hard work, and, entirely inexperienced as we were, we made but little headway. As the day wore on, the darkness and silence grew very oppressive, and made us start nervously at the least thing. The sudden arrival of our donkey with its cart gave me a dreadful fright. The friendly beast greeted us with a joyous bray and rubbed its shaggy sides against us in the most companionable way. In the flickering light of my lamp I caught sight of its long ears waving over me — I don't believe I had seen three donkeys before in my life; there were none where I came from — and heard that demoniac shriek, and I verily believe I thought the evil one had come for me in person. I know that I nearly fainted.

That donkey was a discerning animal. I think it knew when it first set eyes on us that we were not going to overwork it; and we didn't. When, toward evening, we quit work, after narrowly escaping being killed by a large stone that fell from the roof in consequence of our neglect to brace it up properly, our united efforts had resulted in barely filling two of the little carts, and we had earned, if I recollect aright, something like sixty cents each. The fall of the roof robbed us of all desire to try mining again. It knocked the lamps from our hats, and, in darkness that could almost be felt, we groped our way back to the light along the track, getting more badly frightened as we went. The last stretch of way we ran, holding each other's hands as though we were not men and miners, but two frightened children in the dark.

As we emerged from the damp gap in the mountain side, the sunset was upon the hills. Peaceful sounds came up from the valley where the shadows lay deep. Gangs of men were going home from the day's toil to their evening rest. It seemed to me that I had been dead and had come back to life. The world was never so wondrous fair. My companion stood looking out over the landscape with hungry eyes. Neither of us spoke, but when the last gleam had died out in the window of the stone church we went straight to the company's store and gave up our picks. I have never set foot in a coal mine since, and have not the least desire to do so.

I was back in the harness of the carpenter-shop when, in the middle of July, the news struck down

in our quiet community like a bombshell that
France had declared war on Prussia; also that
Denmark was expected to join her forces to those
of her old ally and take revenge for the great robbery of 1864. I dropped my tools the moment I
heard it, and flew rather than ran to the company's
office to demand my time; thence to our boarding-
house to pack. Adler reasoned and entreated, called
it an insane notion, but, when he saw that nothing
would stop me, lent a hand in stuffing my trunk,
praying pathetically between pulls that his countrymen would make short work of me, as they certainly
would of France. I heeded nothing. All the hot
blood of youth was surging through me. I remembered the defeat, the humiliation of the flag I loved,
— aye! and love yet, for there is no flag like the flag
of my fathers, save only that of my children and of
my manhood, — and I remembered, too, Elizabeth,
with a sudden hope. I would be near her then, and
I would earn fame and glory. The carpenter would
come back with shoulder-straps. Perhaps then, in
the castle . . . I shouldered my trunk and ran for
the station. Such tools, clothes, and things as it
would not hold I sold for what they would fetch,
and boarded the next train for Buffalo, which was
as far as my money would take me.

I cannot resist the temptation at this point to
carry the story thirty years forward to last winter,

in order to point out one of the queer happenings which long ago caused me to be known to my friends as "the man of coincidences." I have long since ceased to consider them as such, though in this one there is no other present significance than that it decided a point which I had been turning over in

"I found the valley deserted and dead."

my own mind, of moment to me and my publisher. I was lecturing in Pittsburg at the time, and ran up to take another look at Brady's Bend. I found the valley deserted and dead. The mills were gone. Disaster had overtaken them in the panic of 1873, and all that remained of the huge plant was a tottering stump of the chimney and clusters of vacant houses dropping to pieces here and there. Young trees grew out of the cold ashes in the blast-furnace. All about was desolation. Strolling down by the river with the editor of the local paper in East Brady, which had grown into a slow little railroad town, my eye fell upon a wrecked hut in which I recognized the company's office. The shutters were gone, the door hung on one hinge, and the stairs had rotted away, but we climbed in somehow. It was an idle quest, said my companion; all the books and papers had been sold the summer before to a Pittsburg junkman, who came with a cart and pitch-forked them into it as so much waste paper. His trail was plain within. The floor was littered with torn maps and newspapers from the second term of President Grant. In a rubbish heap I kicked against something more solid and picked it up. It was the only book left in the place: the "draw-book" for the years 1870–72; and almost the first name I read was my own, as having received, on July 19, 1870, $10.63 in settlement of my account with the Brady's Bend Company when I started for the war. My companion stared. I wrapped up the book and took it away with me. I considered that I had a moral right to it; but if anybody questions it, it is at his service.

Buffalo was full of Frenchmen, but they did not receive me with a torchlight procession. They even

E

shrugged their shoulders when good old Pater Bret-
ton took up my cause and tried to get me forwarded
at least to New York.   The one patriot I found to
applaud my high resolve was a French pawnbroker,
who, with many compliments and shoulder pattings,
took my trunk and all its contents, after I had paid
my board out of it, in exchange for a ticket to New
York.   He took my watch, too, but that didn't keep
time.   I remember seeing my brush go with a grim
smile.   Having no clothes to brush, I had no need
of it any longer.   That pawnbroker was an artist.
The year after, when I was in Buffalo again, it
occurred to me to go in and see if I could get back
any of my belongings.   I was just a bit ashamed of
myself, and represented that I was a brother of the
young hothead who had gone to the war.   I thought
I discovered a pair of trousers that had been mine
hanging up in his store, but the Frenchman was
quicker than I.   His eyes followed mine, and he
took instant umbrage: —

"So your brother vas one shump, vas he?" he
yelled.   "Your brother vas a long sight better man
zan you, mine frient.   He go fight for la France.
You stay here.   Get out!"   And he put me out,
and saved the day and the trousers.

It was never a good plan for me to lie.   It never
did work out right, not once.   I have found the
only safe plan to be to stick to the truth and let the

house come down if it must. It will come down anyhow.

I reached New York with just one cent in my pocket, and put up at a boarding-house where the charge was one dollar a day. In this no moral obliquity was involved. I had simply reached the goal for which I had sacrificed all, and felt sure that the French people or the Danish Consul would do the rest quickly. But there was evidently something wrong somewhere. The Danish Consul could only register my demand to be returned to Denmark in the event of war. They have my letter at the office yet, he tells me, and they will call me out with the reserves. The French were fitting out no volunteer army that I could get on the track of, and nobody was paying the passage of fighting men. The end of it was that, after pawning my revolver and my top-boots, the only valuable possessions I had left, to pay for my lodging, I was thrown on the street, and told to come back when I had more money. That night I wandered about New York with a gripsack that had only a linen duster and a pair of socks in it, turning over in my mind what to do next. Toward midnight I passed a house in Clinton Place that was lighted up festively. Laughter and the hum of many voices came from within. I listened. They spoke French. A society of Frenchmen having their annual dinner, the watchman in the block told me. There at last was my chance. I went up the steps and rang the bell. A flunkey in a dress-suit opened, but when he saw that I was not a guest, but to all appearances a tramp, he tried to put me out. I, on my part, tried to explain. There was an altercation, and two gentlemen of the society appeared. They listened impatiently to what I had to say, then, without a word, thrust me into the street and slammed the door in my face.

It was too much. Inwardly raging, I shook the dust of the city from my feet, and took the most direct route out of it, straight up Third Avenue. I walked till the stars in the east began to pale, and then climbed into a wagon that stood at the curb to sleep. I did not notice that it was a milk-wagon. The sun had not risen yet when the driver came, unceremoniously dragged me out by the feet, and dumped me into the gutter. On I went with my gripsack, straight ahead, until toward noon I reached Fordham College, famished and footsore. I had eaten nothing since the previous day, and had vainly tried to make a bath in the Bronx River do for breakfast. Not yet could I cheat my stomach that way.

The college gates were open, and I strolled wearily in, without aim or purpose. On a lawn some young men were engaged in athletic exercises, and I stopped to look and admire the beautiful shade-trees and the imposing building.   So at least it seems to me at this distance.   An old monk in a cowl, whose noble face I sometimes recall in my dreams, came over and asked kindly if I was not hungry.   I was in all conscience fearfully hungry, and I said so, though I did not mean to.   I had never seen a real live monk before, and my Lutheran training had not exactly inclined me in their favor.   I ate of the food set before me, not without qualms of conscience, and with a secret suspicion that I would next be asked to abjure my faith, or at least do homage to the Virgin Mary, which I was firmly resolved not to do. But when, the meal finished, I was sent on my way with enough to do me for supper, without the least allusion having been made to my soul, I felt heartily ashamed of myself.   I am just as good a Protestant as I ever was.   Among my own I am a kind of heretic even, because I cannot put up with the apostolic succession; but I have no quarrel with the excellent charities of the Roman Church, or with the noble spirit that animates them.   I learned that lesson at Fordham thirty years ago.

Up the railroad track I went, and at night hired out to a truck-farmer, with the freedom of his haymow for my sleeping quarters.   But when I had hoed cucumbers three days in a scorching sun, till my back ached as if it were going to break, and the farmer guessed that he would call it square for three shillings, I went farther. A man is not necessarily a philanthropist, it seems, because he tills the soil. I did not hire out again. I did odd jobs to earn my meals, and slept in the fields at night, still turning over in my mind how to get across the sea. An incident of those wanderings comes to mind while I am writing. They were carting in hay, and when night came on, somewhere about Mount Vernon, I gathered an armful of wisps that had fallen from the loads, and made a bed for myself in a wagon-shed by the roadside. In the middle of the night I was awakened by a loud outcry. A fierce light shone in my face. It was the lamp of a carriage that had been driven into the shed. I was lying between the horse's feet unhurt. A gentleman sprang from the carriage, more frightened than I, and bent over me. When he found that I had suffered no injury, he put his hand in his pocket and held out a silver quarter.

" Go," he said, " and drink it up."

" Drink it up yourself!" I shouted angrily. " What do you take me for?"

They were rather high heroics, seeing where I was, but he saw nothing to laugh at. He looked earnestly at me for a moment, then held out his hand and shook mine heartily. " I believe you," he said; " yet you need it, or you would not sleep here.

Now will you take it from me?" And I took the money.

The next day it rained, and the next day after that, and I footed it back to the city, still on my vain quest. A quarter is not a great capital to subsist on in New York when one is not a beggar and has no friends. Two days of it drove me out again to find at least the food to keep me alive; but in those two days I met the man who, long years after, was to be my honored chief, Charles A. Dana, the editor of the *Sun*. There had been an item in the *Sun* about a volunteer regiment being fitted out for France. I went up to the office, and was admitted to Mr. Dana's presence. I fancy I must have appealed to his sense of the ludicrous, dressed in top-boots and a linen duster much the worse for wear, and demanding to be sent out to fight. He knew nothing about recruiting. Was I French? No, Danish; it had been in his paper about the regiment. He smiled a little at my faith, and said editors sometimes did not know about everything that was in their papers. I turned to go, grievously disappointed, but he called me back.

"Have you," he said, looking searchingly at me "have you had your breakfast?"

No, God knows that I had not; neither that day nor for many days before. That was one of the things I had at last learned to consider among the

superfluities of an effete civilization. I suppose I
had no need of telling it to him, for it was plain to
read in my face. He put his hand in his pocket
and pulled out a dollar.

" There," he said, " go and get your breakfast;
and better give up the war."

Give up the war! and for a breakfast. I spurned
the dollar hotly.

" I came here to enlist, not to beg money for
breakfast," I said, and strode out of the office, my
head in the air but my stomach crying out miser-
ably in rebellion against my pride. I revenged
myself upon it by leaving my top-boots with the
" uncle," who was my only friend and relative here,
and filling my stomach upon the proceeds. I had
one good dinner anyhow, for when I got through
there was only twenty-five cents left of the dollar I
borrowed upon my last article of " dress." That I
paid for a ticket to Perth Amboy, near which place
I found work in Pfeiffer's clay-bank.

Pfeiffer was a German, but his wife was Irish and
so were his hands, all except a giant Norwegian
and myself. The third day was Sunday, and was
devoted to drinking much beer, which Pfeiffer,
with an eye to business, furnished on the premises.
When they were drunk, the tribe turned upon the
Norwegian, and threw him out. It seems that this
was a regular weekly occurrence. Me they fired

out at the same time, but afterward paid no atten
tion to me. The whole crew of them perched on
the Norwegian and belabored him with broomsticks
and bale-sticks until they roused the sleeping Ber-
serk in him. As I was coming to his relief, I saw
the human heap heave and rock. From under it
arose the enraged giant, tossed his tormentors aside
as if they were so much chaff, battered down the
door of the house in which they took refuge, and
threw them all, Mrs. Pfeiffer included, through the
window. They were not hurt, and within two
hours they were drinking more beer together and
swearing at one another endearingly. I concluded
that I had better go on, though Mr. Pfeiffer regret-
ted that he never paid his hands in the middle of
the month. It appeared afterward that he objected
likewise to paying them at the end of the month, or
at the beginning of the next. He owes me two
days' wages yet.

CHAPTER III

I GO TO WAR AT LAST AND SOW THE SEED OF FUTURE CAMPAIGNS

AT sunset on the second day after my desertion of Pfeiffer I walked across a footbridge into a city with many spires, in one of which a chime of bells rang out a familiar tune. The city was New Brunswick. I turned down a side street where two stone churches stood side by side. A gate in the picket fence had been left open, and I went in looking for a place to sleep. Back in the churchyard I found what I sought in the brownstone slab covering the tomb of, I know now, an old pastor of the Dutch Reformed Church, who died full of wisdom and grace. I am afraid that I was not overburdened with either, or I might have gone to bed with a full stomach too, instead of chewing the last of the windfall apples that had been my diet on my two days' trip; but if he slept as peacefully under the slab as I slept on it, he was doing well. I had for once a dry bed, and brownstone keeps warm long after the sun has set. The night dews and the snakes, and the dogs that kept sniffing and growl-

"The dead were much better company."

ing half the night in the near distance, had made me tired of sleeping in the fields. The dead were much better company. They minded their own business, and let a fellow alone.

Before sun-up I was on the tow-path looking for a job. Mules were in demand there, not men. The drift caught me once more, and toward evening cast me up at a country town then called Little Washington, now South River. How I got there I do not now remember. My diary from those days says nothing about it. Years after, I went back over that road and accepted a "lift" from a farmer going my way. We passed through a toll-gate, and I wondered how the keeper came to collect uneven money. We were two men and two horses. When I came back the day after, I found out. So many cents, read the weather-beaten sign that swung from the gate, for team and driver, so many for each additional beast. I had gone through as an additional beast.

A short walk from Little Washington I found work in Pettit's brick-yard at $22 a month and board. That night, when I turned in after a square meal, in an old wagon I had begged for a bed, I felt like a capitalist. I took to the wagon because one look within the barracks had shown them to be impossible. Whether it was that, or the fact that most of the other hands were Germans, who felt in duty bound to celebrate each victory over the French as it was reported day by day, and so provoked me to wrath — from the first we didn't get on. They made a point whenever they came back from their celebrations in the village, of dragging my wagon, with me fast asleep in it, down into the river, where by and by the tide rose and searched me out. Then I had to swim for it. That was of less account. Our costume was not elaborate, — a pair of overalls, a woollen shirt, and a straw hat, that was all, and a wetting was rather welcome than otherwise; but they dubbed me Bismarck, and that was not to be borne. My passionate protest only made them laugh the louder. Yet they were not an ill-natured lot, rather the reverse. Saturday afternoon was our wash-day, when we all sported together in peace and harmony in the river. When we came out, we spread our clothes to dry on the roof of the barracks, while we burrowed each in a hill of white sand, and smoked our pipes far into the night, with only our heads and the hand that held the pipe sticking out. That was for protection against mosquitoes. It must have been a sight, one of those Saturday night confabs, but it was solid comfort after the week's work.

Bricks are made literally while the sun shines. The day begins with the first glimmer of light in the east, and is not over till the "pits" are worked out. It was my task to cart clay in the afternoon to fill them up again. It was an idle enough kind of job. All I had to do was to walk alongside my horse, a big white beast with no joints at all except where its legs were hinged to the backbone, back it up to the pit, and dump the load. But, walking so in the autumn sun, I fell a-dreaming. I forgot claybank and pit. I was back in the old town — saw her play among the timber. I met her again on the Long Bridge. I held her hands once more in that last meeting — the while I was mechanically backing my load up to the pit and making ready to dump it. Day-dreams are out of place in a brick-yard. I forgot to take out the tail-board. To my amazement, I beheld the old horse skating around, making frantic efforts to keep its grip on the soil, then slowly rise before my bewildered gaze, clawing feebly at the air as it went up and over, backwards into the pit, load, cart and all.

I wish for my own reputation that I could truly say I wept for the poor beast. I am sure I felt for it, but the reproachful look it gave me as it lay there on its back, its four feet pointing skyward, was too much. I sat upon the edge of the pit and shouted with laughter, feeling thoroughly ashamed of my levity. Mr. Pettit himself checked it, run-ning in with his boys and demanding to know what I was doing. They had seen the accident from the office, and at once set about getting the horse out. That was no easy matter. It was not hurt at all, but it had fallen so as to bend one of the shafts of the truck like a bow. It had to be sawed in two to get the horse out. When that was done, the heavy ash stick, rebounding suddenly, struck one of the boys, who stood by, a blow on the head that laid him out senseless beside the cart.

It was no time for laughter then. We ran for water and restoratives, and brought him to, white and weak. The horse by that time had been lifted to his feet and stood trembling in every limb, ready to drop. It was a sobered driver that climbed out of the pit at the tail end of the procession which bore young Pettit home. I spent a miserable hour hanging around the door of the house waiting for news of him. In the end his father came out to comfort me with the assurance that he would be all right. I was not even discharged, though I was deposed from the wagon to the command of a truck of which I was myself the horse. I "ran out" brick from the pit after that in the morning.

More than twenty years after, addressing the students of Rutgers College, I told them of my experience in the brick-yard which was so near them. At the end of my address a gentleman came up to me and said, with a twinkle in his eye:

"So that was you, was it? My name is Pettit, and I work the brick-yard now. I helped my father get that horse out of the pit, and I have cause to remember that knock on the head." He made me promise sometime to tell him what happened to me since, and if he will attend now he will have it all.

I had been six weeks in the brick-yard when one day I heard of a company of real volunteers that was ready to sail for France, and forthwith the war fever seized me again. That night I set out for Little Washington, and the next morning's steamer bore me past the brick-yard, where the German hands dropped their barrows and cheered me on with a howl of laughter that was yet not all derision. I had kept my end up with them and they knew it. They had lately let my sleeping-car alone in the old barn. Their shouts rang in my ears, nevertheless, when I reached New York and found that the volunteers were gone, and that I was once more too late. I fell back on the French Consul then, but was treated very cavalierly there. I suppose I became a nuisance, for when I called the twelfth or twentieth time at the office in Bowling Green, he waxed wroth with sudden vehemence and tried to put me out.

Then ensued the only fight of the war in which I was destined to have a part, and that on the wrong side. My gorge rose at these continual insults. I grabbed the French Consul by the nose, and in a moment we were rolling down the oval stairs together, clawing and fighting for all we were worth. I know it was inexcusable, but consider the provocation; after all I had sacrificed to serve his people, to be put out the second time like a beggar and a tramp! I had this one chance of getting even, and that I took it was only human. The racket we made on the stairs roused the whole house. All the clerks ran out and threw themselves upon me. They tore me away from the sacred person of the

Consul and thrust me out into the street bleeding and with a swollen eye to rage there, comforted only by the assurance that without a doubt both his were black. I am a little ashamed — not very much — of the fact that it comforts me even now to think of it. He really did me a favor, that Consul; but he was no good. He certainly was not.

It is to be recorded to the credit of my resolution, if not of my common sense, that even after that I made two attempts to get over to France. The one was with the captain of a French man-of-war that lay in the harbor. He would not listen to me at all. The other, and the last, was more successful. I actually got a job as stoker on a French steamer that was to sail for Havre that day in an hour. I ran all the way down to Battery Place, where I had my valise in a boarding-house, and all the way back, arriving at the pier breathless, in time to see my steamer swing out in the stream beyond my reach. It was the last straw. I sat on the stringpiece and wept with mortification. When I arose and went my way, the war was over, as far as I was concerned. It was that in fact, as it speedily appeared. The country which to-day, after thirty years of trial and bereavement, is still capable of the Dreyfus infamy, was not fit to hold what was its own. I am glad now that I did not go, though I cannot honestly say that I deserve any credit for it.

All my money was gone, and an effort I made to join a railroad gang in the Spuyten Duyvil cut came to nothing. Again I reënforced my credit with my revolver and the everlasting top-boots, but the two or three dollars they brought at the pawn-shop were soon gone, and once more I was turned out in the street. It was now late in the fall. The brick-making season was over. The city was full of idle men. My last hope, a promise of employment in a human-hair factory, failed, and, homeless and penniless, I joined the great army of tramps, wandering about the streets in the daytime with the one aim of somehow stilling the hunger that gnawed at my vitals, and fighting at night with vagrant curs or outcasts as miserable as myself for the protection of some sheltering ash-bin or door-way. I was too proud in all my misery to beg. I do not believe I ever did. But I remember well a basement window at the down-town Delmonico's, the silent appearance of my ravenous face at which, at a certain hour in the evening, always evoked a generous supply of meat-bones and rolls from a white-capped cook who spoke French. That was the saving clause. I accepted his rolls as instalments of the debt his country owed me, or ought to owe me, for my unavailing efforts in its behalf.

It was under such auspices that I made the acquaintance of Mulberry Bend, the Five Points, and the rest of the slum, with which there was in the years to come to be a reckoning. For half a lifetime afterward they were my haunts by day and by night, as a police reporter, and I can fairly lay claim, it seems to me, to a personal knowledge of the evil I attacked. I speak of this because, in a batch of reviews of "A Ten Years' War"[1] which came yesterday from my publishers to me there is one which lays it all to "maudlin sensitiveness" on my part.

Lunching at Delmonico's.

"The slum," says this writer, "is not at all so unspeakably vile," and measures for relief based on my arraignment "must be necessarily abortive." Every once in a while I am asked why I became

[1] Now, "The Battle with the Slum."

a newspaper man. For one thing, because there were writers of such trash, who, themselves comfortably lodged, have not red blood enough in their veins to feel for those to whom everything is denied, and not sense enough to make out the facts when they see them, or they would not call playgrounds, schoolhouses, and better tenements "abortive measures." Some one had to tell the facts; that is one reason why I became a reporter. And I am going to stay one until the last of that ilk has ceased to discourage men from trying to help their fellows by the shortest cut they can find, whether it fits in a theory or not. I don't care two pins for all the social theories that were ever made unless they help to make better men and women by bettering their lot. I have had cranks of that order, who rated as sensible beings in the ordinary affairs of life, tell me that I was doing harm rather than good by helping improve the lot of the poor; it delayed the final day of justice we were waiting for. Not I. I don't propose to wait an hour for it, if I can help bring it on; and I know I can.

There! I don't believe I have read fifteen reviews of any of my books. Life is too short; but I am glad I did not miss that one. Those are the fellows for whom Roosevelt is not a good enough reformer; who chill the enthusiasm of mankind with a deadly chill, and miscall it method — science.

The science of how not to do a thing — yes! They make me tired.

There was until last winter a doorway in Chatham Square, that of the old Barnum clothing store, which I could never pass without recalling those nights of hopeless misery with the policeman's periodic "Get up there! move on!" reënforced by a prod .of his club or the toe of his boot. I slept there, or tried to when crowded out of the tenements in the Bend by their utter nastiness. Cold and wet weather had set in, and a linen duster was all that covered my back. There was a woollen blanket in my trunk which I had from home — the one, my mother had told me, in which I was wrapped when I was born; but the trunk was in the "hotel" as security for money I owed for board, and I asked for it in vain. I was now too shabby to get work, even if there had been any to get. I had letters still to friends of my family in New York who might have helped me, but hunger and want had not conquered my pride. I would come to them, if at all, as their equal, and, lest I fall into temptation, I destroyed the letters. So, having burned my bridges behind me, I was finally and utterly alone in the city, with the winter approaching and every shivering night in the streets reminding me that a time was rapidly coming when such a life as I led could no longer be endured.

Not in a thousand years would I be likely to forget the night when it came. It had rained all day, a cold October storm, and night found me, with the chill downpour unabated, down by the North River, soaked through and through, with no chance for a supper, forlorn and discouraged. I sat on the bulwark, listening to the falling rain and the swish of the dark tide, and thinking of home. How far it seemed, and how impassable the gulf now between the "castle" with its refined ways, between her in her dainty girlhood and me sitting there, numbed with the cold that was slowly stealing away my senses with my courage. There was warmth and cheer where she was. Here —— An overpowering sense of desolation came upon me. I hitched a little nearer the edge. What if — ? Would they miss me much or long at home if no word came from me? Perhaps they might never hear. What was the use of keeping it up any longer with, God help us, everything against and nothing to back a lonely lad?

And even then the help came. A wet and shivering body was pressed against mine, and I felt rather than heard a piteous whine in my ear. It was my companion in misery, a little outcast black-and-tan, afflicted with fits, that had shared the shelter of a friendly doorway with me one cold night and had clung to me ever since with a loyal affection that was the one bright spot in my hard life. As my hand stole mechanically down to caress it, it crept upon my knees and licked my face, as if it meant to tell me that there was one who understood; that I was not alone. And the love of the faithful little beast thawed the icicles in my heart. I picked it up in my arms and fled from the tempter; fled to where there were lights and men moving, if they cared less for me than I for them — anywhere so that I saw and heard the river no more.

In the midnight hour we walked into the Church Street police station and asked for lodging. The rain was still pouring in torrents. The sergeant spied the dog under my tattered coat and gruffly told me to put it out, if I wanted to sleep there. I pleaded for it in vain. There was no choice. To stay in the street was to perish. So I left my dog out on the stoop, where it curled up to wait for me. Poor little friend! It was its last watch. The lodging-room was jammed with a foul and stewing crowd of tramps. A loud-mouthed German was holding forth about the war in Europe, and crowding me on my plank. Cold and hunger had not sufficed to put out the patriotic spark within me. It was promptly fanned into flame, and I told him what I thought of him and his crew. Some Irishmen cheered and fomented trouble, and the doorman came in threatening to lock us all up. I smothered my disgust at the place as well as I could, and slept, wearied nearly to death.

In the middle of the night I awoke with a feeling that something was wrong. Instinctively I felt for the little gold locket I wore under my shirt, with a part of the precious curl in it that was my last link with home. It was gone. I had felt it there the last thing before I fell asleep. One of the tramp lodgers had cut the string and stolen it. With angry tears I went up and complained to the sergeant that I had been robbed. He scowled at me over the blotter, called me a thief, and said that he had a good mind to lock me up. How should I, a tramp boy, have come by a gold locket? He had heard, he added, that I had said in the lodging-room that I wished the French would win, and he would only be giving me what I deserved if he sent me to the Island. I heard and understood. He was himself a German. All my sufferings rose up before me, all the bitterness of my soul poured itself out upon him. I do not know what I said. I remember that he told the doorman to put me out. And he seized me and threw me out of the door, coming after to kick me down the stoop.

My dog had been waiting, never taking its eyes off the door, until I should come out. When it saw me in the grasp of the doorman, it fell upon him at once, fastening its teeth in his leg. He let go of me with a yell of pain, seized the poor little beast by the legs, and beat its brains out against the stone steps.

The Fight on the Police Station Steps.

At the sight a blind rage seized me. Raving like a madman, I stormed the police station with paving-stones from the gutter. The fury of my on-set frightened even the sergeant, who saw, perhaps, that he had gone too far, and he called two policemen to disarm and conduct me out of the precinct anywhere so that he got rid of me. They marched me to the nearest ferry and turned me loose. The ferry-master halted me. I had no money, but I gave him a silk handkerchief, the last thing about me that had any value, and for that he let me cross to Jersey City. I shook the dust of New York from my feet, vowing that I would never return, and, setting my face toward the west, marched straight out the first railroad track I came to.

And now, right here, begins the part of my story that is my only excuse for writing down these facts, though it will not appear for a while yet. The outrage of that night became, in the providence of God, the means of putting an end to one of the foulest abuses that ever disgraced a Christian city, and a mainspring in the battle with the slum as far as my share in it is concerned. My dog did not die unavenged.

I walked all day, following the track, and in the afternoon crossed the long trestlework of the Jersey Central Railroad over Newark Bay, with my face set toward Philadelphia. I had friends there, distant relatives, and had at last made up my mind to go to them and ask them to start me afresh. On the road which I had chosen for myself I had come to the jumping-off place. Before night I found company in other tramps who had been over the road before and knew just what towns to go around and which to walk through boldly. Rahway, if I remember rightly, was one of those to be severely shunned. I discovered presently that I was on the great tramps' highway, with the column moving south on its autumn hegira to warmer climes. I cannot say I fancied the company. Tramps never had any attraction for me, as a sociological problem or otherwise. I was compelled, more than once, to be of and with them, but I shook their company as quickly as I could. As for the "problem" they are supposed to represent, I think the workhouse and the police are quite competent to deal with that, provided it is not a Tammany police. It does not differ appreciably from the problem of human laziness in any other shape or age. We got some light on that, which ought to convince anybody, when under Mayor Strong's administration we tried to deal intelligently with vagrancy. One-half of the homeless applicants for night shelter were fat, well-nourished young loafers who wouldn't work. That is not my statement, but the report of the doctor who saw them stripped, taking their bath. The bath and the investigation presently decreased their numbers, until in a week scarcely anything was left of the "problem" that had bothered us so.

Four days I was on the way to Philadelphia, living on apples and an occasional meal earned by doing odd jobs. At night I slept in lonely barns that nearly always had a board ripped out — the tramps' door. I tried to avoid the gang, but I was not always successful. I remember still with a shudder an instance of that kind. I was burrowing in a haymow, thinking myself alone. In the night a big storm came up. The thunder shook the old barn, and I sat up wondering if it would be blown away. A fierce lightning-flash filled it with a ghostly light, and showed me within arm's length a white and scared face with eyes starting from their sockets at the sight of me. The next moment all was black darkness again. My heart stood still for what seemed the longest moment of my life. Then there came out of the darkness a quaking voice asking, " Is anybody there ? " For once I was glad to have a live tramp about. I really thought it was a ghost.

The last few miles to Camden I rode in a cattle-car, arriving there at night, much the worse for the wear of it on my linen duster. In the freight-yard I was picked up by a good-hearted police captain who took me to his station, made me tell him my story, and gave me a bed in an unused cell, the door of which he took the precaution to lock on the outside. But I did not mind. Rather that a hundred times than the pig-sty in the New York station-house. In the morning he gave me breakfast and money to get my boots blacked and to pay my fare across the Delaware. And so my homeless wanderings came, for the time being, to an end. For in Philadelphia I found in the Danish Consul, Ferdinand Myhlertz, and his dear wife, friends indeed as in need. The City of Brotherly Love found heart and time to welcome the wanderer, though at the time it was torn up by the hottest kind of fight over the question whether or not to disfigure the beautiful square at Broad and Market streets by putting the new municipal building there.

When, after two weeks' rest with my friends, they sent me on my way to an old schoolmate in Jamestown, N.Y., clothed and in my right mind, I was none the worse for my first lesson in swimming against the current, and quite sure that next time I should be able to breast it. Hope springs eternal at twenty-one. I had many a weary stretch ahead before I was to make port. But with youth and courage as the equipment, one should win almost any fight.

CHAPTER IV

WORKING AND WANDERING

WINTER came quickly up by the northern lakes, but it had no terror for me. For once I had shelter and enough to eat. It found me felling trees on Swede Hill, where a considerable settlement of Scandinavians was growing up. I had tried my hand at making cradles in a furniture-shop, but at two dollars and forty cents per dozen there was not much profit in it. So I took to the woods and learned to swing an axe in the American fashion that had charmed me so at Brady's Bend. I liked it much better, anyway, than being in the house winter and summer. It is well that we are fashioned that way, some for indoors and some for outdoors, for so the work of the world is all done; but it has always seemed to me that the indoor folk take too big a share of credit to themselves, as though there were special virtue in that, though I think that the reverse is the case. At least it seems more natural to want to be out in the open where the sun shines and the winds blow. When I was not chopping wood I was helping with the ice har-

vess on the lake or repairing the steamer that ran
in summer between Jamestown and Mayville. My
home was in Dexterville, a mile or so out of town,
where there lived a Danish family, the Romers, at
whose home I was made welcome. The friendship
which grew up between us has endured through life
and been to me a treasure. Gentler and truer
hearts than those of Nicholas and John Romer
there are not many.

I shared my room with another countryman,
Anthony Ronne, a young axe-maker, who, like myself, was in hard luck. The axe-factory had burned
down, and, with no work in sight, the outlook for
him was not exactly bright. He had not my way
of laughing it off, but was rather disposed to see the
serious side of it. Probably that was the reason we
took to each other; the balance was restored so.
Maybe he sobered me down somewhat. If any one
assumes that in my rôle of unhappy lover I went
about glooming and glowering on mankind, he
makes a big mistake. Besides, I had not the least
notion of accepting that rôle as permanent. I was
out to twist the wheel of fortune my way when I
could get my hands upon it. I never doubted that
I should do that sooner or later, if only I kept doing
things. That Elizabeth should ever marry anybody
but me was preposterously impossible, no matter
what she or anybody said.

Was this madness? They half thought so at home when they caught a glimpse of it in my letters. Not at all. It was conviction — the conviction that shapes events and the world to its ends. I know what I am talking about. If any one doubts it, and thinks his a worse case than mine, let him try my plan. If he cannot muster up courage to do it, it is the best proof in the world that she was right in refusing him.

To return to my chum; he, on his part, rose to the height even of "going out," but not with me. There was a physical obstacle to that. We had but one coat between us, a turned black kersey, worn very smooth and shiny also on the wrong side, which I had bought of a second-hand dealer in Philadelphia for a dollar. It was our full-dress, and we took turns arraying ourselves in it for the Dexterville weekly parties. These gatherings interested me chiefly as outbreaks of the peculiar American humor that was very taking to me, in and out of the newspapers. Dancing being tabooed as immoral and contaminating, the young people had recourse to particularly energetic kissing games, which more than made up for their deprivation on the other score. It was all very harmless and very funny, and the winter wore away pleasantly enough in spite of hard luck and hard work when there was any

With the early thaw came change. My friends moved away to Buffalo, and I was left for two months the sole occupant of the Romer homestead. My last job gave out about that time, and a wheelbarrow express which I established between Dexterville and the steamboat landing on the lake refused to prosper. The idea was good enough, but I was ahead of my time: travel on the lake had not yet begun. With my field thus narrowed down, I fell back on my gun and some old rat-traps I found in the woodshed. I became a hunter and trapper. Right below me was the glen through which the creek ran on its way to the sawmills and furniture-shops of Jamestown. It was full of musk-rats that burrowed in its banks between the roots of dead hemlocks and pines. There I set my traps and baited them with carrots and turnips. The manner of it was simple enough. I set the trap on the bottom of the creek and hung the bait on a stick projecting from the bank over it, so that to get at it the rat had to step on the trap. I caught lots of them. Their skins brought twenty cents apiece in the town, so that I was really quite independent. I made often as much as a dollar overnight with my traps, and then had the whole day to myself in the hills, where I waylaid many a fat rabbit or squirrel and an occasional bird.

The one thing that marred my enjoyment of this

life of freedom was my vain struggle to master the
art of cookery in its elements. To properly get the
hang of that, and of housekeeping in general, two
heads are needed, as I have found out since — one of
them with curls and long eyelashes. Then it is fine

"There I set my traps."

fun; but it is not good for man to tackle that job
alone. Goodness knows I tried hard enough. I remember the first omelet I made. I was bound to
get it good. So I made a muster-roll of all the good
things Mrs. Romer had left in the house, and put
them all in. Eggs and strawberry jam and raisins
and apple-sauce, and some sliced bacon — the way

I had seen mother do with "egg pancakes." But though I seasoned it liberally with baking-powder to make it rise, it did not rise. It was dreadfully heavy and discouraging, and not even the strawberry jam had power to redeem it. To tell the truth, it was not a good omelet. It was hardly fit to eat. The jam came out to better advantage in the sago I boiled, but there was too much of it. It was only a fruit-jar full, but I never saw anything swell so. It boiled out of the pot and into another and another, while I kept pouring on water until nearly every jar in the house was full of sago that stood around until moss grew on it with age. There is much contrariness in cooking. When I tapped my maples with the rest — there were two big trees in front of the house — and tried to make sugar, I was prepared to see the sap boil away; but when I had labored a whole day and burned half a cord of wood, and had for my trouble half a teacupful of sugar, which made me sick into the bargain, I concluded that that game was not worth the candle, and gave up my plans of becoming a sugar-planter on a larger scale.

It was at this time that I made my first appearance on the lecture platform. There was a Scandinavian society in Jamestown, composed chiefly of workingmen whose fight with life had left them little enough time for schooling. They were anxious to learn, however, and as I was set on teaching where I saw the chance, the thing came of itself. I had been mightily interested in the Frenchman Figuier's account of the formation and development of the earth, and took that for my topic. Twice a week, when I had set my traps in the glen, I went to town and talked astronomy and geology to interested audiences that gazed terror stricken at the loathsome saurians and the damnable pterodactyl which I sketched on the blackboard. Well they might. I spared them no gruesome detail, and I never could draw, anyhow. However, I rescued them from those beasts in season, and together we hauled the earth through age-long showers of molten metal into the sunlight of our day. I sometimes carried home as much as two or three dollars, after paying for gas and hall, with the tickets ten cents apiece, and I saw wealth and fame ahead of me, when sudden wreck came to my hopes and my career as a lecturer.

It was all because, having got the earth properly constructed and set up, as it were, I undertook to explain about latitude and longitude. Figures came in there, and I was never strong at mathematics. My education in that branch had run into a snag about the middle of the little multiplication table. A boy from the "plebs" school challenged me to fight, as I was making my way to recitation, trying

to learn the table by heart. I broke off in the
middle of the sixes to wallop him, and never got
any farther. The class went on that day without
me, and I never overtook it. I made but little
effort. In the Latin School, which rather prided
itself upon being free from the commercial taint,
mathematics was held to be in the nature of an
intrusion, and it was a sort of good mark for a boy
that he did not take to it, if at the same time he
showed aptitude for language. So I was left to
deplore with Marjorie Fleming to the end of my
days the inherent viciousness of sevens and eights,
as "more than human nature can endure." It is
one of the ironies of life that I should have had to
take up work into which the study of statistics
enters largely. But the powers that set me the
task provided a fitter back than mine for that
burden. As I explained years ago in the preface
to " How the Other Half Lives," the patient friendship of Dr. Roger S. Tracy, the learned statistician
of the Health Department, has smoothed the rebel-
lious kinks out of death-rates and population statistics, as of so many other knotty problems which we
have worked out together.

But I am getting out of my longitude, as I did
then. When I had groped about long enough trying to make my audience understand what I only
half understood myself, an old sea-captain arose in

his place and said that any man who would make a mess of so simple a thing as latitude and longitude evidently knew nothing at all.   It happened to be the one thing he knew about.   Popular favor is a fickle thing.   The audience that had but now been applauding my efforts to organize the earth took his word for it without waiting for an explanation and went out in a body, scouting even the ichthyosaurus as a prehistoric fake.

I made a valiant effort to stem the tide, but came to worse grief than before.   My only listener was a Swedish blacksmith who had attended the creation and development of the earth from the beginning with unshaken faith, though he was a member of the Lutheran church, with the pastor and deacons of which I had waged a bitter newspaper war over the "sin" of dancing.   But when I said, on the authority of Figuier, that an English man-of-war had once during an earthquake been thrown into the city of Callao and through the roof of a church, between the walls of which it remained standing upright on its keel, he got up and went too.   He circulated the story in town with various embellishments.   The deacons aforesaid seized upon it as welcome ammunition, construing it into an insult to the church, and there was an end to my lecturing.

The warm spring weather, together with these disappointments, bred in me the desire to roam.

I packed away my traps and started for Buffalo
with my grip, walking along the lake. It set in
with a drizzling rain, and I was soon wet to the
skin. Where the Chautauqua summer school
grounds are now I surprised a flock of wild ducks
near the shore, and was lucky enough to wound
one with my revolver. But the wind carried it
out of my reach, and I trudged on supperless,
through Mayville, where the lights were beginning
to shine in the windows. Not one of them was
for me. All my money had gone to pay back debts
to my Dexterville landlady. The Danes had a
good name in Jamestown, and we were all very
jealous of it. We would have starved, every one
of us, rather than leave unpaid debts behind. As
Mrs. Ben Wah many years after put it to me, " it
is no disgrace to be poor, but it is sometimes very
inconvenient." I found it so when, worn out with
walking, I crawled into an abandoned barn halfway to Westfield and dug down in the hay, wet
through and hungry as a bear. It stormed and
rained all night, and a rat or a squirrel fell from the
roof on my face. It felt like a big sprawling hand,
and woke me up in a great fright.

The sun was shining upon a peaceful Sabbath
when I crawled out of my hole and saw to my dismay that I had been sleeping in a pile of old hay
seed that had worked through and through my wet

clothes until I was a sight. An hour's patient plucking and a bath in a near-by pond restored me to something like human shape, and I held my entry into Westfield. The people were going to church in their holiday clothes, and eyed the uncouth stranger askance. I travelled the whole length of the town thinking what to do next. My stomach decided for me. There was a house standing in a pretty garden with two little cast-iron negro boys for hitching-posts at the steps. I rang the bell, and to an old lady who opened the door I offered to chop wood, fetch water, or do anything there was to do in exchange for breakfast. She went in and brought out her husband, who looked me over and said that if I was willing to do his chores I need go no farther. I was tired and famished, and the place was so restful that I said yes at once. In ten minutes I was eating my breakfast in the kitchen, duly installed as Dr. Spencer's hired man.

I think of the month I spent in the doctor's house with mingled feelings of exasperation and amusement. If I had not learned to milk a cow there, probably Octavia Ely would never have come into my life, horrid nightmare that she was. Octavia Ely was a Jersey cow with a brass tag in her ear, whose attacks upon the domestic peace of my house in after years even now fill me with rage. In the

twelve months of her sojourn with us she had
fifteen different kinds of disease, every one of
which advertised itself by the stopping of her milk.
When she had none, she never once gave down the
milk without grudging it.   With three of us to
hold her legs and tail lest she step in the pail or
switch our ears, she would reach back and eat the
vest off my back where I sat milking her.   But
she does not belong in this story, thank goodness!
If she had never belonged to me or mine, I should
be a better man to-day; she provoked me so.
However, I cannot reasonably lay the blame for
her on the doctor.   His cow was friendly enough.
It was Sport, the old dog, that made the heaviest
and at the same time a most ludicrous item in my
duties as hired man.   Long past the age of sport
of any kind, he spent his decadent years in a state
of abject fear of thunder and lightning.   If only
a cloud darkened the sun, Sport kept up a ceaseless
pilgrimage between his corner and the kitchen
door to observe the sky, sighing most grievously
at the outlook.   At the first distant rumble — this
was in the month of May, when it thundered almost
every day — he became perfectly rigid with terror.
It was my duty then to carry him down into the
cellar and shut him in the wood-box, where he
was out of the way of it all.   Poor Sport laid his
head against my shoulder and wept great tears that

wrung peals of laughter from me and from the boys who always hung around to see the show.

One of these was just beginning the struggle with his Homer, which I knew by heart almost, and it may have been the discovery that I was able to steer him through it between chores, as well as to teach him some tricks of fencing, that helped make the doctor anxious that I should promise to stay with him always. He would make me rich, he said. But other ambitions than to milk cows and plant garden truck were stirring in me. To be rich was never among them. I had begun to write essays for the magazines, choosing for my topic, for want of any other, the maltreatment of Denmark by Prussia, which rankled fresh in my memory, and the duty of all Scandinavians to rise up and avenge it. The Scandinavians would not listen when I wrote in Danish, and my English outpourings never reached the publishers. I dis-covered that I lacked words — they didn't pour; at which, in general discontentment with myself and all things, I pulled up stakes and went to Buffalo. Only, this time I rode in a railway train, with money in my pocket.

For all that, Buffalo received me with no more circumstance than it had done when I came there penniless, on the way to the war, the year before. I piled boards in a lumber-yard until I picked a quarrel with a tyrant foreman on behalf of a lot of green Germans whom he maltreated most shamefully. Then I was put out. A cabinet-maker in the "Beehive," a factory building out in Niagara Street, hired me next to make bedsteads, and took me to board with him. In the top story of the factory we fitted up a bedroom that was just large enough for one sitting and two standing, so long as the door was not opened; then one of the two had to get out. It mattered little, for the only visitor I had was a half-elderly countryman of mine whom they had worked so hard in his childhood that he had never had a chance to go to school. We two labored together by my little lamp, and it was great fun to see him who had never known how to read and write his own Danish make long strides in the strange tongue he spoke so singularly well. When we were both tired out, we would climb up on the roof and lie there and look out over the lake and the city where the myriad lights were shining, and talk of the old home and old times.

Sometimes the new would crowd them out in spite of all. I remember that Fourth of July when the salute from Fort Porter woke me up at sunrise and fired me with sudden patriotic ardor. I jumped out of bed and grabbed my revolver. There was a pile of packing-boxes in the yard below, and, know ing that there was no one around whom I could hurt, I made it my target and fired away all my ammunition at it. It made a fine racket, and I was happy. A couple of days later, when I was down in the yard, it occurred to me to look at the boxes to ascertain what kind of a score I had made. A very good one. All the bullets had hit. The boxes looked like so many sieves. Incidentally I found out that they were not empty, as I had supposed, but filled with glass fruit-jars.

I had eventually to give that job up also, because my boss was "bad pay." He was pretty much all bad, I guess. I do think his house was the most disorderly one I have ever come across. Seven ill-favored children clamored about the table, fighting with their even more ill-favored mother. She used to single out the one she wished to address by slamming a handful of string-beans, or whatever greens might be at hand, across the table at him. The youngster would fire it back, and so they were *en rapport* with each other. The father was seldom sober at meals. When he "felt funny," he would stealthily pour a glass of water down the nearest child's back and then sit and chuckle over the havoc he had wrought. There followed a long and woful wail and an instant explosion from the mother in this wise. I can hear her now. It was always the same : —

" Gott-himmel-donnerwetter-noch-emal-ich-will-de-mal-hole-du-spitzbub-eselskerl - wart'- nur-ich - schlag-de-noch-todt-potz-sacrement ! "

Whereupon, from sheer exhaustion all round, there was peace for at least five minutes.

Which reminds me of meeting Adler, my chum from Brady's Bend, in Buffalo. He had come up to get a $1500 place, as he informed me. That would about satisfy him. That such jobs were waiting by the score for an educated German in this barbarous land he never doubted for a moment. In the end he went to work in a rolling-mill at a dollar a day. Adler was ever a stickler for etiquette. In Brady's Bend we had very little of it. At meal-times a flock of chickens used to come into the summer kitchen where we ate, and forage around, to Adler's great disgust. One day they deliberately flew up on the table, and fell to fighting with the boarders for the food. A big Shanghai rooster trod in the butter and tracked it over the table. At the sight Adler's rage knew no bounds. Seizing a half-loaf of bread, he aimed it at the rooster and felled him in his tracks. The flock of fowl flew squawking out of the door. The women screamed, and the men howled with laughter. Adler flourished another loaf and vowed vengeance upon bird or beast that did not let the butter alone.

I have been often enough out of patience with

the ways of the labor men which seem to me to be the greatest hindrance to the success of their cause; but I am not in danger of forgetting the other side which makes that cause — if for no other reason, because of an experience I had in Buffalo that year. In a planing-mill in which I had found employment I contracted with the boss to plane doors, sandpaper them, and plug knot-holes at fifteen cents a door. It was his own offer, and I did the work well, better than it had been done before, so he said himself. But when he found at the end of the week that I had made $15 where my slow-coach predecessor had made only ten, he cut the price down to twelve cents. I objected, but in the end swallowed my anger and, by putting on extra steam and working overtime, made $16 the next week. The boss examined the work very carefully, said it was good, paid my wages, and cut down the price to ten cents. He did not want his men to make over $10 a week, he said; it was not good for them. I quit then, after giving him my opinion of him and of the chances of his shop. I do not know where he may be now, but wherever he is, I will warrant that my prediction came true. There is in Danish an old proverb, " Falsk slaar sin egen Herre paa Hals," which is to say that chickens come home to roost, and that right in the end does prevail over might. The Lord Chief Justice over all is not to be tricked. If the labor men will only remember that, and devote, let us say, as much time to their duties as to fighting for their rights, they will get them sooner. Which is not saying that there is not a time to strike. Witness my experience with the planing-mill man.

I struck not only against him, but against the whole city of Buffalo. I shook the dust of it from my feet and went out to work with a gang on a new railroad then being built through Cattaraugus County — the Buffalo and Washington, I think. Near a village called Coonville our job was cut out for us. We were twenty in the gang, and we were to build the line across an old dry river-bed at that point. In the middle of the river there had once been a forest-clad island. This we attacked with pickaxe and spade and carried it away piecemeal in our wheelbarrows. It fell in with the hottest weather of the year. Down in the hollow where no wind blew it was utterly unbearable. I had never done such work before, and was not built for it. I did my best to keep up with the gang, but my chest heaved and my heart beat as though it would burst. There were nineteen Irishmen in the gang — big, rough fellows who had picked me out, as the only " Dutchman," as the butt for their coarse jokes; but when they saw that the work was plainly too much for me, the other side of this curiously contradictory, mischief-loving, and big-hearted people came out. They invented a thousand excuses to get me out of the line. Water was certainly not their daily diet, but they fell victims, one and all, to the most ravening thirst, which required the despatching of me every hour to the spring a quarter of a mile away to fill the pail. If they could not empty it quickly enough, they managed to upset it, and, to cover up the fraud, cursed each other roundly for their clumsiness. Between whiles they worried me as ever with their horse-play; but I had seen the real man behind it, and they might have called me Bismarck, had they chosen, without offence.

The heat, the work, and the slave-driver of a foreman were too much for them even, and before the end of a week the gang was broken and scattered wide. I was on the road again looking for work on a farm. It was not to be had. Perhaps I did not try very hard. Sunday morning found me spending my last quarter for breakfast in an inn at Lime Lake. When I had eaten, I went out in the fields and sat with my back against a tree, and listened to the church-bells that were ringing also, I knew, in my home four thousand miles away. I saw the venerable Domkirke, my father's gray head in his pew, and Her, young and innocent, in the women's seats across the aisle. I heard the old pastor's voice in the solemn calm, and my tears fell upon her picture that had called up the vision. It was as if a voice spoke to me and said to get up and be a man; that if I wanted to win Elizabeth, to work for her was the way, and not idling my days away on the road. And I got right up, and, setting my face toward Buffalo, went by the shortest cut back to my work.

I walked day and night, pursued in the dark by a hundred skulking curs that lurked behind trees until I came abreast of them and then sallied

Our Old Pastor.

out to challenge my progress. I stoned them and went on. Monday's setting sun saw me outside Buffalo, tired, but with a new purpose. I had walked fifty miles without stopping or eating. I slept under a shed that night, and the very next day found work at good wages on some steamers the Erie Railroad was then building for the Lake Superior

H

trade. With intervals of other employment when
for any reason work in the ship-yard was slack, I
kept that up all winter, and became quite opulent,
even to the extent of buying a new suit of clothes,
the first I had had since I landed. I paid off all
my debts, and quarrelled with all my friends about
religion. I never had any patience with a person
who says "there is no God." The man is a fool,
and therefore cannot be reasoned with. But in
those days I was set on converting him, as my
viking forefathers did when from heathen they
became Christians — by fire and sword if need be.
I smote the infidels about me hip and thigh, but
there were a good many of them, and they kept
springing up, to my great amazement. Probably
the constant warfare imparted a tinge of fierceness
to that whole period of my life, for I remember that
one of my employers, a Roman Catholic builder,
discharged me for disagreeing with him about the
saints, telling me that I was "too blamed independent, anyhow." I suspect I must have been a
rather unlovely customer, take it all together.
Still, every once in a while it boils up in me yet
against the discretion that has come with the years,
and I want to slam in after the old fashion. Seems
to me we are in danger of growing stale with all
our soft speeches nowadays.

Things enough happened to take down my self-

esteem a good many pegs. It was about this time
I made up my mind to go into the newspaper busi
ness. It seemed to me that a reporter's was the
highest and noblest of all callings; no one could
sift wrong from right as he, and
punish the wrong. In that I was
right. I have not changed my
opinion on that point one whit,
and I am sure I never shall. The
power of fact is the mightiest
lever of this or of any day. The
reporter has his hand upon it,
and it is his grievous fault if he
does not use it well. I thought
I would make a good reporter.
My father had edited our local
newspaper, and such little help

When I worked in the
Buffalo Ship-yard.

as I had been of to him had given me a taste for
the business. Being of that mind, I went to the
Courier office one morning and asked for the editor.
He was not in. Apparently nobody was. I wandered through room after room, all empty, till at last
I came to one in which sat a man with a paste-pot
and a pair of long shears. This must be the editor;
he had the implements of his trade. I told him my
errand while he clipped away.

"What is it you want?" he asked, when I had
ceased speaking and waited for an answer.

"Work," I said.

"Work!" said he, waving me haughtily away with the shears; "we don't work here. This is a newspaper office."

I went, abashed. I tried the *Express* next. This time I had the editor pointed out to me. He was just coming through the business office. At the door I stopped him and preferred my request. He looked me over, a lad fresh from the shipyard, with horny hands and a rough coat, and asked: —

"What are you?"

"A carpenter," I said.

The man turned upon his heel with a loud, rasping laugh and shut the door in my face. For a moment I stood there stunned. His ascending steps on the stairs brought back my senses. I ran to the door, and flung it open. "You laugh!" I shouted, shaking my fist at him, standing halfway up the stairs, "you laugh now, but wait —" And then I got the grip of my temper and slammed the door in my turn. All the same, in that hour it was settled that I was to be a reporter. I knew it as I went out into the street.

CHAPTER V

I GO INTO BUSINESS, HEADLONG

SOMEWHAT suddenly and quite unexpectedly, a business career opened for me that winter. Once I had tried to crowd into it uninvited, but the result was not good. It was when I had observed that, for the want of the window reflectors which were much in use in the old country, American ladies were at a disadvantage in their homes in not being able to make out undesirable company at a distance, themselves unseen, and conveniently forgetting that they were "in." This civilizing agency I set about supplying forthwith. I made a model and took it to a Yankee business man, to whom I explained its use. He listened attentively, took the model, and said he had a good mind to have me locked up for infringing the patent laws of other lands; but because I had sinned from ignorance he would refrain. His manner was so impressive that he really made me uneasy lest I had broken some kind of a law I knew not of. From the fact that not long after window reflectors began to make their appearance in Buffalo, I infer that, whatever

the enactment, it did not apply to natives, or else
that he was a very fearless man, willing to take the
risk from which he would save me — a sort of commercial philanthropist. However, by that time I
had other things to think of, being a drummer and
a very energetic one.

It came about in this way: some countrymen of
mine had started a coöperative furniture-factory
in Jamestown, where there were water-power and
cheap lumber. They had no capital, but just below
was the oil country, where everybody had money,
slathers of it. New wells gushed every day, and
boom towns were springing up all along the Allegheny valley. Men were streaming into it from
everywhere, and needed furniture. If once they
got the grip on that country, reasoned the furniture-
makers, they would get rich quickly with the rest.
The thing was to get it. To do that they needed
a man who could talk. Perhaps they remembered
the creation of the world the year before. At all
events, they sent up to Buffalo and asked me if I
would try.

I slammed my tool-box shut and started for
Jamestown on the next train. Twenty-four hours
later saw me headed for the oil country, equipped
with a mighty album and a price-list. The album
contained pictures of the furniture I had for sale.
All the way down I studied the price-list, and when

I reached Titusville I knew to a cent what it cost
my employers per foot to make ash extension
tables. I only wish they had known half as well.

My first customer was a grumpy old shopkeeper
who needed neither tables nor bedsteads, so he
said. But I had thought it all over and made up
my mind that the first blow was half the battle.
Therefore I knew better. I pushed my album
under his nose, and it fell open at the extension
tables. Cheap, I said, and rattled off the price. I
saw him prick up his ears, but he only growled that
probably they were no good.

What! my extension tables no good? I dared
him to try them, and he gave me an order for a
dozen, but made me sign an agreement that they
were to be every way as represented. I would have
backed my tables with an order for the whole shop,
so sure was I that they could not be beaten. The
idea! With the fit of righteous indignation upon
me, I went out and sold every other furniture-
dealer in Titusville a bill of tables; not one of
them escaped. At night, when I had sent the
order home, I set out for Oil City, so as to lose no
valuable time.

It was just the same there. For some reason
they were suspicious of the extension tables, yet
they wanted nothing else. I had to give ironclad
guarantees that they were as represented, which I

did impatiently enough. There was a thunder-
storm raging at the time. The lightning had
struck a tank, and the burning oil ran down a hill

and set the
town on fire.
One end of it
was burning
while I was
canvassing the
other, mental-
ly calculating
how many ex-
tension tables
would be
needed to re-
place those
that were lost.
People did not
seem to have
heard of any
other kind of
furniture in
that country.
Walnut bed-
steads, marble-

"One end of the town was burning while I was
canvassing the other."

top bureaus, turned washstands — they passed them
all by to fall upon the tables with shrill demand. I
made out their case to suit the facts, as I swept

down through that region, scattering extension tables right and left. It was the excitement, I reasoned, the inrush of population from everywhere; probably everybody kept boarders, more every day; had to extend their tables to seat them. I saw a great opportunity and resolutely grasped it. If it was tables they wanted, tables it should be. I let all the rest of the stock go and threw myself on the tables exclusively. Town after town I filled with them. Night after night the mails groaned under the heavy orders for extension tables I sent north. From Allegheny City alone an order of a thousand dollars' worth from a single reputable dealer went home, and I figured in my note-book that night a commission of $50 for myself plus my salary.

I could know nothing of the despatches that were hot on my trail ever since my first order came from Titusville, telling me to stop, let up on the tables, come home, anything; there was a mistake in the price. They never overtook me. My pace was too hot for that. Anyhow, I doubt if I would have paid any attention to them. I had my instructions and was selling according to orders. Business was good, getting better every day. The firm wrote to my customers, but they merely sent back copies of the iron-clad contract. They had seen my instructions, and they knew it was all right.   It was not until I brought up, my last penny gone, in Rochester, near the Ohio line, that the firm established communication with me at last.   Their instructions were brief : to come home and sell no more tables.   They sent $10, but gave me no clew to their curious decision, with things booming as they were.

Being in the field I considered that, whatever was up, I had a better command of the situation. I decided that I would not go home, — at least not until I had sold a few more extension tables while they were in such demand.   I made that $10 go farther than $10 ever went before.   It took me a little way into Ohio, to Youngstown, and then back to Pennsylvania, to Warren and Meadville and Corry.   My previous training in going hungry for days came in handy at last.   In the interests of commerce, I let my dinners go.   So I was enabled to make a final dash to Erie, where I planted my last batch of tables before I went home, happy.

I got home in time to assist in the winding up of the concern.   The iron-clad contracts had done the business.   My customers would not listen to explanations.   When told that the price of those tables was lower than the cost of working up the wood, they replied that it was none of their business.   They had their contracts.   The Allegheny man threatened suit, if I remember rightly, and the firm gave up. Nobody blamed me, for I had sold according to orders; but instead of $450 which I had figured out as my commission, I got seventy-five cents. It was half of what my employer had. He divided squarely, and I could not in reason complain.

I sat in the restaurant where he had explained the situation to me, and tried to telescope my ambitions down to the seventy-five-cent standard, when my eyes fell upon a copy of *Harper's Weekly* that lay on the table. Absent-mindedly I read an advertisement in small type, spelling it over idly while I was trying to think what to do next.

"Wanted," it read, "by the Myers Manufacturing Company, agents to sell a patent flat and fluting iron. Samples 75 cents."

The address was somewhere in John Street, New York. Samples seventy-five cents! I repeated it mechanically. Why, that was just the size of my pile. And right in my line of canvassing, too! In ten minutes it was on the way to New York and I had secured a provisional customer in the cook at the restaurant for an iron that would perform what this one promised, iron the skirt and flute the flounce too. In three days the iron came and proved good. I started in canvassing Jamestown with it, and in a week had secured orders for one hundred and twenty, upon which my profit would be over $80.

Something of business ways must have stuck to
me, after all, from my one excursion into the realm
of trade; for when it came to delivering the goods
and I had no money, I went boldly to a business
man whose wife was on my books, and offered, if
he would send for the irons, to pay for them as I
took them out of the store. He made no bones
about it, but sent for the irons and handed them
over to me to pay for when I could. So men are
made. Commercial character, as it is rated on
'change, I had none before that; but I had after.
How could I disappoint a man like that?

The confidence of the community I had not lost
through my too successful trip as a drummer, at all
events. Propositions came speedily to me to "travel
in" pianos and pumps for local concerns. It never
rains but it pours. An old schoolmate who had
been ordained a clergyman wrote to me from Denmark to find him a charge among the Danish settlements out West. But neither pumps, pianos, nor
parsons had power to swerve me from my chosen
course. With them went bosses and orders; with
the flat-iron cherished independence. When I
had sold out Jamestown, I made a bee-line for Pittsburg, a city that had taken my fancy because of its
brisk business ways. They were brisk indeed.
Grant's second campaign for the Presidency was
in full swing. On my second night in town I went

"I went to hear Horace Greeley address an open-air meeting."

to hear Horace Greeley address an open-air meeting. I can see his noble old head yet above the crowd, and hear his opening appeal. Farther I never got. A marching band of uniformed shouters for Grant had cut right through the crowd. As it passed I felt myself suddenly seized; an oilcloth cape was thrown over my head, a campaign cap jammed after, and I found myself marching away with a torch on my shoulder to the tune of a brass band just ahead. How many others of Mr. Greeley's hearers fared as I did I do not know. The thing seemed so ludicrous (and if I must march I really cared very little whether it was for Greeley or Grant) that I stuck it out, hoping as we went to come somewhere upon my hat, which had been lost in the sudden attack; but I never saw it again.

Speaking of parading, my old desire to roam, that kept cropping out at intervals, paid me a characteristic trick at this time. I was passing through a horse-market when I saw a fine-looking, shapely young horse put up at what seemed a ridiculously low price. Eighteen dollars was the bid, and it was about to be knocked down at that. The October sun was shining warm and bright. A sudden desire to get on the horse and ride out into the wide world, away from the city and the haunts of men, never to come back, seized me. I raised the bid to $19. Almost before I knew, the beast was knocked down to me and I had paid over the money. It left me with exactly $6 to my name.

Leading the animal by the halter, I went down the street and sat on the stoop of the Robinson House to think. With every step, perplexities I hadn't thought of sprang up. In the first place, I could not ride. I had always wanted to, but had never learned. Even if I had been able to, where was I going, and to do what? I couldn't ride around and sell flat-irons. The wide world seemed suddenly a cold and far-off place, and $6 but small backing in an attack upon it, with a hungry horse waiting to be fed. That was only too evident.

'The wide world seemed suddenly a cold and far-off place."

The beast was tearing the hitching-post with its teeth in a way that brooked no delay. Evidently it had a healthy appetite. The conclusion was slowly dawning upon me that I had made a fool of myself, when the man who had bid $18 came by and saw me sitting there. He stopped to ask what was the matter, and I told him frankly. He roared and gave me $18 for the beast. I was glad enough to give it up. I never owned a horse before or since, and I had that less than fifteen minutes; but it was the longest quarter of an hour since I worked in the coal-mine.

The flat-iron did not go in Pittsburg. It was too cheap. During a brief interval I peddled campaign books, but shortly found a more expensive iron, and had five counties in western Pennsylvania allotted to me as territory. There followed a winter of great business. Before it was half over I had achieved a bank account, though how I managed it is a mystery to me till this day. Simple as the reckoning of my daily trade ought to be, by no chance could I ever make it foot up as it should. I tried honestly every night, but the receipts would never square with the expenditures, do what I might. I kept them carefully apart in different pockets, but mixed they would get in spite of all. I had to call it square, however far the footing was out of the way, or sit up all night, which I would not do. I remember well the only time I came out even. I was so astonished that I would not believe it, but had to go all over the account again. That night I slept the sleep of the just. The next morning, when I was starting out on my route with a clean conscience and a clean slate, a shopkeeper rapped on his window as I went by to tell me that

I had given him the previous day a twenty-dollar bill for a ten, in making change. After that I gave up trying.

I was no longer alone. From Buffalo my old chum Ronne had come, hearing that I was doing well, to join me, and from Denmark an old school-fellow, whose life at twenty-two had been wrecked by drink and who wrote begging to be allowed to come. His mother pleaded for him too, but it was not needed. He had enclosed in his letter the strongest talisman of all, a letter written by Elizabeth in the long ago when we were children together. I have it yet. He came, and I tried hard to break him of his failing. But I had undertaken a job that was too big for me. Upon my return from a Western trip I found that he had taken to drinking again, and in his cups had enlisted. His curse followed him into the army. He rose to the rank of sergeant, only to fall again and suffer degradation. The other day he shot himself at the post where he was stationed, after nearly thirty years of service. Yet in all his ups and downs he never forgot his home. While his mother lived he helped support her in far-off Denmark; and when she was gone, no month passed that he did not send home the half of his wages for the support of his crippled sister in the old town. Charles was not bad. He was a poor, helpless, unhappy boy, who came to me

for help, and I had none to give, God pity him and
me.

The Western trip I spoke of was my undoing.
Puffed up by my success as a salesman, I yielded in
an evil hour to the blandishments of my manufac-
turers, and accepted the general agency of the State
of Illinois, with headquarters in Chicago.   It sounded
well, but it did not work well.   Chicago had not yet
got upon its feet after the great fire; and its young
men were too sharp for me.   In six weeks they had
cleaned me out bodily, had run away with my irons
and with money they borrowed of me to start them
in business.   I returned to Pittsburg as poor as
ever, to find that the agents I had left behind in my
Pennsylvania territory had dealt with me after the
same fashion.   The firm for which I worked had
connived at the frauds.   My friends had left me.
The one I spoke of was in the army.   Ronne had
given up in discouragement, and was at work in a
rolling-mill.   In the utter wreck of all my hopes I
was alone again.

Angry and sore, I went up the Allegheny River,
with no definite purpose in mind except to get away
from everybody I knew.   At Franklin I fell ill with
a sneaking fever.   It was while I lay helpless in a
lonely tavern by the riverside that the crushing blow
fell.   Letters from home, sent on from Pittsburg,
told me that Elizabeth was to be married.   A cav-

alry officer who was in charge of the border police, a dashing fellow and a good soldier, had won her heart. The wedding was to be in the summer. It was then the last week in April. At the thought I turned my face to the wall, and hoped that I might die.

But one does not die of love at twenty-four. The days that passed slowly saw me leave my sick-bed and limp down to the river on sunny days, to sit and watch the stream listlessly for hours, hoping nothing, grasping nothing, except that it was all over. In all my misadventures that was the one thing I had never dreamed of. If I did, I as quickly banished the thought as preposterous. That she should be another's bride seemed so utterly impossible that, sick and feeble as I was, I laughed it to scorn even then; whereat I fell to reading the fatal letter again, and trying to grasp its meaning. It made it all only the more perplexing that I should not know who he was or what he was. I had never heard of him before, in that town where I thought I knew every living soul. That he must be a noble fellow I knew, or he could not have won her; but who—why—what—what had come over everything in such a short time, and what was this ugly dream that was setting my brain awhirl and shutting out the sunlight and the day? Presently I was in a relapse, and it was all darkness to me, and oblivion.

When at last I got well enough to travel, I set my face toward the east, and journeyed on foot through the northern coal regions of Pennsylvania by slow stages, caring little whither I went, and earning just enough by peddling flat-irons to pay my way. It was spring when I started; the autumn tints were on the leaves when I brought up in New York at last, as nearly restored as youth and the long tramp had power to do. But the restless energy that had made of me a successful salesman was gone. I thought only, if I thought at all, of finding some quiet place where I could sit and see the world go by that concerned me no longer. With a dim idea of being sent into the farthest wilds as an operator, I went to a business college on Fourth Avenue and paid $20 to learn telegraphing. It was the last money I had. I attended the school in the afternoon. In the morning I peddled flat-irons, earning money for my board, and so made out.

One day, while I was so occupied, I saw among the "want" advertisements in a newspaper one offering the position of city editor on a Long Island City weekly to a competent man. Something of my old ambition stirred within me. It did not occur to me that city editors were not usually obtained by advertising, still less that I was not competent, hav ing only the vaguest notions of what the functions of a city editor might be. I applied for the job, and got it at once. Eight dollars a week was to be my salary; my job, to fill the local column and attend to the affairs of Hunter's Point and Blissville generally, politics excluded. The editor attended to that. In twenty-four hours I was hard at work writing up my then most ill-favored bailiwick. It is none too fine yet, but in those days, when every nuisance crowded out of New York found refuge there, it stunk to heaven.

Certainly I had entered journalism by the back door, very far back at that, when I joined the staff of the *Review*. Signs of that appeared speedily, and multiplied day by day. On the third day of my employment I beheld the editor-in-chief being thrashed down the street by an irate coachman whom he had offended, and when, in a spirit of loyalty, I would have cast in my lot with him, I was held back by one of the printers with the laughing comment that that was his daily diet and that it was good for him. That was the only way any one ever got any satisfaction or anything else out of him. Judging from the goings on about the office in the two weeks I was there, he must have been extensively in debt to all sorts of people who were trying to collect. When, on my second deferred pay-day, I met him on the stairs, propelled by his washer-woman, who brought her basket down on his head with every step he took, calling upon the populace (the stairs were outside the building) to witness just punishment meted out to him for failing to pay for the washing of his shirts, I rightly concluded that the city editor's claim stood no show. I left him owing me two weeks' pay, but I freely forgive him. I think I got my money's worth of experience. I did not let grass grow under my feet as "city editor." Hunter's Point had received for once a thorough raking over, and I my first lesson in hunting the elusive item and, when found, making a note of it.

Except for a Newfoundland pup which some one had given me, I went back over the river as poor as I had come. The dog proved rather a doubtful possession as the days went by. Its appetite was tremendous, and its preference for my society embarrassingly unrestrained. It would not be content to sleep anywhere else than in my room. If I put it out in the yard, it forthwith organized a search for me in which the entire neighborhood was compelled to take part, willy-nilly. Its manner of doing it boomed the local trade in hair-brushes and mantel bric-à-brac, but brought on complications with the landlord in the morning that usually resulted in the departure of Bob and myself for other pastures. Part with him I could not; for Bob loved me. Once I tried, when it seemed that there was no choice. I had been put out for perhaps the tenth time, and I had no more money left to provide for our keep. A Wall Street broker had advertised for a watch-dog, and I went with Bob to see him. But when he would have counted the three gold pieces he offered into my hand, I saw Bob's honest brown eyes watching me with a look of such faithful affection that I dropped the coins as if they burned, and caught him about the neck to tell him that we would never part. Bob put his huge paws on my shoulders, licked my face, and barked such a joyous bark of challenge to the world in general that even the Wall Street man was touched.

" I guess you are too good friends to part," he said. And so we were.

We left Wall Street and its gold behind to go out and starve together. Literally we did that in the days that followed. I had taken to peddling books, an illustrated Dickens issued by the Harpers, but I barely earned enough by it to keep life in us and a transient roof over our heads. I call it transient because it was rarely the same two nights together, for causes which I have explained. In the day Bob made out rather better than I. He could always coax a supper out of the servant at the basement gate by his curvetings and tricks, while I pleaded vainly and hungrily with the mistress at the front door. Dickens was a drug in the market. A curious fatality had given me a copy of " Hard

Times " to canvass with. I think no amount of good fortune could turn my head while it stands in my bookcase. One look at it brings back too vividly that day when Bob and I had gone, desperate and breakfastless, from the last bed we might know for many days, to try to sell it and so get the means to keep us for another twenty-four hours.

It was not only breakfast we lacked. The day before we had had only a crust together. Two days without food is not good preparation for a day's canvassing. We did the best we could. Bob stood by and wagged his tail persuasively while I did the talking; but luck was dead against us, and " Hard Times " stuck to us for all we tried. Evening came and found us down by the Cooper Institute, with never a cent. Faint with hunger, I sat down on the steps under the illuminated clock, while Bob stretched himself at my feet. He had beguiled the cook in one of the last houses we called at, and his stomach was filled. From the corner I had looked on enviously. For me there was no supper, as there had been no dinner and no breakfast. To-morrow there was another day of starvation. How long was this to last? Was it any use to keep up a struggle so hopeless? From this very spot I had gone, hungry and wrathful, three years before when the dining Frenchmen for whom I wanted to fight thrust me forth from their company. Three wasted years! Then I had one cent in my pocket, I remembered. To-day I had not even so much. I was bankrupt in hope

"Hard Times."

and purpose. Nothing had gone right; nothing would ever go right; and, worse, I did not care. I drummed moodily upon my book. Wasted! Yes, that was right. My life was wasted, utterly wasted.

A voice hailed me by name, and Bob sat up, looking attentively at me for his cue as to the treatment of the owner of it. I recognized in him the principal of the telegraph school where I had gone until my money gave out. He seemed suddenly struck by something.

"Why, what are you doing here?" he asked. I told him Bob and I were just resting after a day of canvassing.

"Books!" he snorted. "I guess they won't make you rich. Now, how would you like to be a reporter, if you have got nothing better to do? The manager of a news agency down town asked me to-day to find him a bright young fellow whom he could break in. It isn't much — $10 a week to start with. But it is better than peddling books, I know."

He poked over the book in my hand and read the title. "Hard Times," he said, with a little laugh. "I guess so. What do you say? I think you will do. Better come along and let me give you a note to him now."

As in a dream, I walked across the street with him to his office and got the letter which was to make me, half-starved and homeless, rich as Crœsus, it seemed to me. Bob went along, and before I departed from the school a better home than I could give him was found for him with my benefactor. I

was to bring him the next day.   I had to admit that
it was best so.   That night, the last which Bob
and I spent together, we walked up and down
Broadway, where there was quiet, thinking it over.
What had happened had stirred me profoundly.
For the second time I saw a hand held out to save
me from wreck just when it seemed inevitable;
and I knew it for His hand, to whose will I was
at last beginning to bow in humility that had been a
stranger to me before.   It had ever been my own
will, my own way, upon which I insisted.   In the
shadow of Grace Church I bowed my head against the
granite wall of the gray tower and prayed for strength
to do the work which I had so long and arduously
sought and which had now come to me; the while
Bob sat and looked on, saying clearly enough with
his wagging tail that he did not know what was
going on, but that he was sure it was all right.
Then we resumed our wanderings.   One thought,
and only one, I had room for.   I did not pursue it;
it walked with me wherever I went: She was not
married yet.   Not yet.   When the sun rose, I
washed my face and hands in a dog's drinking-
trough, pulled my clothes into such shape as I could,
and went with Bob to his new home.   That parting
over, I walked down to 23 Park Row and delivered
my letter to the desk editor in the New York News
Association, up on the top floor.

He looked me over a little doubtfully, but evidently impressed with the early hours I kept, told me that I might try. He waved me to a desk, bidding me wait until he had made out his morning book of assignments; and with such scant ceremony was I finally introduced to Newspaper Row, that had been to me like an enchanted land. After twenty-seven years of hard work in it, during which I have been behind the scenes of most of the plays that go to make up the sum of the life of the metropolis, it exercises the old spell over me yet. If my sympathies need quickening, my point of view adjusting, I have only to go down to Park Row at eventide, when the crowds are hurrying homeward and the City Hall clock is lighted, particularly when the snow lies on the grass in the park, and stand watching them awhile, to find all things coming right. It is Bob who stands by and watches with me then, as on that night.

The assignment that fell to my lot when the book was made out, the first against which my name was written in a New York editor's book, was a lunch of some sort at the Astor House. I have forgotten what was the special occasion. I remember the bearskin hats of the Old Guard in it, but little else. In a kind of haze, I beheld half the savory viands of earth spread under the eyes and nostrils of a man who had not tasted food for the third day.

I did not ask for any.   I had reached that stage of
starvation that is like the still centre of a cyclone,
when no hunger is felt.   But it may be that a touch
of it all crept into my report ; for when the editor
had read it, he said briefly : —

"You will do.   Take that desk, and report at ten
every morning, sharp."

That night, when I was dismissed from the office,
I went up the Bowery to No. 185, where a Danish
family kept a boarding-house up under the roof.   I
had work and wages now, and could pay.   On the
stairs I fell in a swoon and lay there till some one
stumbled over me in the dark and carried me in.
My strength had at last given out.

So began my life as a newspaper man.

CHAPTER VI

IN WHICH I BECOME AN EDITOR AND RECEIVE
MY FIRST LOVE LETTER

I HAD my hands full that winter. The profession
I had entered by so thorny a path did not prove to
be a bed of roses. But I was not looking for roses.
I doubt if I would have known what to do with
them had there been any. Hard work and hard
knocks had been my portion heretofore, and I was
fairly trained down to that. Besides, now that the
question where the next meal was to come from
did not loom up whichever way I looked, the thing
for me was to be at work hard enough and long
enough to keep from thinking. With every letter
from home I expected to hear that she was married,
and then — I never got any farther. A furious kind
of energy took possession of me at the mere idea,
and I threw myself upon my work in a way that
speedily earned for me the name of a good reporter.
"Good" had reference to the quantity of work
done rather than to the quality of it. That was of
less account than our ability to "get around" to our
assignments; necessarily so, for we mostly had **six**

or seven of an evening to attend, our route extend-
ing often from Harlem clear down to the Bowery.
So that they were nearly "on a line," we were supposed to have no cause of complaint.   Our office
sold news to morning and evening papers both, and
our working day, which began at 10 A.M., was seldom over until one or two o'clock the next morning.
Three reporters had to attend to all the general
news of the city that did not come through the
regular department channels.

A queerly assorted trio we were: "Doc" Lynch,
who had graduated from the medical school to
Bohemia, following a natural bent, I suppose;
Crafts, a Maine boy of angular frame and prodigious
self-confidence; and myself.   Lynch I have lost
sight of long ago.   Crafts, I am told, is rich and
prosperous, the owner of a Western newspaper.
That was bound to happen to him.   I remember
him in the darkest days of that winter, when to
small pay, hard work, and long hours had been
added an attack of measles that kept him in bed in
his desolate boarding-house, far from kindred and
friends.   "Doc" and I had run in on a stolen visit
to fill their place as well as we might.   We sat
around trying to look as cheerful as we could and
succeeding very poorly; but Crafts's belief in himself and his star soared above any trivialities of
present discouragement.   I see him now rising on

his elbow and transfixing the two of us with long,
prophetic forefinger : —

"The secret of my success," he said, impressively,
"I lay to —"

We never found out to what he laid it, for we
both burst out laughing, and Crafts, after a passing
look of surprise, joined in.   But that finger prophe-
sied truly.   His pluck won the day, and won it
fairly.   They were two good comrades in a tight
place.   I shouldn't want any better.

Running around was only working off steam, of
which we had plenty.   The long rides, on Harlem
assignments, in horse-cars with straw in the bottom
that didn't keep our feet from freezing until all feeling in them was gone, were worse, a good deal.
At the mere thought of them I fall to nursing my
toes for reminiscent pangs.   However, I had at least
enough to eat.   At the downtown Delmonico's and
the other swell restaurants through the windows of
which I had so often gazed with hungry eyes, I now
sometimes sat at big spreads and public dinners,
never without thinking of the old days and the poor
fellows who might then be having my hard luck.
It was not so long since that I could have forgotten.
I bit a mark in the Mulberry Bend, too, as my professional engagements took me that way, promising
myself that the day should come when I would have
time to attend to it.   For the rest, if I had an hour

to spare, I put it in at the telegraph instrument. I had still the notion that it might not be labor lost. And though I never had professional use for it, it did come handy to me as a reporter more than once. There is scarcely anything one can learn that will not sooner or later be useful to a newspaper man, if he is himself of the kind that wants to be useful.

Along in the spring some politicians in South Brooklyn who had started a weekly newspaper to boom their own fortunes found themselves in need of a reporter, and were told of a "young Dutchman" who might make things go. I was that "Dutchman." They offered me $15 a week, and on May, 20, 1874, I carried my grip across the river, and, all unconscious that I was on the turning tide in my fortunes, cast in my lot with "Beecher's crowd," as the boys in the office said derisively when I left them.

In two weeks I was the editor of the paper. That was not a vote of confidence, but pure economy on the part of my owners. They saved forty dollars a week by giving me twenty-five and the name of editor. The idea of an editor in anything but the name I do not suppose had ever entered their minds. Theirs was an "organ," and for the purposes for which they had started it they thought themselves abundantly able to run it. I, on my part, quickly grew high notions of editorial inde-

K

pendence. Their purposes had nothing to do with it. The two views proved irreconcilable. They clashed quite regularly, and perhaps it was as much that they were tired of the editor as that the paper was a drag upon them that made them throw it up after the fall elections, in which they won. The press and the engine were seized for debt. The last issue of the *South Brooklyn News* had been put upon the street, and I went to the city to make a bargain with the foundryman for the type. It was in the closing days of the year. Christmas was at the door, with its memories. Tired and disheartened, I was on my way back, my business done, as the bells rang in the Holy Eve. I stood at the bow of a Fulton Street ferryboat listening sadly to them, and watched the lights of the city kindling alongshore. Of them all not one was for me. It was all over, and I should have to strike a new trail. Where would that lead? What did it matter, anyhow? Nobody cared. Why should I?

A beautiful meteor shot out of the heavens overhead and spanned the river with a shining arc. I watched it sail slowly over Williamsburg, its trail glowing bright against the dark sky, and mechanically the old wish rose to my lips. It was a superstition with us when we were children that if we were quick enough to " wish out " before the star was extinguished, the wish would come true. I had tried a hundred times, always to fail; but for once I had ample time. A bitter sigh smothered the wish, half uttered. My chance had come too late. Even now she might be another man's wife, and I — I had just made another failure of it, as usual.

It had never happened in all the holiday seasons I had been away that a letter from home had reached me in time for Christmas Eve, and it was a sore subject with me. For it was ever the dearest in the year to me, and is now. But that evening, when I came home, in a very ill humor, for the first time I found the coveted letter. It told me of the death of my two older brothers and of my favorite aunt. In a postscript my father added that Lieutenant B——, Elizabeth's affianced husband, had died in the city hospital at Copenhagen. She herself was living among strangers. She had chosen her lover when the family demanded of her that she give him up as a hopeless invalid. They thought it all for her good. Of her I should have expected nothing less. But she shall tell the story of that herself.

I read the letter through, then lay down upon my bed and wept. When I arose, it was to go to the owners of my paper with a proposition to buy it. They laughed at me at first; asked to see my money. As a reporter for the news bureau I had saved up $75, rather because I had no time to spend it than with any definite notion of what I was going to do with it. This I offered to them, and pointed out that the sale of the old type, which was all that was left of the paper beside the good-will, would bring no more. One of them, more reasonable than the rest — the one who had gener-ally paid the scores while the others took the tricks — was disposed to listen. The upshot of it was that I bought the paper for $650, giving notes for the rest, to be paid when I could. If I could not, they were not much out. And then, again, I might succeed.

I did; by what effort I hesitate to set down here lest I be not believed. The *News* was a big four-page sheet. Literally every word in it I wrote myself. I was my own editor, reporter, publisher, and advertising agent. My pen kept two printers busy all the week, and left me time to canvass for advertisements, attend meetings, and gather the news. Friday night the local undertaker, who advertised in the paper and paid in kind, took the forms over to New York, where the presswork was done. In the early morning hours I shouldered the edition — it was not very large in those days — and carried it from Spruce Street down to Fulton Ferry, and then home on a Fifth Avenue car. I recall with what inward rage I submitted to being held up by every chance policeman and prodded facetiously in the ribs with remarks about the " old man's millions," etc. Once or twice it boiled over and I was threatened with summary arrest. When I got home, I slept on the counter with the edition for my pillow, in order to be up with the first gleam of daylight to skirmish for newsboys. I gathered them in from street and avenue, compelled them to come in if they were not willing, and made such inducements for them that shortly South Brooklyn resounded with the cry of " News " from sunrise to sunset on Saturday. The politicians who had been laughing at my " weekly funeral " beheld with amazement the paper thrust under their noses at every step. They heard its praises, or the other thing, sung on every hand. From their point of view it was the same thing: the paper was talked of. Their utmost effort had failed of that. When, on June 5, Her birthday, I paid down in hard cash what was left of the purchase sum and hoisted the flag over an independent newspaper, freed from debt, they came around with honeyed speeches to make friends. I scarcely heard them. Deep down in my soul a voice kept repeating unceasingly: Elizabeth is free! She is free, free! That night, in the seclusion of my den, clutching grimly the ladder upon which I had at last got my feet, I resolved that I would reach the top, or die climb·

ing. The morning sun shone through my window and found me sleepless, pouring out my heart to her, four thousand miles away.

I carried the letter to the post-office myself, and waited till I saw it started on its long journey. I stood watching the carrier till he turned the corner; then went back to my work.

To that work there had been added a fresh spur just when I was at last free from all trammels.

Brother Simmons.
[The Rev. Ichabod Simmons.]

The other strongest of human emotions had been stirred within me. In a Methodist revival — it was in the old Eighteenth Street Church — I had fallen under the spell of the preacher's fiery eloquence. Brother Simmons was of the old circuit-riders' stock, albeit their day was long past in our staid community. He had all their power, for the spirit burned within him; and he brought me to the altar quickly, though in my own case conversion refused to work the prescribed amount of agony. Perhaps it was because I had heard Mr. Beecher question the correctness of the prescription. When a man travelling in the road found out, he said, that he had gone wrong, he did not usually roll in the dust and agonize over his mistake; he just turned around and went the other way. It struck me so, but none the less with deep conviction. In fact, with the heat of the convert, I decided on the spot to throw up my editorial work and take to preaching. But Brother Simmons would not hear of it.

"No, no, Jacob," he said; "not that. We have preachers enough. What the world needs is consecrated pens."

Then and there I consecrated mine. I wish I could honestly say that it has always come up to the high ideal set it then. I can say, though, that it has ever striven toward it, and that scarce a day has passed since that I have not thought of the charge then laid upon it and upon me.

The immediate result was a campaign for reform that made the town stare. It struck the politicians first. They were Democrats, and I was running a Democratic paper. I did it *con amore*, too, for it was in the days of the scandals of Grant's second term, and the disgrace of it was foul. So far we were agreed. But it happened that the chief obstacle to Democratic success in the Twenty-second Ward, where my paper was located, was the police captain of the precinct, John Mackellar, who died the other day as Deputy Chief of the Borough of Brooklyn. Mackellar was a Republican of a pronounced type and a good deal of a politician besides. Therefore he must go. But he was my friend. I had but two in the entire neighborhood who really cared for me — Edward Wells, clerk in a drug-store across the street, who was of my own age, and Mackellar. Between us had sprung up a strong attachment, and I could not think of having Mackellar removed, particularly as he had done nothing to deserve it. He was a good policeman. I told the bosses so. They insisted; pleaded political expedience. I told them I would not allow it, and when they went ahead in spite of me, told the truth about it in my paper. The Twenty-second was really a Republican ward. The attitude of the *News* killed the job.

The Democratic bosses were indignant.

" How can we run the ward with you acting that way? " they asked. I told them I did not care if they didn't. I could run it better myself, it seemed.

They said nothing. They had other resources. The chief of them — he was a judge — came around and had a friendly talk with me. He showed me that I was going against my own interest. I was just starting out in life. I had energy, education. They were qualities that in politics were convertible into gold, much gold, if I would but follow him and his fortunes.

" I never had an education," he said. " I need you. If you will stick to me, I will make you rich."

I think he meant it. He certainly could have done so had he chosen. He himself died rich. He was not a bad fellow, as bosses go. But I did not like boss politics. And the bait did not tempt me. I never wanted to be rich. I am afraid it would make me grasping; I think I am built that way. Anyhow, it is too much bother. I wanted to run my own paper, and I told him so.

" Well," he said, " you are young. Think it over."

It was some time after that I read in a newspaper, upon returning from a hunting trip to Staten Island, that I had been that day appointed an interpreter in my friend the judge's court, at a salary of $100 a month. I went to him and asked him what it meant.

" Well," he said, " we need an interpreter. There are a good many Scandinavians and Germans in my district. You know their language? "

" But," I protested, " I have no time to go interpreting police court cases. I don't want the office."

He pushed me out with a friendly shoulder-pat. " You go back and wait till I send for you. We can lump the cases, and we won't need you every day."

In fact, they did not need me more than two or

three times that month, at the end of which I drew
my pay with many qualms of conscience. My services were certainly not worth the money I received.
Such is the soothing power of public "pap": on the
second pay-day, though I had performed even less
service, I did not feel nearly so bad about it. My
third check I drew as a matter of course. I was
"one of the boys" now, and treated with familiarity
by men whom I did not like a bit, and who, I am
sure, did not like me. But the cordiality did not
long endure. It soon appeared that the interpreter
in the judge's court had other duties than merely to
see justice done to helpless foreigners; among them
to see things politically as His Honor did. I did
not. A ruction followed speedily — I think it was
about our old friend Mackellar — that wound up by
his calling me an ingrate. It was a favorite word
of his, as I have noticed it is of all bosses, and it
meant everything reprehensible. He did not discharge me; he couldn't. I was as much a part of
the court as he was, having been appointed under a
State law. But the power of the Legislature that
had created me was invoked to kill me, and, for
appearance's sake, the office. Before it adjourned,
the same Legislature resurrected the office, but not
me. So contradictory is human nature that by that
time I was quite ready to fight for my "rights."
But for once I was outclassed. The judge and the

Legislature were too many for me, and I retired as gracefully as I could.

So ceased my career as a public officer, and forever. It was the only office I ever held, and I do not want another. I am ashamed yet, twenty-five years after, of having held that one. Because, however I try to gloss it over, I was, while I held it, a sinecurist, pure and simple.

However, it did not dampen my zeal for reform in the least. That encompassed the whole range of my little world; nor would it brook delay even for a minute. It did not consider ways and means, and was in nowise tempered with discretion. Looking back now, it seems strange that I never was made to figure in the police court in those days in another capacity than that of interpreter. Not that I did anything for which I should have been rightly jailed. But people will object to being dragged by the hair even in the ways of reform. When the grocer on my corner complained that he was being ruined by "beats" who did not pay their bills and thereby compelled him to charge those who did pay more, in order that he might live, I started in at once to make those beats pay up. I gave notice, in a plain statement of the case in my editorial columns, that they must settle their scores for the sake of the grocer and the general good, or I would publish their names. I was as good as my word. I not only published the list of them, but how much and how long they owed it, and called upon them to pay or move out of the ward.

Did they move? Well, no! Perhaps it was too much to expect. They were comfortable. They stayed to poison the mind of the town against the man who was lying awake nights to serve it; in which laudable effort they were ably seconded by the corner grocer. I record without regret the subsequent failure of that tradesman. There were several things wrong with the details of my campaign, — for one thing, I had omitted to include him among the beats, — but in its large lines we can all agree that it was right. It was only another illustration of the difficulty of reducing high preaching to practice. Instead of society hailing me as its saviour, I grew personally unpopular. I doubt if I had another friend in the world beside the two I have mentioned. But the circulation of my paper grew enormously. It was doubled and trebled week by week — a fact which I accepted as public recognition of the righteousness of my cause. I was wrong in that. The fact was that ours was a community of people with a normally healthy appetite for knowing one's neighbor's business. I suppose the thing has been mistaken before by inexperience for moral enthusiasm, and will be again.

I must stop here to tell the reason why I would

not convict the meanest thief on circumstantial
evidence. I would rather let a thousand go free
than risk with one what I risked and shudder yet
to think of. There had been some public excitement that summer about mad dogs, especially spitz-
dogs. A good many persons had been bitten, and
the authorities of Massachusetts, if I remember
rightly, had put that particular breed under the
ban as dangerous at all times. There was one
always prowling about the lot behind my office,
through which the way led to my boarding-house,
and, when it snapped at my leg in passing one
day, I determined to kill it in the interest of public
safety. I sent my office-boy out to buy a handful of
buckshot, and, when he brought it, set about loading
both barrels of the fowling-piece that stood in my
office. While I was so occupied, my friend the
drug-clerk came in, and wanted to know what I was
up to. Shooting a dog, I said, and he laughed:—

"Looks as though you were going gunning for
your beats."

I echoed his laugh thoughtlessly enough; but
the thing reminded me that it was unlawful to
shoot within the city limits, and I sent the boy up
to the station to tell the captain to never mind if
he heard shooting around: I was going out for a
dog. With that I went forth upon my quest.

The dog was there; but he escaped before I

could get a shot at him.   He dodged, growling and snapping, among the weeds, and at last ran into a large enclosed lot in which there were stacks of lumber and junk and many hiding-places.   I knew that he could not get out, for the board fence was high and tight.   So I went in and shut the door after me, and had him.

I should have said before that among my enemies was a worthless fellow, a hanger-on of the local political machine, who had that afternoon been in the office annoying me with his loud and boisterous talk.   He was drunk, and as there were some people to see me, I put him out.   He persisted in coming back, and I finally told him, in the hearing of a dozen persons, to go about his business, or some serious harm would befall him.   If I connected any idea with it, it was to call a policeman; but I left them to infer something worse, I suppose.   Getting arrested was not very serious business with him. He went out, swearing.

It was twilight when I began my still-hunt for the spitz in the lumber lot, and the outlines of things were more or less vague ; but I followed the dog about until at last I made him out standing on a pile of boards a little way off.   It was my chance. I raised the gun quickly and took aim.   I had both barrels cocked and my finger on the trigger, when something told me quite distinctly not to shoot; to put down the gun and go closer. I did so, and found, not the dog as I thought, but my enemy whom I had threatened but an hour or two before, asleep at full length on the stack, with his coat rolled under his head for a pillow. It was his white shirt-bosom which I had mistaken in the twilight for the spitz dog.

He never knew of his peril. I saw my own at a glance, and it appalled me. Stranger that I was, hated and denounced by many who would have posed as victims of my violence; with this record against me of threatening the man whom I would be accused of having slain an hour later; with my two only friends compelled to give evidence which would make me out as artfully plotting murder under the shield of a palpable invention — for who ever heard of any one notifying the police that he was going to shoot a dog? — with no family connection or previous good character to build a defence upon: where would have been my chance of escape? What stronger chain of circumstantial evidence could have been woven to bring me, an innocent man, to the gallows? I have often wished to forget that evening by the sleeping man in the lumber lot. I cannot even now write calmly about it. Many months passed before I could persuade myself to touch my gun, fond as I had always been of carrying it through the woods.

Of all this the beats knew nothing. They kept up their warfare of backbiting and of raising petty ructions at the office when I was not there, until I hit upon the plan of putting Pat in charge. Pat was a typical Irish coal-heaver, who would a sight rather fight than eat. There was a coal office in the building, and Pat was generally hanging around, looking for a job. I paid him a dollar a week to keep the office clear of intruders, and after that there was no trouble. There was never any fighting, either. The mere appearance of Pat in the doorway was enough, to his great disgust. It was a success as far as preserving the peace of the office was concerned. But with it there grew up, unknown to me, an impression that personally I would not fight, and the courage of the beats rose correspondingly. They determined to ambush me and have it out with me. One wintry Saturday night, when I was alone in the office closing up the business of the week, they met on the opposite corner to see me get a thrashing. One of their number, a giant in stature, but the biggest coward of the lot, was to administer it. He was fitted out with an immense hickory club for the purpose, and to nerve his arm they filled him with drink.

My office had a large window running the whole length of the front, with a sill knee-high that made a very good seat when chairs were scarce. Only one had to be careful not to lean against the window. It was made of small panes set in a slight wooden framework, which every strong wind blew out or in, and I was in constant dread lest the whole thing should collapse. On that particular night the window was covered with a heavy hoarfrost, so that it was quite impossible to see from outside what was going on within, or *vice versa*. From my seat behind the desk I caught sight through the door, as it was opened by a chance caller, of the gang on the opposite corner, with Jones and his hickory club, and knew what was coming. I knew Jones, too, and awaited his début as a fighter with some curiosity.

He came over, bravely enough, after the fifth or sixth drink, opened the door, and marched in with the tread of a grenadier. But the moment it fell to behind him, he stood and shook so that the club fairly rattled on the floor. Outside the gang were hugging their sides in expectation of what was coming.

"Well, Jones," I said, "what is it?"

He mumbled something so tremulously and incoherently that I felt really sorry for him. Jones was not a bad fellow, though he was in bad company just then. I told him so, and that it would be best for him to go out quietly, or he might hurt himself. He seemed to be relieved at the suggestion, and

L

when I went from behind the counter and led him toward the door, he went willingly enough. But as I put my hand on the latch he remembered his errand, and, with a sudden plucking up of courage at the thought of the waiting gang, he raised the stick to strike at me.

Honestly, I didn't touch the man with a finger. I suppose he stumbled over the sill, as I had sometimes done in my sober senses. Whatever the cause, he fell against the window, and out with him it went, the whole of the glass front, with a crash that resounded from one end of the avenue to the other, and brought neighbors and policemen, among them my friend the captain, on a run to the store. In the midst of the wreck lay Jones, moaning feebly that his back was broken. The beats crowded around with loud outcry.

" He threw him out of the window," they cried. " We saw him do it!   Through window and all, threw him bodily!   Did he not, Jones ? "

Jones, who was being picked up and carried into my office, where they laid him on the counter while they sent in haste for a doctor, nodded that it was so.   Probably he thought it was.   I cannot even blame the beats.   It must have seemed to them that I threw him out.   They called upon the captain with vehement demand to arrest me for murder.   I looked at him; his face was serious.

"Why, I didn't touch him," I said indignantly. "He must have fallen."

"Fallen!" they shouted. "We saw him come flying through. Fallen! Look at the window!" And indeed it was a sorry sight.

Dr. Howe came with his instrument box, and the crowd increased. The doctor was a young man who had been very much amused by my battle with the beats, and, though he professed no special friendship for me, had no respect for the others. He felt the groaning patient over, punched him here and there, looked surprised, and felt again. Then he winked one eye at the captain and me.

"Jones," he said, "get up! There is nothing the matter with you. Go and get sober."

The beats stood speechless.

"He came right through this window," they began. "We saw him—"

"Something has come through the window, evidently," said the captain, with asperity, "and broken it. Who is to pay for it? If you say it was Jones, it is my duty to hold you as witnesses, if Mr. Riis makes a charge of disorderly conduct against him, as I suppose he will." He trod hard on my toe. "A man cannot jump through another man's window like that. Here, let me—"

But they were gone. I never heard from them again. But ever after the reputation clung to me of being a terrible fighter when roused. Jones swore to it, drunk or sober. Twenty witnesses backed him up. I was able to discharge Pat that week. There was never an ill word in my street after that. I suppose my renown as a scrapper survives yet in the old ward. As in the other case, the chain of circumstantial evidence was perfect. No link was missing. None could have been forged to make it stronger.

I wouldn't hang a dog on such evidence. And I think I am justified in taking that stand.

The summer and fall had worn away, and no word had come from home. Mother, who knew, gave no sign. Every day, when the letter-carrier came up the street, my hopes rose high until he had passed. The letter I longed for never came. It was farthest from my thoughts when, one night in the closing days of a hot political campaign, I went to my office and found it lying there. I knew by the throbbing of my heart what it was the instant I saw it. I think I sat as much as a quarter of an hour staring dumbly at the unopened envelope. Then I arose slowly, like one grown suddenly old, put it in my pocket, and stumbled homeward, walking as if in a dream. I went up to my room and locked myself in.

It lies before me as I write, that blessed letter, the first love-letter I had ever received; much faded and worn, and patched in many places to keep it together. The queer row of foreign stamps climbing over one another — she told me afterward that

The Letter.

she had no idea how many were needed for a letter to America, and was afraid to ask, so she put on three times more than would have been enough — and the address in her fair round hand,

MR. JACOB A. RIIS,
Editor South Brooklyn News,
Fifth Avenue cor. Ninth Street,
Brooklyn, N. Y.,
North America,

the postmark of the little town of Hadersleben, where she was teaching school, the old-fashioned shape of the envelope — they all then and there entered into my life and became part of it, to abide

forever with light and joy and thanksgiving.   How
much of sunshine one little letter can contain!   Six
years seemed all at once the merest breath of time
to have waited for it.   Toil, hardship, trouble —
with that letter in my keep?   I laughed out loud at
the thought.   The sound of my own voice sobered
me.   I knelt down and prayed long and fervently
that I might strive with all my might to deserve the
great happiness that had come to me.

The stars were long out when my landlord, who
had heard my restless walk overhead, knocked to
ask if anything was the matter.   He must have
seen it in my face when he opened the door, for he
took a sidelong step, shading his eyes from the
lamp to get a better look, and held out his hand.

"Wish you joy, old man," he said heartily.
"Tell us of it, will you?"   And I did.

It is true that all the world loves a lover.   It
smiled upon me all day long, and I smiled back.
Even the beats looked askance at me no longer.
The politicians who came offering to buy the
influence of my paper in the election were allowed to escape with their lives.   I wrote — I
think I wrote to her every day.   At least that is
what I do now when I go away from home.   She
laughs when she tells me that in the first letter I
spoke of coming home in a year.   Meanwhile, according to her wish, we were to say nothing about

it. In the second letter I decided upon the following spring. In the third I spoke of perhaps going in the winter. The fourth and fifth preferred the early winter. The sixth reached her from Hamburg, on the heels of a telegram announcing that I had that day arrived in Frisia.

What had happened was that just at the right moment the politicians had concluded, upon the evidence of the recent elections, that they could not allow an independent paper in the ward, and had offered to buy it outright. I was dreadfully overworked. The doctor urged a change. I did not need much urging. So I sold the paper for five times what I had paid for it, and took the first steamer for home. Only the other day, when I was lecturing in Chicago, a woman came up and asked if I was the Riis she had travelled with on a Hamburg steamer twenty-five years before, and who was going home to be married. She had never forgotten how happy he was. She and the rest of the passengers held it to be their duty to warn me that "She" might not turn out as nice as I thought she was.

"I guess we might have spared ourselves the trouble," she said, looking me over.

Yes, they might. But I shall have to put off telling of that till next time. And I shall let Elizabeth, my Elizabeth now, tell her part of it in her own way.

CHAPTER VII

How well I remember the days of which my husband has written — our childhood in the old Danish town where to this day, in spite of my love for America, the air seems fresher, the meadows greener, the sea more blue, and where above it all the skylark sings his song clearer, softer, and sweeter than anywhere else in the world! I — it is too bad that we cannot tell our own stories without all the time talking about ourselves, but it is so, and there is no help for it. Well, then, I was a happy little girl in those days. Though my own father, a county lawyer, had died early and left my dear mother without any means of support for herself and three children except what she earned by teaching school and music, it did not make life harder for me, for I had been since I was three years old with mother's youngest and loveliest sister and her husband. They were rich and prosperous. They brought me up as their own, and never had a child a kinder father and mother or a more beautiful home than I had with my uncle and

aunt. Besides, I was naturally a happy child.
Life seemed full of sunshine, and every day
dawned with promise of joy and pleasure. I remember often saying to my aunt, whom, by the
way, I called mother, " I am
so happy I don't know what
to do!"

So I skipped and danced
about among the lumber in
the sight of Jacob Riis, till,
in sheer amazement, he cut
his finger off. *He* says admiration, not amazement, but I
have my own ideas about
that. I see him yet with his
arm in a sling and a defiant
look, making his way across
the hall at dancing-school to
engage me as his partner. I

Elizabeth's Mother.

did not appreciate the compliment in the least, for
I would a good deal rather have had Charles, who
danced well and was a much nicer looking boy.
Besides, Charles's sister Valgerda had told me in
confidence how Jacob had said to Charles that he
would marry me when I was a woman, or die. And
was there ever such assurance? From the day I
learned of this, I treated Jacob with all the coolness
and contempt of which my naturally kindly disposi-

tion was capable. When he spoke to me I answered him hardly a word, and took pains to show my preference for Charles or some other boy. But it seemed to make no difference to him.

I was just seventeen when I received my first love-letter from Jacob. Like the dutiful fellow he was, he sent it through his mother, to my mother, who read it before giving it to me. She handed it to me with the words: " I need not tell you that neither father nor I would ever give our consent to an engagement between you two till Jacob had some good position." Way down in my heart there was a small voice whispering: " Well, if I loved him I wouldn't ask anybody." But the letter was a beautiful one, and after these many years I know that every word in it was prompted by true, unselfish love. I cried over it and answered it as best I could, and then after a while forgot about it and was happy as ever with my studies, my music, and plenty of dances and parties to break the routine. Jacob had gone away to America.

Before I was twenty years old I met one who was to have a great influence on my life. He was a dashing cavalry officer, much older than I, and a frequent visitor at our home. And here I must tell that my own dear mother had died when I was fifteen years old, and my brother and sister had come to live with us in Ribe. There was house-room and

heart-room for us all there.   They were very good
to us, my uncle and aunt, and I loved them as if
they were indeed my parents.   They spared no
expense in our bringing up.   Nothing they gave
their only son was too good for us.   Our home was
a very beautiful and happy one.

Elizabeth's Home — "The Castle."

It was in the summer of 1872 that I met Raymond.   That is not a Danish name, but it was his.
He came to our little town as next in command of a
company of gendarmes — mounted frontier police.
In the army he had served with my mother's brother,
and naturally father and mother, whose hospitable

home welcomed every distinguished stranger, did everything to make his existence, in what must to a man of the world have been a dull little town, less' lonely than it would otherwise have been.   He had a good record, had been brave in the war, was the finest horseman in all the country, could skate and dance and talk, and, best of all, was known to be a good and loving son to his widowed mother, and greatly beloved by his comrades.   So he came into my life and singled me out before the other girls at the balls and parties where we frequently met. Strange as it may seem, for I was not a pretty girl, I had many admirers among the young men in our town.   Perhaps there wasn't really any admiration about it; perhaps it was just because we knew each other as boys and girls and were brought up to-gether.   Most of the young men in our town were college students who had gone to school in Ribe and came back at vacation time to renew old friend-ships and have a good time with old neighbors.   I danced well, played the piano well, and was full of life, and they all liked to come in our house, where there were plenty of good things of all kinds.   So I really ought not to say that I, who frequently cried over the length of my nose, had admirers.   I should rather say good friends, who saw to it in their kind-ness that I never was a wall-flower at a ball, or lacked favors at a cotillon.

But he was so different.   The others were young like myself.   He had experience.   He was a man, handsome and good, just such a man as would be likely to take the fancy of a girl of my age.   And he, who had seen so many girls prettier and better than I, singled me out of them all; and I — well, I was proud of the distinction, and I loved him.

How well I remember the clear winter day when he and I skated and talked, and talked and skated, till the moon was high in the heavens, and my brother was sent out to look for me!   I went home that evening the happiest girl in the world, so I thought; for he had called me "a beautiful child," and told me that he loved me.   And father and mother had given their consent to our engagement. Never did the sun shine so brightly, never did the bells ring out so clearly and appealingly in the old Cathedral, and surely never was the world so beautiful as on the Sunday morning after our engagement when I awoke early in my dear little room. Oh, how I loved the whole world and every one in it! how good God was, how kind and loving my father and mother and brother and sisters!   How I would love to be good to every one around me, and thus in a measure show my gratitude for all the happiness that was mine!

So passed the winter and spring, with many preparations for our new home and much planning for our future life. In a town like ours, where every-body knew all about everybody else from the day they were born till the day they died, it was only reasonable to suppose that somebody had told my betrothed about Jacob Riis's love for me. I had hoped that Jacob would learn to look at me in a different light, but from little messages which came to me off and on from the New World, I knew that he was just as faithful as ever to his idea that we were meant for one another, and that "I might say him No time and time again, the day would come when I would change my mind." But in the first happy days of our engagement I confess that I did not think very much about him, except for mention-ing him once or twice to my friend as a good fellow, but such a queer and obstinate one, who some day would see plainly that I was not half as good as he thought, and learn to love some other girl who was much better.

But one day there came a letter from America, and so far was Jacob from my thoughts at that moment that, when my lieutenant asked me from whom did I think that American letter came, I answered in perfect good faith that I could not imagine, unless it were from a former servant of ours who lived over there.

"No servant ever wrote that address," said Ray-mond, dryly. It was from Jacob, and filled with good wishes for us both. He listened to it in silence. I said how glad I was to find that at last he looked upon me merely as a friend. "You little know how to read between the lines," was his sober comment. He was very serious, almost sad it seemed to me.

In the early summer came the first cloud on my sunlit sky. One evening, when we were invited to a party of young people at our doctor's house, word was sent from Raymond that he was sick and could not come, but that I must on no account stay home. But I did. For me there was no pleasure without him, no, not anywhere in the world. He recovered soon, however; but after that, short spells of illness, mostly heavy colds, were the rule. He was a strong man and had taken pride in being able to do things which few other men could do without harm coming to them; for instance, to chop a hole in the ice and go swimming in midwinter. But exposure to the chill, damp air of that North Sea country and the heavy fogs that drifted in from the ocean at night, when he rode alone, often many miles over the moor on his tours of inspection, had undermined his splendid constitution, and before the summer was over the doctors pronounced my dear one a sufferer from bronchial consumption, and told us that his only chance lay in his seeking a milder climate. I grieved at the thought of separation for a whole winter, perhaps longer, and at his suffering; but I felt sure that he would come back to me from Switzerland a well man.

So we parted. That winter we lived in our letters. The fine climate in Montreux seemed to do him good, and his messages were full of hope that all would be well. Not so with my parents. They had been told by physicians who had treated Raymond that his case was hopeless; that he might live years, perhaps, in Switzerland, but that in all probability to return to Denmark would be fatal to him. They told me so, and I could not, would not, believe them. It seemed impossible that God would take him away from me. They also told me that on no condition must I think of marrying him, because either I should be a widow soon after marriage, or else I should be a sick-nurse for several years. So they wished me to break the engagement while he was absent.

This and much more was said to me. And I, who had always been an obedient daughter and never crossed their will in any way, for the first time in my life opposed them and told them that never should anybody separate me from the one I loved until God himself parted us. Mother reminded me of my happy childhood, and of how much she and my foster-father had done for me, and that now they had only my happiness in view — a fact which I might not understand till I was older, she said, but must now take on trust. Beside which, Raymond would be made to feel as if a load were taken off his mind if of my free will I broke our engagement and left him free from any responsibility toward me. But all the time his letters told me that he loved me better than ever, and I lived only in the hope of his home-coming. So I refused to listen to them. They wrote to him; told him what the doctor said and appealed to him to set me free. And he, loyal and good as he was, gave me back my promise. He believed he would get well. But he knew he could not return to Ribe. He had resigned his command and gone back to the rank and pay of a plain lieutenant. He could not offer me now such a home as I was used to these many years; and as he was so much older than I, he thought it his duty to tell me all this. And all the time he knew, oh, so well! that I would never leave him, come what might, sickness, poverty, or death itself. I was bound to stand by him to the last.

That was a hard winter. Father and mother, who could not look into my heart and see that I still loved them as dearly as ever — I know so well they meant it all for the best — called me ungrateful and told me that I was blind and would not see what made for my good, and that therefore they

M

must take their own measures for my happiness. So they offered me the choice between giving up the one I loved or leaving the home that had been mine so long. I chose the last, for I could not do otherwise. I packed my clothes and said good-by to my friends, of whom many treated me with coldness, since they, too, thought I must be ungrateful to those who had done so much for me. Homeless and alone I went to Raymond's brother, who had a little country home near the city of Copenhagen. With him and his young wife I stayed until one day my Raymond returned, much better apparently, yet not the same as before. Suffering, bodily and mental, had left its traces upon his face and frame, but his love for me was greater than ever, and he tried hard to make up to me all I lost; as if I had really lost anything in choosing him before all the world.

We were very happy at first in the joy of being together. But soon he suffered a relapse, and decided to go to the hospital for treatment. He never left it again, except once or twice for a walk with me. All the long, beautiful summer days he spent in his room, the last few months in bed. Many friends came to see him, and as for me, I spent all my days with him, reading softly to him or talking with him. And I never gave up hope of his getting better some day. He probably knew that his time was short, but I think that he did not

have the heart to tell me. Sometimes he would
say, "I wonder whether your people would take
you back to your home if I died." Or, "If I
should die, and some other man who loved you,
and who you knew was good and faithful, should
ask you to marry him, you ought to accept him,
even if you did not love him." I never could bear
to hear it or to think of it then.

One raw, dark November morning I started on
the long walk from his mother's house, where I
had stayed since he took to his bed, to go and
spend the day with him as usual. By this time I
was well acquainted with every one in the hospital.
The nurses were good to me. They took off my
shoes and dried and warmed them for me, and
some brought me afternoon coffee, which otherwise was contraband in the sick-rooms. But this
morning the nurse in charge of Raymond's ward
turned her back upon me and pretended not to
hear me when I bid her good-morning. When I
entered his room, it was to find the lifeless body of
him who only a few hours before had bidden me a
loving and even cheerful good-night.

Oh! the utter loneliness of those days; the longing for mother and home! But no word came from
Ribe then. My dear one was laid to rest, with the
sweet, resigned smile on his brave face, and I
stayed for a while with his people, not being quite

able to look into the future. My father had meanwhile made provision for me at Copenhagen. When
I was able to think clearly, I went to the school
in which my education had been "finished" in the
happy, careless days, and through its managers
secured a position in Baron von D——'s house,
not far from my old home, but in the province that

Elizabeth as I found her again.

was taken from Denmark
by Germany the winter I
played in the lumber-yard.
My employers were kind
to me, and my three girl
pupils soon were the firm
friends of the quiet little
governess with the sad face.
We worked hard together,
to forget if I could. But
each day I turned my face
to the west toward Ribe,
and my heart cried out for my happy childhood.

At last mother sent for me to come to them in
the summer vacation. Oh, how good it was to go
home again! How nice they all were, and what
quiet content I felt, though I knew I should never
forget! The six weeks went by like a dream. On
the last day, as I was leaving, mother gave me a
letter from Jacob Riis, of whom I had not thought
for a long while. It was a letter of proposal, and I

was angry. I answered it, however, as nicely as I could, and sent the letter to his mother. Then I returned to my three pupils in their pleasant country home, and soon we were busy with our studies and our walks. But I felt lonelier than ever, longed more than ever for the days that had been and would never return. I could not sleep, and grew pale and thin. And ever Raymond's words about a friend, good and faithful, who loved me truly, came back to me. Did he mean Jacob, who had surely proved constant, and like me, had suffered much? He was lonely and I was lonely, oh! so lonely! What if I were to accept his offer, and when he came home go back with him to his strange new country to share his busy life, and in trying to make him happy, perhaps find happiness myself? Unless I asked him to come, he would probably never return. The thought of how glad it would make his parents if they could see him again, now that they had buried two fine sons, almost tempted me.

Yet again, it was too soon, too soon. I banished the thought with angry impatience. But in the still night watches it came and knocked again. Jacob need not come home just now. We might write and get acquainted, and get used to the idea of each other, and his old people could look forward to the joy of having him return in a year or two.

At last, one night, I got up at two o'clock, sat down at my desk, and wrote to him in perfect sincerity all that was in my mind concerning him, and that if he still would have me, I was willing to go with him to America if he would come for me some time. Strange to say, Jacob's mother had never sent the letter in which I refused him a second time. Perhaps she thought his constancy and great love would at last touch my heart, longing as it was for somebody to cling to. So that he got my last letter first. But instead of waiting several years, he came in a few weeks. He was always that way.

And now, after twenty-five happy years——

ELISABETH.[1]

I cut the rest of it off, because I am the editor and want to begin again here myself, and what is the use of being an editor unless you can cut " copy "?   Also, it is not good for woman to allow her to say too much. She has already said too much about that letter. I have got it in my pocket, and I guess I ought to know. " Your own Elisabeth " — was not that enough? For him, with his poor, saddened life, peace be to its memory! He loved her. That covers all. How could he help it?

---

[1] That is right. Up to this the printer has had his way. Now we will have ours, she and I, and spell her name properly. Together we shall manage him.

If they did not think I had lost my senses before, they assuredly did when that telegram reached Ribe. Talk about the privacy of the mails (the telegraph is part of the post-office machinery there), official propriety, and all that — why, I don't suppose that telegraph operator could get his coat on quick enough to go out and tell the amazing news. It would not have been human nature, certainly not Ribe human nature. Before sundown it was all over town that Jacob Riis was coming home, and coming for Elisabeth. Poor girl! It was in the Christmas holidays, and she was visiting there. She had been debating in her own mind whether to tell her mother, and how; but they left her precious little time for debate. In a neighborhood gathering that night one stern, uncompromising dowager transfixed her with avenging eye.

"They say Jacob Riis is coming home," she observed. Elisabeth knitted away furiously, her cheeks turning pink for all she made believe she did not hear.

"They say he is coming back to propose to a certain young lady again," continued the dowager, pitilessly, her voice rising. There was the stillness of death in the room. Elisabeth dropped a stitch, tried to pick it up, failed, and fled. Her mother from her seat observed with never-failing dignity that it blew like to bring on a flood. You could almost hear the big cathedral bell singing in the tower. And the subject was changed.

But I will warrant that Ribe got no wink of sleep that night, the while I fumed in a wayside Holstein inn.   In my wild rush to get home I had taken the wrong train from Hamburg, or forgot to change, or something.   I don't to this day know what.   I know that night coming on found me stranded in a little town I had never heard of, on a spur of the road I didn't know existed, and there I had to stay, raging at the railroad, at the inn, at everything.   In the middle of the night, while I was tossing sleepless on the big four-poster bed, a drunken man who had gone wrong fell into my room with the door and a candle.   That man was my friend.   I got up and kicked him out, called the landlord and blew him up, and felt much better.   The sun had not risen when I was posting back to the junction, counting the mile-posts as we sped, watch in hand.

If mother thought we had all gone mad together, there was certainly something to excuse her.   Here she had only a few weeks before forwarded with a heavy heart to her son in America Elisabeth's flat refusal to hear him, and when she expected gloom and despair, all at once his letters overflowed with a hysterical happiness that could only hail from a disordered mind.   To cap it all, Christmas Eve brought her the shock of her life.   Elisabeth, sitting near her in the old church and remorsefully watching her weep for her buried boys, could not resist the impulse to steal up behind, as they were going out, and whisper into her ear, as she gave her a little vicarious hug: "I have had news from Jacob. He is *very* happy." The look of measureless astonishment on my mother's face, as she turned, recalled to her that she could not know, and she hurried away, while mother stood and looked after her, for the first time in her life, I verily believe, thinking hard things of a fellow-being — and of her! Oh, mother! could you but have known that that hug was for your boy!

Counting hours no longer, but minutes, till I should claim it myself, I sat straining my eyes in the dark for the first glimmer of lights in the old town, when my train pulled up at a station a dozen miles from home. The guard ran along and threw open the doors of the compartments. I heard voices and the cry: —

"This way, Herr Doctor! There is room in here," and upon the step loomed the tall form of our old family physician. As I started up with a cry of recognition, he settled into a seat with a contented —

"Here, Overlaerer, is one for you," and I was face to face with my father, grown very old and white. My heart smote me at the sight of his venerable head.

"I was face to face with my father."

"Father!" I cried, and reached out for him. I think he thought he saw a ghost. He stood quite still, steadying himself against the door, and his face grew very pale. It was the doctor, ever the most jovial of men, who first recovered himself.

"Bless my soul!" he cried, "bless my soul if here

is not Jacob, come back from the wilds as large as life! Welcome home, boy!" and we laughed and shook hands. They had been out to see a friend in the country and had happened upon my train.

At the door of our house, father, who had picked up two of my brothers at the depot, halted and thought.

"Better let me go in first," he said, and, being a small man, put the door of the dining-room between me and mother, so that she could not see me right away.

"What do you think — " he began, but his voice shook so that mother rose to her feet at once. How do mothers know?

"Jacob!" she cried, and, pushing past him, had me in her embrace.

That was a happy tea-table. If mother's tears fell as she told of my brothers, the sting was taken out of her grief. Perhaps it was never there. To her there is no death of her dear ones, but rejoicing in the midst of human sorrow that they have gone home where she shall find them again. If ever a doubt had arisen in my mind of that home, how could it linger? How could I betray my mother's faith, or question it?

Perfectly happy were we; but when the tea-things were removed and I began to look restlessly at my watch and talk of an errand I must go, a shadow of anxiety came into my father's eyes. Mother looked

at me with mute appeal. They were still as far
from the truth as ever. A wild notion that I had
come for some other man's daughter had entered
their minds, or else, God help me, that I had lost
mine. I kissed mother and quieted her fears.

"I will tell you when I come back;" and when
she would have sent my brothers with me: "No!
this walk I must take alone. Thank God for it."

So I went over the river, over the Long Bridge
where I first met Her, and from the arch of which
I hailed the light in her window, the beacon that
had beckoned me all the years while two oceans
surged between us; under the wild-rose hedge
where I had dreamed of her as a boy, and presently
I stood upon the broad stone steps of her father's
house, and rang the bell.

An old servant opened the door, and, with a grave
nod of recognition, showed me into the room to the
left, — the very one where I had taken leave of her
six years before, — then went unasked to call "Miss
Elisabeth." It was New Year's Eve, and they were
having a card party in the parlor.

"Oh, it isn't—?" said she, with her heart in her
mouth, pausing on the threshold and looking appealingly at the maid. It was the same who years before had told her how I kept vigil under her window.

"Yes! it is!" she said, mercilessly, "it's him,"
and she pushed her in.

Bringing the "Loved-up" Flowers.

I think it was I who spoke first.

"Do you remember when the ice broke on the big ditch and I had you in my arms, so, lifting you over?"

"Was I heavy?" she asked, irrelevantly, and we both laughed.

Father's reading-lamp shone upon the open Bible when I returned. He wiped his spectacles and looked up with a patiently questioning "Well, my boy?" Mother laid her hand upon mine.

"I came home," I said unsteadily, "to give you Elisabeth for a daughter. She has promised to be my wife."

Mother clung to me and wept. Father turned the leaves of the book with hands that trembled in spite of himself, and read: —

"Not unto us, O Lord, not unto us, but unto Thy name give glory for thy mercy — "

His voice faltered and broke.

The old town turned out, to the last man and woman, and crowded the Domkirke on that March day, twenty-five years ago when I bore Her home my bride. From earliest morning the street that led to "the Castle" had seen a strange procession of poor and aged women pass, carrying flowers grown in window-gardens in the scant sunlight of the long Northern winter — "loved up," they say

in Danish for "grown"; in no other way could it
be done. They were pensioners on her mother's
bounty, bringing their gifts to the friend who was
going away. And it was their flowers she wore when
I led her down the church aisle my wife, my own.

The Castle opened its doors hospitably at last to
the carpenter's lad. When they fell to behind us,
with father, mother, and friends waving tearful
good-bys from the steps, and the wheels of the mail-

"Out into the open country, into the wide world, — our life's journey
had begun."

coach rattled over the cobblestones of the silent
streets where old neighbors had set lights in their
windows to cheer us on the way, — out into the open
country, into the wide world, — our life's journey
had begun. Looking steadfastly ahead, over the
bleak moor into the unknown beyond, I knew in
my soul that I should conquer. For her head was
leaning trustfully on my shoulder and her hand was
in mine; and all was well.

CHAPTER VIII

EARLY MARRIED LIFE; I BECOME AN ADVERTISING
BUREAU; ON THE "TRIBUNE"

It was no easy life to which I brought home my
young wife. I felt it often with a secret pang when
I thought how few friends I had to offer her for
those she had left, and how very different was the
whole setting of her new home. At such times I
set my teeth hard and promised myself that some
day she should have the best in the land. She
never with word or look betrayed if she, too, felt the
pang. We were comrades for better or worse from
the day she put her hand in mine, and never was
there a more loyal and faithful one. If, when in
the twilight she played softly to herself the old airs
from home, the tune was smothered in a sob that was
not for my ear, and shortly our kitchen resounded
with the most tremendously energetic housekeeping
on record, I did not hear. I had drunk that cup to
the dregs, and I knew. I just put on a gingham
apron and turned in to help her. Two can battle
with a fit of homesickness much better than one,
even if never a word is said about it. And it can very

rarely resist a man with an apron on. I suppose he looks too ridiculous.

Besides, housekeeping in double harness was a vastly different matter from going it single. Not that it was plain sailing by any manner of means. Neither of us knew anything about it; but we were there to find out, and exploring together was fine fun. We started fair by laying in a stock of everything there was in the cook-book and in the grocery, from "mace," which neither of us knew what was, to the prunes which we never got a chance to cook because we ate them all up together before we could find a place where they fitted in. The deep councils we held over the disposal of those things, and the strange results which followed sometimes! Certain rocks we were able to steer clear of, because I had carefully charted them in the days of my bachelorhood. In the matter of sago, for instance, which swells so when cooked. You would never believe it. But there were plenty of unknown reefs. I mind our first chicken. I cannot to this day imagine what was the matter with that strange bird. I was compelled to be at the office that afternoon, but I sent my grinning "devil" up to the house every half-hour for bulletins as to how it was getting on. When I came home in the gloaming, it was sizzling yet, and my wife was regarding it with a strained look and with cheeks which the fire had dyed a most lovely red. I can see her now. She was just too charming for anything. With the chicken something was wrong. As I said, I don't know what it was, and I don't care. The skin was all drawn tight over the bones like the covering on an umbrella frame, and there was no end of fat in the pan that we didn't know what to do with. But our supper of bread and cheese that night was a meal fit for a king. My mother, who was a notable cook, never made one so fine. It is all stuff about mothers doing those things better. Who cares, anyhow? Have mothers curls of gold and long eyelashes, and have they arch ways? And do they pout, and have pet names? Well, then, are not these of the very essence of cookery, all the dry books to the contrary notwithstanding? Some day some one will publish a real cook-book for young housekeepers, but it will be a wise husband with the proper sense of things, not a motherly person at all, who will write it. They make things that are good enough to eat, but that is not the best part of cooking by long odds.

There is one housekeeping feat of which Elisabeth says she is ashamed yet. I am not. I'll bet it was fine. It was that cake we took so much trouble with. The yeast went in all right, but something else went wrong. It was not put to soak, or to sizzle, in the oven, or whatever it was. Like my

N

single-blessed pancake, it did not rise, and in the
darkness before I came home she smuggled it out of
the house; only to behold, with a mortification that
endures to this day, the neighbor-woman who had
taken such an interest in our young housekeeping,
examining it carefully in the ash-barrel next morning. People *are* curious. But they were welcome
to all they could spy out concerning our household.
They discovered there, if they looked right, the
sweetest and altogether the bravest little housekeeper in all the world. And what does a cake
matter, or a hen, or twenty, when only the housekeeper is right?

In my editorial enthusiasm for the new plan there
was no doubtful note. The "beats" got a rest for
a season while I transferred my attention to the
boarding-house. My wife teases me yet with those
mighty onslaughts on the new enemy. Having
clearly made him out by the light of our evening
lamp, I went for him with might and main, determined to leave no boarding-house through the
length and breadth of the land, or at least of South
Brooklyn. "Ours," I cried, weekly "to fulfil its
destiny, must be a nation of homes. Down with
the boarding-house!" and the politicians applauded.
They were glad to be let alone. So were the beats
who were behind in their bills, and whose champion
I had unexpectedly become. A doughty champion,

too, a walking advertisement of my own prescription; for I grew fat and strong, whereas I had been lean and poor. I was happy, that was it; very, very happy, and full of faith in our ability to fight our way through, come what might. Nor did it require the gift of a prophet to make out that trying days were coming; for my position, again as the paid editor of my once "owners," the politicians, was rapidly becoming untenable. It was an agreement entered into temporarily. When it should lapse, what then? I had pledged myself when I sold the paper not to start another for ten years in South Brooklyn. So I would have to begin life over again in a new place. I gave the matter but little thought. I suppose the old folks, viewing it all from over there, thought it trifling with fate. It was not. It was a trumpet challenge to it to come on, all that could crowd in. Two, we would beat the world.

Before I record the onset that ensued, I must stop to tell of another fight, one which in my soul I regret, though it makes me laugh even now. Nonresistance never appealed to me except in the evildoer who has been knocked down for cause. I suppose it is wicked, but I promised to tell the truth, and — I always did like Peter for knocking off the ear of the high priest's servant. If only it had been the high priest's own ear! And so when the Rev. Mr. — no, I will not mention names; he was

Brother Simmons's successor, that is what grieves me — when he found fault with the *News* for being on sale Sundays, if I remember rightly, and preached about it, announcing that "never in the most anxious days of the war had he looked in a newspaper on the Sabbath"; and when ill luck would have it that on the same Sunday I beheld his Reverence, who was a choleric man, hotly stoning a neighbor's hen from his garden, I drew editorial parallels which were not soothing to the reverend temper. What really ailed Mr.—— was that he was lacking in common sense, or he would never have called upon me with his whole board of deacons in the quiet of the Sunday noon, right after church, to demand a retraction. I have no hope that a sense of the humor of the thing found its way into the clerical consciousness when I replied that I never in the most exciting times transacted business on Sunday; for if it had, we would have been friends for life. But I know that it "struck in" in the case of the deacons. They went out struggling with their mirth behind their pastor's back. I think he restrained himself with difficulty from pronouncing the major excommunication against me, with bell, book, and candle, then and there.

About that time I saw advertised for sale a stereopticon outfit, and bought it without any definite idea of what to do with it. I suppose it ought to be set down as foolishness and a waste of money. And yet it was to play an important part in the real life-work that was waiting for me. Without the knowledge which the possession of it gave me, that work could not have been carried out as it was. That is not to say that I recommend every man to have a magic lantern in his cellar, or the promiscuous purchase of all sorts of useless things as though the world were a kind of providential rummage sale. I should rather say that no effort to in any way add to one's stock of knowledge is likely to come amiss in this world of changes and emergencies, and that Providence has a way of ranging itself on the side of the man with the strongest battalions of resources when the emergency does come. In other words, that to "trust God and keep your powder dry" is the plan for all time.

The process of keeping mine dry came near blowing up the house. My two friends, Mackellar and Wells, took a sympathetic interest in the lantern proceedings, which was well, because, being a druggist, Wells knew about making the gas and could prevent trouble on that tack. It was before the day of charged tanks. The gas we made was contained in wedge-shaped rubber bags, in a frame with weights on top that gave the necessary pressure. Mackellar volunteered to be the weight, and sat on the bags, at our first séance, while Wells superintended the gas and I read the written directions. We were getting along nicely when I came to a place enjoining great caution in the distribution of the weight. "You are working," read the text, "with two gases which, if allowed to mix in undue proportion, have the force and all the destructive power of a bombshell." Mackellar, all ear, from fidgeting fell into a tremble on his perch. He had not dreamed of this; neither had we. I steadied him with an imperative gesture.

"Sit still," I commanded. "Listen! 'If, by any wabbling of the rack, the pressure were to be suddenly relieved, the gas from one bag might be sucked into the other, with the result of a disastrous explosion.'"

We stood regarding each other in dumb horror. Mackellar was deathly pale.

"Let me off, boys," he pleaded faintly. "I've got to go to the station to turn out the men." He made a motion to climb down.

Wells had snatched the book from me. "Jack! for your life don't move!" he cried, and pointed to the next paragraph in the directions: —

"Such a thing has happened when the frame has been upset, or the weight in some other way suddenly shifted."

Mac sat as if frozen to stone. Ed and I sneaked out of the back door on tiptoe to make for down-

stairs, three steps at a time.   In less time than it
takes to tell it we were back, each with an armful of
paving-stones, which we piled up beside our ago-
nized comrade, assuring him volubly that there was
no danger if he would only sit still, still as a mouse,
till we came back.   Then we were off again.   The
third trip gave us stones enough, and with infinite
care we piled them, one after another, upon the rack
as the Captain eased up, until at last he stood upon
the floor, a freed and saved man.   It was only then
that it occurred to us that we might have turned off
the gas in the first place, and so saved ourselves all
our anguish and toil.

I can say honestly that I tried the best I knew
how to get along with the politicians I served, but
in the long run it simply could not be done.   They
treated me fairly, bearing no grudges.   But it is one
thing to run an independent newspaper, quite another to edit an "organ."   And there is no deceiving
the public.   Not that I tried.   Indeed, if anything,
the shoe was on the other foot.   We parted company eventually to our mutual relief, and quite
unexpectedly I found my lantern turning the bread-
winner of the family.   The notion of using it as a
means of advertising had long allured me.   There
was a large population out on Long Island that
traded in Brooklyn stores and could be reached in
that way.   In fact, it proved to be so.   I made

money that fall travelling through the towns and villages and giving open-air exhibitions in which the
"ads" of Brooklyn merchants were cunningly inter-
larded with very beautiful colored views, of which I
had a fine collection.   When the season was too far
advanced to allow of this, I established myself in a
window at Myrtle Avenue and Fulton Street and
appealed to the city crowds with my pictures.   So
I filled in a gap of several months, while our people
on the other side crossed themselves at my having
turned street fakir.   At least we got that impression
from their letters.   They were not to blame.   That
is their way of looking at things.   A chief reason
why I liked this country from the very beginning was
that it made no difference what a man was doing, so
long as it was some honest, decent work.   I liked
my advertising scheme.   I advertised nothing I
would not have sold the people myself, and I gave
it to them in a way that was distinctly pleasing and
good for them; for my pictures were real work of
art, not the cheap trash you see nowadays on street
screens.

The city crowds were always appreciative.   In
the country the hoodlums made trouble occasionally.
We talk a great deal about city toughs.   In nine
cases out of ten they are lads of normal impulses
whose resources have all been smothered by the
slum; of whom the street and its lawlessness, and

the tenement that is without a home, have made
ruffians. With better opportunities they might
have been heroes. The country hoodlum is oftener
what he is because his bent is that way, though he,
too, is not rarely driven into mischief by the utter
poverty — æsthetically I mean — of his environment.
Hence he shows off in his isolation so much worse
than his city brother. It is no argument for the
slum. It makes toughs, whereas the other is one
in spite of his country home. That is to say, if the
latter is really a home. There is only one cure
then — an almighty thrashing.

There ought to be some ex-hoodlums left in Flushing to echo that sentiment, even after a quarter of a
century. From certain signs I knew, when I hung
my curtain between two trees in the little public
park down by the fountain with the goldfish, that
there was going to be trouble. My patience had
been pretty well worn down, and I made preparations. I hired four stout men who were spoiling for
a fight, and put good hickory clubs into their hands,
bidding them restrain their natural desire to use
them till the time came. My forebodings were not
vain. Potatoes, turnips, and eggs flew, not only at
the curtain, but at the lantern and me. I stood it
until the Castle of Heidelberg, which was one of my
most beautiful colored views, was rent in twain by a
rock that went clear through the curtain. Then I

gave the word.   In a trice the apparatus was
gathered up and thrown into a wagon that was waiting, the horses headed for Jamaica.   We made one
dash into the crowd, and a wail arose from the
bruised and bleeding hoodlums that hung over the
town like a nightmare, while we galloped out of it,
followed by cries of rage and a mob with rocks and
clubs.   But we had the best team in town, and soon
lost them.

Vengeance?   No!   Of course there was the
ruined curtain and those eggs to be settled for; but,
on the whole, I think we were a kind of village
improvement society for the occasion, though we
did not stay to wait for a vote of thanks.   I am sure
it was our due all the same.

Along in the summer of 1877 Wells and I hatched
out a scheme of country advertising on a larger
scale, of which the lantern was to be the vehicle.
We were to publish a directory of the city of Elmira.
How we came to select that city I have forgotten,
but the upshot of that latest of my business ven-
tures I am not likely to forget soon.   Our plan was
to boom the advertising end of the enterprise by a
nightly street display in the interest of our patrons.
We had barely got into town when the railroad
strikes of that memorable summer reached Elmira.
There had been dreadful trouble, fire and bloodshed,
in Pennsylvania, and the citizens took steps at once

to preserve the peace. A regiment of deputy sheriffs were sworn in, and the town was put under semi-martial law. Indeed, soldiers with fixed bayonets guarded every train and car that went over the bridge between the business section of the town and the railroad shops across the Chemung River.

Our ill luck — or good; when a thing comes upon you so unexpectedly as did that, I am rather disposed to consider it a stroke of good fortune, however disguised — would have it that the building we had chosen to hang our curtain on was right at the end of this bridge which seemed to be the danger point. From the other end the strikers looked across the river, hourly expected to make a movement of some kind, exactly what I don't know. I know that the whole city was on pins and needles about it, while we, all unconscious that we were the object of sharp scrutiny, were vainly trying to string our sixteen-foot curtain. There was a high wind that blew it out over the river despite all our efforts to catch and hold it. Twice it escaped our grasp. We could see a crowd of strikers watching us on the other side. The deputies who held our end of the bridge saw them too. We were strangers; came from no one knew where. They must have concluded that we were in league with the enemy and signalling to him. When for the third time our big white flag was wafted toward the shops, a committee of citizens came up from the street and let us know in as few words as possible that any other place would be healthier for us just then than Elmira.

In vain we protested that we were noncombatants and engaged in peaceful industry. The committee pointed to the flag and to the crowd at the farther end of the bridge. They eyed our preparations for making gas askance, and politely but firmly insisted that the next train out of town was especially suited for our purpose. There was nothing to be done. It was another case of circumstantial evidence, and in the absence of backing of any kind we did the only thing we could; packed up and went. It was not a time for trifling. The slaughter of a number of militiamen in a Pennsylvania round-house that was set on fire by the strikers was fresh in the public mind. But it was the only time I have been suspected of sympathy with violence in the settlement of labor disputes. The trouble with that plan is that it does not settle anything, but rakes up fresh injuries to rankle indefinitely and widen the gap between the man who does the work and the man who hires it done so that he may have time to attend to his own. Both workmen, they only need to understand each other and their common interests to see the folly of quarrelling. To do that they must know one another; but a blow and a kick are a poor introduction. I am not saying that the provocation is not sometimes great; but better not. It does not do any good, but a lot of harm. Besides, if we haven't got to the point yet where we can settle our disputes peaceably by discussion, the fault is not all the employers by any manner of means.

We jumped out of the ashes into the fire, as it turned out. At Scranton our train was held up. There were torpedoes on the track; rails torn up or something. For want of something better to do, we went out to take a look at the town. At the head of the main street was a big crowd. Untaught by experience, we bored our way through it to where a line of men with guns, some in their shirt-sleeves, some in office coats, some in dusters, were blocking advance to the coal company's stores. The crowd hung sullenly back, leaving a narrow space clear in front of the line. Within it a man — I learned afterward that he was the Mayor of the town — was haranguing the people, counselling them to go back to their homes quietly. Suddenly a brick was thrown from behind me and struck him on the head.

I heard a word of brief command, the rattle of a score of guns falling into as many extended hands, and a volley was fired into the crowd point blank. A man beside me weltered in his blood. There was an instant's dead silence, then the rushing of a thousand feet and wild cries of terror as the mob broke and fled. We ran with it. In all my life I never ran so fast. I would never have believed that I could do it. Ed teased me to the day of his death about it, insisting that one might have played marbles on my coat-tails, they flew out behind so. But he was an easy winner in that race. The riots were over, however, before they had begun, and perhaps a greater calamity was averted. It was the only time I was ever under fire, except once when a crazy man came into Mulberry Street years after and pointed a revolver at the reporters. I regret to say that I gave no better account of myself then, and for a man who was so hot to go to war I own it is a bad showing. Perhaps it was as well I didn't go, even on that account. I might have run the wrong way when it came to the scratch.

We were not yet done suffering undeserved indignities on that trip, for when we got as far as Stanhope, on the Morris and Essex road, our money had given out. I offered the station-master my watch as security for the price of two tickets to New York, but he bestowed only a contemptuous glance upon it and remarked that there were a good many fakirs running about the country palming off " snide " gold watches on people. Our lantern outfit found no more favor with him, and we were compelled to tramp it to the village in Schooley's Mountains where my wife was then summering with our baby. We walked all night, and when at dawn we arrived, had the mortification of being held up by the farmer's dog, who knew nothing about us. He walked alongside of me all that day, as I was pushing the baby-carriage up hill, eying me with a look that said plainly enough I had better not make a move to sneak away with the child. Wells went on to the city to replenish our funds.

And here I take leave of this loyal friend in the story of my life. A better one I never had. He lived to grow rich in possessions, but his wealth was his undoing. It is one of the sore spots in my life — and there are many more than I like to think of — that when he needed me most I was not able to be to him what I would and should have been. We had drifted too far apart then, and the influence I had over him once I had myself surrendered. It was so with Charles. It was so with Nicolai. They come, sometimes when I am alone, and nod to me out of the dim past: "You were not tempted. You should have helped!" Yes, God help me! it is true. I am more to blame than they. I should have helped and did not. What would I not give that I could unsay that now! Two of them died by their own hand, the third in Bloomingdale.

I had been making several attempts to get a foothold on one of the metropolitan newspapers, but
always without success. That fall I tried the *Tribune*, the city editor of which, Mr. Shanks, was
one of my neighbors, but was told, with more frankness than flattery, that I was "too green." Very
likely Mr. Shanks had been observing my campaign against the beats and thought me a dangerous man in those days of big libel suits. I should
have done the same thing. But a few weeks after he
changed his mind and invited me to come on the
paper and try my hand. So I joined the staff of
the *Tribune* five years after its great editor had
died, a beaten and crushed man, one of the most
pathetic figures in American political history.

They were not halcyon days, those winter
months of reporting for the *Tribune*. I was on
trial, and it was hard work and very little pay, not
enough to live on, so that we were compelled to
take to our little pile to make ends meet. But
there was always a bright fire and a cheery welcome for me at home, so what did it matter? It
was a good winter despite the desperate stunts
sometimes set me. Reporters on general work do
not sleep on flowery beds of ease. I remember
well one awful night when word came of a dreadful disaster on the Coney Island shore. Half of it
had been washed away by the sea, the report ran,

with houses and people. I was sent out to get at
the truth of the thing. I started in the early twilight and got as far as Gravesend. The rest of the
way I had to foot it through snow and slush knee-
deep in the face of a blinding storm, and got to
Sheepshead Bay dead beat, only to find that the ice
and the tide had shut off all approach to the island.

I did the next best thing; I gathered from the
hotel-keepers of the Bay an account of the wreck
on the beach that lacked nothing in vividness,
thanks to their laudable desire not to see an enter-
prising reporter cheated out of his rightful "space."
Then I hired a sleigh and drove home through the
storm, wet through — "I can hear the water yet
running out of your boots," says my wife — wet
through and nearly frozen stiff, but tingling with
pride at my feat.

The *Tribune* next day was the only paper
that had an account of the tidal wave on the island.
But something about it did not seem to strike the
city editor just right. There was an unwonted
suavity in his summons when he called me to his
desk which I had learned to dread as liable to conceal some fatal thrust.

"So you went to the island last night, Mr. Riis,"
he observed, regarding me over the edge of the
paper.

"No, sir! I couldn't get across; nobody could."

o

"Eh!" He lowered the paper an inch, and took a better look: "this very circumstantial account—"

"Was gathered from the hotel-keepers in Sheepshead Bay, who had seen it all. If there had been a boat not stove by the ice, I would have got across somehow."

Mr. Shanks dropped the paper and considered me almost kindly. I saw that he had my bill for the sleigh-ride in his hand.

"Right!" he said. "We'll allow the sleigh. We'll allow even the stove, to a man who owns he didn't see it, though it is pretty steep." He pointed to a paragraph which described how, after the wreck of the watchman's shanty, the kitchen stove floated ashore with the house-cat alive and safe upon it. I still believe that an unfriendly printer played me that trick.

"Next time," he added, dismissing me, "make them swear to the stove. There is no accounting for cats."

But, though I did not hear the last of it in the office for a long time, I know that my measure was taken by the desk that day. I was trusted after that, even though I had made a mistake.

In spite of it, I did not get on. There was not a living in it for me, that was made plain enough. We were too many doing general work. After six months of hard grubbing I decided that I had better seek my fortune elsewhere. Spring was coming, and it seemed a waste of time to stay where I was. I wrote out my resignation and left it on the city editor's desk. Some errand took me out of the office. When I returned it lay there still, unopened. I saw it, and thought I would try another week. I might make a strike. So I took the note away and tore it up, just as Mr. Shanks entered the room.

That evening it set in snowing at a great rate. I had been uptown on a late assignment, and was coming across Printing-House Square, running at top speed to catch the edition. The wind did its part. There is no corner in all New York where it blows as it does around the *Tribune* building. As I flew into Spruce Street I brought up smack against two men coming out of the side door. One of them I knocked off his feet into a snowdrift. He floundered about in it and swore dreadfully. By the voice I knew that it was Mr. Shanks. I stood petrified, mechanically pinning his slouch hat to the ground with my toe. He got upon his feet at last and came toward me, much wrought up.

" Who in thunder — " he growled angrily and caught sight of my rueful face. I was thinking I might as well have left my note on his desk that morning, for now I was going to be discharged anyhow.

" Is that the way you treat your city editor, Riis?" he asked, while I handed him his hat.

"It was the wind, sir, and I was running — "

"Running! What is up that set you going at that rate?"

I told him of the meeting I had attended — it was of no account — and that I was running to catch the edition. He heard me out.

"And do you always run like that when you are out on assignments?"

"When it is late like this, yes. How else would I get my copy in?"

"Well, just take a reef in when you round the corner," he said, brushing the snow from his clothes. "Don't run your city editor down again." And he went his way.

It was with anxious forebodings I went to the office the next morning. Mr. Shanks was there before me. He was dictating to his secretary, Mr. Taggart, who had been witness of the collision of the night before, when I came in. Presently I was summoned to his desk, and went there with sinking heart. Things had commenced to look up a bit in the last twenty-four hours, and I had hoped yet to make it go. Now, it was all over.

"Mr. Riis," he began stiffly, "you knocked me down last night without cause."

"Yes, sir! But I — "

"Into a snowdrift," he went on, unheeding. "Nice thing for a reporter to do to his commanding officer.

Now, sir! this will not do. We must find some way of preventing it in the future. Our man at Police Headquarters has left. I am going to send you up there in his place. You can run there all you want to, and you will want to all you can. It is a place

Copyright, 1900, by Detroit Phothograpic Company.
Mulberry Street.

that needs a man who will run to get his copy in and tell the truth and stick to it. You will find plenty of fighting there. But don't go knocking people down — unless you have to."

And with this kind of an introduction I was sent off to Mulberry Street, where I was to find my life-work. It is twenty-three years since the day I took

my first walk up there and looked over the ground
that has since become so familiar to me. I knew it
by reputation as the hardest place on the paper, and
it was in no spirit of exultation that I looked out
upon the stirring life of the block. If the truth be
told, I think I was, if anything, a bit afraid. The
story of the big fight the *Tribune* reporter was having on his hands up there with all the other papers
had long been echoing through newspaperdom, and
I was not deceived. But, after all, I had been doing
little else myself, and, having given no offence, my
cause would be just. In which case, what had I to
fear? So in my soul I commended my work and
myself to the God of battles who gives victory, and
took hold.

Right here, lest I make myself appear better than
I am, I want to say that I am not a praying man in
the sense of being versed in the language of prayer
or anything of that kind. I wish I were. So, I
might have been better able to serve my unhappy
friends when they needed me. Indeed, those who
have known me under strong provocation — provocation is *very* strong in Mulberry Street — would
scorn such an intimation, and, I am sorry to say,
with cause. I was once a deacon, but they did not
often let me lead in prayer. My supplications ordinarily take the form of putting the case plainly to
Him who is the source of all right and all justice,

and leaving it so. If I were to find that I could not do that, I should decline to go into the fight, or, if I had to, should feel that I were to be justly beaten. In all the years of my reporting I have never omitted this when anything big was on foot, whether a fire, a murder, a robbery, or whatever might come in the way of duty, and I have never heard that my reports were any the worse for it. I know they were better. Perhaps the notion of a police reporter praying that he may write a good murder story may seem ludicrous, even irreverent, to some people. But that is only because they fail to make out in it the human element which dignifies anything and rescues it from reproach. Unless I could go to my story that way I would not go to it at all. I am very sure that there is no irreverence in it — just the reverse.

So I dived in. But before I did it I telegraphed to my wife : —

"Got staff appointment. Police Headquarters. $25 a week. Hurrah!"

I knew it would make her happy.

CHAPTER IX

LIFE IN MULBERRY STREET

IT was well that I stopped to make explanations before I took hold in my new office. Mighty little time was left me after. What the fight was about to which I fell heir I have long since forgotten. Mulberry Street in those days was prone to such things. Somebody was always fighting somebody else for some fancied injury or act of bad faith in the gathering of the news. For the time being they all made common cause against the reporter of the *Tribune*, who also represented the local bureau of the Associated Press. They hailed the coming of "the Dutchman" with shouts of derision, and decided, I suppose, to finish me off while I was new. So they pulled themselves together for an effort, and within a week I was so badly "beaten" in the Police Department, in the Health Department, in the Fire Department, the Coroner's office, and the Excise Bureau, all of which it was my task to cover, that the manager of the Press Bureau called me down to look me over. He reported to the *Tribune* that he did not think I would do

But Mr. Shanks told him to wait and see. In some
way I heard of it, and that settled it that I was to
win. I might be beaten in many a battle, but how
could I lose the fight with a general like that?

And, indeed, in another week it was their turn
to be called down to give an account of themselves.
The "Dutchman" had stolen a march on them.
I suppose it was to them a very astounding thing,
yet it was perfectly simple. Their very strength,
as they held it to be, was their weakness. They
were a dozen against one, and each one of them
took it for granted that the other eleven were
attending to business and that he need not exert
himself overmuch. A good many years after, I had
that experience as a member of a board of twelve
trustees, each one of whom had lent his name but
not his work to the cause we were supposed to
represent. When we met at the end of that season,
and heard how narrow had been the escape from
calamity due to utter lack of management, a good
Methodist brother put in words what we were each
and every one of us thinking about.

"Brethren," he said, "so far as I can make out,
but for the interposition of a merciful Providence
we should all be in jail, as we deserve. Let us
pray!"

I think that prayer was more than lip-service
with most of us. I know that I registered a vow

that I would never again be trustee of anything without trusteeing it in fact. And I have kept the vow

But to return to Mulberry Street. The immediate result of this first victory of mine was a whirl-
wind onslaught on me, fiercer than anything that

had gone before. I
expected it and met
it as well as I could,
holding my own after
a fashion. When,
from sheer exhaus-
tion, they let up to
see if I was still
there, I paid them
back with two or
three "beats" I had
stored up for the oc-
casion. And then we
settled down to the
ten years' war for the

Tribune Police Bureau.

mastery, out of which I was to come at last fairly
the victor, and with the only renown I have ever
coveted or cared to have, that of being the "boss
reporter" in Mulberry Street. I have so often been
asked in later years what my work was there,[1] and

---

[1] I say *was*; only in the last twelvemonth have I grasped Mr.
Dana's meaning in calling his reporters his "young men." They need
to be that. I, for one, have grown too old.

how I found there the point of view from which
I wrote my books, that I suppose I shall have to
go somewhat into the details of it.

The police reporter on a newspaper, then, is the
one who gathers and handles all the news that
means trouble to some one: the murders, fires,
suicides, robberies, and all that sort, before it gets
into court. He has an office in Mulberry Street,
across from Police Headquarters, where he receives
the first intimation of the trouble through the precinct reports. Or else he does not receive it. The
police do not like to tell the public of a robbery
or a safe "cracking," for instance. They claim that
it interferes with the ends of justice. What they
really mean is that it brings ridicule or censure
upon them to have the public know that they do
not catch every thief, or even most of them. They
would like that impression to go out, for police
work is largely a game of bluff. Here, then, is
an opportunity for the "beats" I speak of. The
reporter who, through acquaintance, friendship, or
natural detective skill, can get that which it is the
policy of the police to conceal from him, wins. It
may seem to many a reader a matter of no great
importance if a man should miss a safe-burglary
for his paper; but reporting is a business, a very
exacting one at that, and if he will stop a moment
and think what it is he instinctively looks at first in

his morning paper, even if he has schooled himself
not to read it through, he will see it differently.
The fact is that it is all a great human drama in
which these things are the acts that mean grief,
suffering, revenge upon somebody, loss or gain.
The reporter who is behind the scenes sees the
tumult of passions, and not rarely a human heroism
that redeems all the rest.   It is his task so to por-
tray it that we can all see its meaning, or at all
events catch the human drift of it, not merely the
foulness and the reek of blood.   If he can do that,
he has performed a signal service, and his murder
story may easily come to speak more eloquently to
the minds of thousands than the sermon preached
to a hundred in the church on Sunday.

Of the advantages that smooth the way to news-
getting I had none.   I was a stranger, and I was
never distinguished for detective ability.   But good
hard work goes a long way toward making up for
lack of genius; and I mentioned only one of the
opportunities for getting ahead of my opponents.
They were lying all about us.   Any seemingly innocent slip sent out from the police telegraph office
across the way recording a petty tenement-house fire
might hide a fire-bug, who always makes shuddering
appeal to our fears; the finding of John Jones sick
and destitute in the street meant, perhaps, a story
full of the deepest pathos.   Indeed, I can think of a

"In which lay dying a French nobleman of proud and ancient name."

dozen now that did. I see before me, as though it
were yesterday, the desolate Wooster Street attic,
with wind and rain sweeping through the bare room
in which lay dying a French nobleman of proud and
ancient name, the last of his house. He was one of
my early triumphs. New York is a queer town.
The grist of every hopper in the world comes to it.
I shall not soon forget the gloomy tenement in Clinton Street where that day a poor shoemaker had
shot himself. His name, Struensee, had brought
me over. I knew there could not be such another.
That was where my Danish birth stood me in good
stead. I knew the story of Christian VII.'s masterful minister; of his fall and trial on the charge of

supplanting his master in the affections of the young and beautiful Queen, sister of George III.   Very old men told yet, when I was a boy, of that dark day when the proud head fell under the execu tioner's axe in the castle square — dark for the people whose champion Struensee had tried to be. My mother was born and reared in the castle at Elsinore where the unhappy Queen, disgraced and an outcast, wrote on the window-pane of her prison cell : "Lord, keep me innocent; make others great." It was all a familiar story to me, and when I sat beside that dead shoemaker and, looking through his papers, read there that the tragedy of a hundred years before was his family story, I knew that I held in my hands the means of paying off all accumu- lated scores to date.

Did I settle in full? Yes, I did.   I was in a fight not of my own choosing, and I was well aware that my turn was coming.   I hit as hard as I knew how, and so did they.   When I speak of "triumphs," it is professionally.   There was no hard-heartedness about it.   We did not gloat over the misfortunes we described.   We were reporters, not ghouls. There lies before me as I write a letter that came in the mail this afternoon from a woman who bit- terly objects to my diagnosis of the reporter's as the highest and noblest of all callings.   She signs her- self "a sufferer from reporters' unkindness," and tells me how in the hour of her deep affliction they have trodden upon her heart. Can I not, she asks, encourage a public sentiment that will make such reporting disreputable? All my life I have tried to do so, and, in spite of the evidence of yellow journalism to the contrary, I think we are coming nearer to that ideal; in other words, we are emerging from savagery. Striving madly for each other's scalps as we were, I do not think that we scalped any one else unjustly. I know I did not. They were not particularly scrupulous, I am bound to say. In their rage and mortification at having underestimated the enemy, they did things unworthy of men and of reporters. They stole my slips in the telegraph office and substituted others that sent me off on a wild-goose chase to the farthest river wards in the midnight hour, thinking so to tire me out. But they did it once too often. I happened on a very important case on such a trip, and made the most of it, telegraphing down a column or more about it from the office, while the enemy watched me helplessly from the Headquarters' stoop across the way. They were gathered there, waiting for me to come back, and received me with loud and mocking ahems! and respectfully sympathetic toots on a tin horn, kept for that purpose. Its voice had a mournful strain in it that was especially exasperating. But when, without paying any attention to them, I busied myself with the wire at

once, and kept at it right along, they scented
trouble, and consulted anxiously among themselves.
My story finished, I went out and sat on my own
stoop and said ahem! in my turn in as many aggravating ways as I could.   They knew they were
beaten then, and shortly they had confirmation of
it.   The report came in from the precinct at 2 A.M.,
but it was then too late for their papers, for there
were no telephones in those days.   I had the only
telegraph wire.   After that they gave up such tricks,
and the *Tribune* saved many cab fares at night; for
there were no elevated railroads, either, in those
days, or electric or cable cars.

On the other hand, this enterprise of ours was
often of the highest service to the public.   When,
for instance, in following up a case of destitution
and illness involving a whole family, I, tracing back
the origin of it, came upon a party at which ham
sandwiches had been the bill of fare, and upon looking up the guests, found seventeen of the twenty-
five sick with identical symptoms, it required no
medical knowledge, but merely the ordinary information and training of the reporter, to diagnose
trichinosis.   The seventeen had half a dozen different doctors, who, knowing nothing of party or ham,
were helpless, and saw only cases of rheumatism or
such like.   I called as many of them as I could
reach together that night, introduced them to one

another and to my facts, and asked them what they
thought then.   What they thought made a sensation in my paper the next morning, and practically
decided the fight, though the enemy was able to
spoil my relish for the ham by reporting the poison-
ing of a whole family with a dish of depraved smelt
while I was chasing up the trichinæ.   However, I
had my revenge.   I walked in that afternoon upon
Dr. Cyrus Edson at his microscope surrounded by
my adversaries, who besought him to deny my story.
The doctor looked quizzically at them and made
reply : —

"I would like to oblige you, boys, but how I can
do it with those fellows squirming under the microscope I don't see.   I took them from the flesh of
one of the patients who was sent to Trinity Hospital to-day.   Look at them yourself."

He winked at me, and, peering into his microscope, I saw my diagnosis more than confirmed.
There were scores of the little beasts curled up and
burrowing in the speck of tissue.   The unhappy
patient died that week.

We had our specialties in this contest of wits.
One was distinguished as a sleuth.   He fed on
detective mysteries as a cat on a chicken-bone.   He
thought them out by day and dreamed them out
by night, to the great exasperation of the official
detectives, with whom their solution was a com-

P

mercial, not in the least an intellectual, affair. They solved them on the plane of the proverbial lack of honor among thieves, by the formula, " You scratch my back, and I'll scratch yours."

Another came out strong on fires. He knew the history of every house in town that ran any risk of being burned; knew every fireman; and could tell within a thousand dollars, more or less, what was the value of the goods stored in any building in the dry-goods district, and for how much they were insured. If he couldn't, he did anyhow, and his guesses often came near the fact, as shown in the final adjustment. He sniffed a firebug from afar, and knew without asking how much salvage there was in a bale of cotton after being twenty-four hours in the fire. He is dead, poor fellow. In life he was fond of a joke, and in death the joke clung to him in a way wholly unforeseen. The firemen in the next block, with whom he made his head-quarters when off duty, so that he might always be within hearing of the gong, wished to give some tangible evidence of their regard for the old re-porter, but, being in a hurry, left it to the florist, who knew him well, to choose the design. He hit upon a floral fire-badge as the proper thing, and thus it was that when the company of mourners was assembled, and the funeral service in progress, there arrived and was set upon the coffin, in the view of all, that triumph of the florist's art, a shield of white roses, with this legend written across it in red immortelles: "Admit within fire lines only." It was shocking, but irresistible. It brought down even the house of mourning.

The incident recalls another, which at the time caused me no little astonishment. A telegram from Long Branch had announced the drowning of a young actor, I think, whose three sisters lived over on Eighth Avenue. I had gone to the house to learn about the accident, and found them in the first burst of grief, dissolved in tears. It was a very hot July day, and to guard against sunstroke I had put a cabbage-leaf in my hat. On the way over I forgot all about it, and the leaf, getting limp, settled down snugly upon my head like a ridiculous green skullcap. Knowing nothing of this, I was wholly unprepared for the effect my entrance, hatless, had upon the weeping family. The young ladies ceased crying, stared wildly, and then, to my utter bewilderment, broke into hysterical laughter. For the moment I thought they had gone mad. It was only when in my perplexity I put up my hand to rub my head, that I came upon the cause of the strange hilarity. For years afterward the thought of it had the same effect upon me that the cabbage-leaf produced so unexpectedly in that grief-stricken home.

I might fill many pages with such stories, but I shall not attempt it. Do they seem mean and trifling in the retrospect? Not at all. They were my work, and I liked it. And I got a good deal of fun out of it from time to time. I mind Dr. Bryant's parrot story. Dr. Joseph D. Bryant was Health Commissioner at the time, and though we rarely agreed about anything — there is something curious about that, that the men I have thought most of were quite often those with whom I disagreed ordinarily about everything — I can say truly that there have been few better Health Commissioners, and none for whom I have had a more hearty respect and liking. Dr. Bryant especially hated reporters. He was built that way; he disliked notoriety for himself and his friends, and therefore, when one of these complained of a neighbor's parrot to the Health Department, he gave strict orders that the story was to be guarded from the reporters, and particularly from me, who had grieved him more than once by publishing things which, in his opinion, I ought to have said nothing about. I heard of it within the hour, and promptly set my wit against the Doctor's to unearth the parrot.

But it would not come out. Dig as I might, I could not get at it. I tried every way, while the Doctor laughed in his sleeve and beamed upon me.

At last, in desperation, I hit upon a bold plan. I
would get it out of the Doctor himself. I knew his
hours for coming to Sanitary Headquarters — from
his clinics, I suppose. He always came up the stairs

Our Office — my Partner, Mr. Ensign at the Desk, I in the Corner.

absorbed in thought, noticing nothing that passed.
I waylaid him in the turn of the dark hall, and before he had time to think plumped at him an —

"Oh, Doctor! about that parrot of your friend —
er-er, oh! what was his name?"

"Alley," said the Doctor, mechanically, and went
in, only half hearing what I said. I made for the
city directory. There were four Alleys in it. In
an hour I had located my man, and the next morning's *Tribune* had a column account of the tragedy
of the parrot.

The Doctor was very angry.   He went to Headquarters and summoned me solemnly before the
assembled Board.   The time had come, he said, to
have an explanation from me as to who it was that
gave me information against orders and the public
interest.   Evidently there was a traitor in camp, by
whatever means I had procured his treachery.

In vain did I try to show the Doctor how unpro-
fessional my conduct would be in betraying my
informant, even how contemptible.   He was inexo-
rable.   This time I should not escape, nor my accom-
plice either.   Out with it, and at once.   With a
show of regretful resignation I gave in.   For once
I would break my rule and " tell on " my informant.
I thought I detected a slight sneer on the Doctor's
lip as he said that was well; for he was a gentleman,
every inch of him, and I know he hated me for telling.   The other Commissioners looked grave.

" Well, then," I said, "the man who gave me the
parrot story was — you, Dr. Bryant."

The Doctor sat bolt upright with a jerk.   " No
bad jokes, Mr. Riis," he said.   " Who gave you the
story ? "

" Why, you did.   Don't you remember ? "   And
I told how I waylaid him in the hall.   His face, as
the narrative ran on, was a study.   Anger, mirth,
offended pride, struggled there; but the humor of
the thing got the upper hand in the end, and the

one who laughed loudest in the Board room was
Dr. Bryant himself. In my soul I believe that he
was not a little relieved, for under a manner of much
sternness he had the tenderest of hearts.

But it was not always I who came out ahead in
the daily encounters which made up the routine of
my day. It was an important part of my task to be
on such terms with the heads of departments that
they would talk freely to us so that we might know
in any given case, or with reference to the policy of
the department, " where we were at." I do not
mean talk for publication. It is a common mistake
of people who know nothing about the newspaper
profession that reporters flit about public men like
so many hawks, seizing upon what they can find to
publish as their lawful prey. No doubt there are
such guerrillas, and they have occasionally more
than justified their existence; but, as applied to the
staff reporters of a great newspaper, nothing could
be farther from the truth. The department reporter
has his field as carefully laid out for him every day
as any physician who starts out on his route, and
within that field, if he is the right sort of man, he is
friend, companion, and often counsellor to the officials with whom he comes in contact — always sup-
posing that he is not fighting them in open war.
He may serve a Republican paper and the President
of the Police Board may be a Democrat of Demo-

crats; yet in the privacy of his office he will talk as freely to the reporter as if he were his most intimate party friend, knowing that he will not publish what is said in confidence. This is the reporter's capital, without which he cannot in the long run do business.

I presume he is sometimes tempted to gamble with it for a stake. I remember well when the temptation came to me once after a quiet hour with Police Commissioner Matthews, who had been telling me the inside history of an affair which just then was setting the whole town by the ears. I told him that I thought I should have to print it; it was too good to keep. No, it wouldn't do, he said. I knew well enough he was right, but I insisted; the chance was too good a one to miss. Mr. Matthews shook his head. He was an invalid, and was taking his daily treatment with an electric battery while we talked and smoked. He warned me laughingly against the consequences of what I proposed to do, and changed the subject.

" Ever try these ? " he said, giving me the handles. I took them, unsuspecting, and felt the current tingle in my finger-tips. The next instant it gripped me like a vice. I squirmed with pain.

"Stop!" I yelled, and tried to throw the things away; but my hands crooked themselves about them like a bird's claws and held them fast. They would not let go. I looked at the Commissioner. He was

studying the battery leisurely, and slowly pulling
out the plug that increased the current.

"For mercy's sake, stop!" I called to him. He
looked up inquiringly.

"About that interview, now," he drawled. "Do
you think you ought to print—"

"Wow, wow! Let go, I tell you!" It hurt
dreadfully. He pulled the thing out another peg.

"You know it wouldn't do, really. Now, if—"
He made as if to still further increase the current.
I surrendered.

"Let up," I begged, "and I will not say a word.
Only let up."

He set me free. He never spoke of it once in all
the years I knew him, but now and again he would
offer me, with a dry smile, the use of his battery as
"very good for the health." I always declined
with thanks.

I got into Mulberry Street at what might well
be called the heroic age of police reporting. It
rang still with the echoes of the unfathomed
Charley Ross mystery. That year occurred the
Stewart grave robbery and the Manhattan Bank
burglary — three epoch-making crimes that each
in its way made a sensation such as New York
has not known since. For though Charley Ross
was stolen in Philadelphia, the search for him centred in the metropolis. The three-million-dollar

burglary within the shadow of Police Headquarters
gave us Inspector Byrnes, who broke up the old

"About that interview, now," he drawled.

gangs of crooks and drove those whom he did not
put in jail over the sea to ply their trade in Europe.
The Stewart grave robbery ended the career of

the ghouls, and the Charley Ross case put a stop
to child-stealing for a generation, by making those
crimes unprofitable.   The public excitement was
so great that it proved impossible for the thieves
to deliver the goods and effect the change for ran-
som.   At intervals for years these cases kept turning up in one new phase or another. You could
never tell where to look for them.   Indeed, I
have to thank the Stewart ghouls for the first public recognition that came to me in those early
years of toil.   Of all the mysteries that ever vexed
a reporter's soul, that was the most agonizing.
The police, most of the time, were as much in the
dark as the rest of us, and nothing was to be got
from that source.   Heaven knows I tried.   In our
desperation we caught at every straw.   One stormy
night in the hottest of the excitement Judge Hilton,
who had offered the $50,000 reward for the stolen
body on behalf of Mrs. Stewart, went to Headquarters and stayed an hour in the detective office.
When he came out, he was attended by two of the
oldest and ablest detectives.   Clearly something big
was on foot.   They were just like so many sphinxes,
and went straight to the carriage that waited at the
Mulberry Street door.   I do not know how it ever
entered my head; perhaps it didn't at all, but was
just done mechanically.   The wind had blown out
the lamp on the steps, and the street was in pro-

found darkness.   As they stepped into the carriage, I, with only the notion in my head that here was news which must be got somehow, went in last and sank down in the vacant seat, pulling the door to after me.   The carriage went on.   To my intense relief, it rounded the corner.   I was undiscovered! But at that moment it came to a sudden stop.

"The carriage went on."

An invisible hand opened the door, and, grasping my collar, gently but firmly propelled me into the street and dropped me there.   Then the carriage went on.   Not a word had been spoken.   They understood and so did I.   It was enough.

But, as I said, I had my revenge.   It came when the opposition reporters, believing the mystery to be near its solution,[1] entered into a conspiracy to

[1] This was, as nearly as I remember, in the autumn of 1879, the year following the robbery.

forestall it and deliberately invented the lines of the
coming dénouement.   Day by day they published
its progress " upon the authority of a high official "
who never existed, announcing that " behind each
one of the grave-robbers stood a detective with
uplifted hand " ready to arrest him when the word
was given.   It was truly the dawn of yellow journalism.   With such extraordinary circumstantiality
were the accounts given that for once my office
wavered in its faith in Ensign and me.   Amos
Ensign was my partner at the time, a fine fellow
and a good reporter.   If we turned out to be wrong,
we were given to understand our careers on the
Tribune would be at an end.   I slept little or
none during that month of intense work and excitement, but spent my days as my nights sifting every
scrap of evidence.   There was nothing to justify the
stories, and we maintained in our paper that they
were lies.   Mr. Shanks himself left the city desk
and came up to work with us.   His head, too,
would fall, we heard, if his faith in the police office
had been misplaced.   The bubble burst at last, and,
as we expected, there was nothing in it.   The *Tribune* was justified.   The opposition reporters were
fined or suspended.   Ensign and I were made
much of in the office.   I have still the bulletin in
which Mr. Shanks spoke of me as the man whose
work had done much to " make the *Tribune* police

reports the best in the city." Sweet comfort for 'the Dutchman"! My salary was raised, but that was of less account. We had saved the day and the desk. After that it was not all pulling up-stream in Mulberry Street. Nothing in this world succeeds like success.

My zeal, activity and faithful recognition of the Tribune rule of exchanging news with no other paper Mr Riis has done much to make

the Tribune Police reports the best in the city.

It naturally gives the City Editor who makes capital by the successes of his associates great satisfaction in announcing Mr Reid's orders as above.

The Bulletin.

Before that I had been once suspended myself for missing something in this very case. I was not to blame, and therefore was angry and refused to make explanations. That night, as I sat sulking in my home in Brooklyn, a big warehouse fire broke out down town. From our house on the hill I watched it grow beyond control, and knew that the boys were hard put to it. It was late, and as I thought of the hastening hours, the police reporter got the better of the man, and I hurried down to take a hand. When I turned up in the office after midnight to write the story, the night editor eyed me curiously.

"I thought, Riis, you were suspended," he said.

For a moment I wavered, smarting under the injustice of it all. But my note-book reminded me.

"I am," I said, "and when I am done with this I am going home till you send for me. But this fire — can I have a desk?"

The night editor got up and came over and shook hands. "Take mine," he said. "There! take it!"

They sent for me the next day.

It is not to be supposed that all this was smooth sailing. Along with the occasional commendations for battles won against "the mob" went constant and grievous complaints of the editors supplied by the Associated Press, and even by some in my own office now and then, of my "style." It was very bad, according to my critics, altogether editorial and presuming, and not to be borne. So I was warned that I must mend it and give the facts, sparing comments. By that I suppose they meant that I must write, not what I thought, but what they probably might think of the news. But, good or bad, I could write in no other way, and kept right on. Not that I think, by any manners of means, that it was the best way, but it was mine. And goodness knows I had no desire to be an editor. I have not now. I prefer to be a reporter and deal with the facts to being an editor and lying about them. In the end the complaints died out. I suppose I was given up as hopeless.

Perhaps there had crept into my reports too much of my fight with the police. For by that time. I had included them in "the opposition." They had not been friendly from the first, and it was best so. I had them all in front then, and an open enemy is better any day than a false friend who may stab you in the back. In the quarter of a century since, I have seldom been on any other terms with the police. I mean with the heads of them. The rank and file, the man with the night-stick as Roosevelt liked to call him, is all right, if properly led. He has rarely been properly led. It may be that, in that respect at least, my reports might have been tempered somewhat to advantage. Though I don't know. I prefer, after all, to have it out, all out. And it did come out, and my mind was relieved; which was something.

Speaking of night-sticks reminds me of seeing General Grant in his to my mind greatest hour, the only time he was ever beaten, and by a police-man. I told his son, Fred Grant, of it when he became a Police Commissioner in the nineties, but I do not think he appreciated it. He was not cast in his great father's mould. The occasion I refer to was after the General's second term in the Presi-dency. He was staying at the Fifth Avenue Hotel when one morning the Masonic Temple was burned. The fire-line was drawn halfway down

"The General said never a word."

the block toward Fifth Avenue, but the police were much hampered by the crowd, and were out of patience when I, standing by, saw a man in a great ulster with head buried deep in the collar, a cigar sticking straight out, coming down the street from the hotel. I recognized him at sight as General Grant. The policeman who blocked his way did not. He grabbed him by the collar, swung him about, and, hitting him a resounding whack across the back with his club, yelled out : —

"What's the matter with you? Don't you see the fire-lines? Chase yourself out of here, and be quick about it."

The General said never a word. He did not stop to argue the matter. He had run up against a sentinel, and when stopped went the other way. That was all. The man had a right to be there; he had none. I was never so much an admirer of Grant as since that day. It was true greatness. A smaller man would have made a row, stood upon his dignity and demanded the punishment of the policeman. As for him, there was probably never so badly frightened a policeman when I told him whom he had clubbed. I will warrant he did not sleep for a week, fearing all kinds of things. No need of it. Grant probably never gave him a thought.

It was in pursuit of the story of a Breton noble

Q

man of hoped-for ancient lineage that I met with
the most disheartening set-back of my experience.
The setting of the case was most alluring. The
old baron — for he was nothing less, though in
Minetta Lane he passed for a cat's-meat man who
peddled his odd ware from door to door — had been
found by the police sick and starving in his wretched
cellar, and had been taken to Bellevue Hospital.
The inevitable *de* suggested the story, and papers
that I found in his trunk — papers most carefully
guarded and cherished — told enough of it to whet
my appetite to its keenest edge. If the owner could
only be made to talk, if his stubborn family pride
could only be overcome, there was every promise
here of a sensation by means of which who could
tell but belated justice might even be done him and
his family — apart from the phenomenal trouncing
I should be administering through him to my rivals.
Visions of conspiracies, court intrigues, confisca-
tions, and what not, danced before my greedy mental vision. I flew rather than walked up to Bellevue
Hospital to offer him my paper and pen in the
service of right and of vengeance, only to find that
I was twenty-four hours late. The patient had
already been transferred to the Charity Hospital as
a bad case. The boat had gone; there would not
be another for several hours. I could not wait, but
it was a comfort, at all events, to know that my

baron was where I could get at him on the morrow.
I dreamed some more dreams of happiness as I
went back, and was content.

As it happened, I was very busy the next day
and for several days after. The week was nearly
spent when I found myself on the boat going up to
the island. At the hospital office they reassured
me with a queer look. Yes; my man was there,
likely to stay there for a little while. The doctor
would presently take me to see him on his rounds.
In one of the big wards I found him at last, num-
bered in the row of beds among a score of other
human wrecks, a little old man, bent and haggard,
but with some of the dignity, I fancied, of his noble
descent upon his white and wrinkled brow. He
sat up in bed, propped by pillows, and listened with
hungry eyes as, in French which I had most carefully polished up for the occasion, I told him my
errand. When at last I paused, waiting anxiously
for an answer, he laid one trembling hand on
mine — I noticed that the other hung limp from
the shoulder — and made, as it seemed, a superhu-
man effort to speak; but only inarticulate, pitiful
sounds came forth. I looked appealingly at the
doctor.

" Dumb," he said, and shook his head. " Paraly-
sis involving the vocal organs. He will never speak
again."

And he didn't. He was buried in the Potter's Field the next week. For once I was too late. The story of the last of my barons remains untold until this hour.

And now that this chapter, somewhat against my planning, has become wholly the police reporter's, I shall have to bring up my *cause célèbre*, though that came a long while after my getting into Mulberry Street. I shall not have so good an opportunity again. It was the occasion of the last of my many battles for the mastery; but, more than that, it illustrates very well that which I have been trying to describe as a reporter's public function. We had been for months in dread of a cholera scourge that summer, when, mousing about the Health Department one day, I picked up the weekly analysis of the Croton water and noticed that there had been for two weeks past "a trace of nitrites" in the water. I asked the department chemist what it was. He gave an evasive answer, and my curiosity was at once aroused. There must be no unknown or doubtful ingredient in the water supply of a city of two million souls. Like Cæsar's wife, it must be above suspicion. Within an hour I had learned that the nitrites meant in fact that there had been at one time sewage contamination; consequently that we were face to face with a most grave problem. How had the water become pol-

luted, and who guaranteed that it was not in that
way even then, with the black death threatening to
cross the ocean from Europe?

I sounded the warning in my paper, then the
Evening Sun, counselled the people to boil the
water pending further discoveries, then took my
camera and went up in the watershed. I spent a
week there, following to its source every stream
that discharged into the Croton River and photographing my evidence wherever I found it. When
I told my story in print, illustrated with the pictures, the town was astounded. The Board of
Health sent inspectors to the watershed, who reported that things were worse a great deal than I
had said. Populous towns sewered directly into
our drinking-water. There was not even a pretence at decency. The people bathed and washed
their dogs in the streams. The public town dumps
were on their banks. The rival newspapers tried
to belittle the evil because their reporters were
beaten. Running water purifies itself, they said.
So it does, if it runs far enough and long enough.
I put that matter to the test. Taking the case of
a town some sixty miles out of New York, one of
the worst offenders, I ascertained from the engineer
of the water-works how long it ordinarily took to
bring water from the Sodom reservoir just beyond,
down to the housekeepers' faucets in the city. Four

days, I think it was. Then I went to the doctors and asked them how many days a vigorous cholera bacillus might live and multiply in running water. About seven, said they. My case was made. There was needed but a single case of the dreaded scourge in any one of a dozen towns or villages that were on the line of travel from the harbor in which a half score ships were under quarantine, to put the metropolis at the mercy of an inconceivable calamity.

There was in all this no attempt at sensation. It was simple fact, as any one could see for himself. The health inspectors' report clinched the matter. The newspapers editorially abandoned their reporters to ridicule and their fate. The city had to purchase a strip of land along the streams wide enough to guard against direct pollution. It cost millions of dollars, but it was the merest trifle to what a cholera epidemic would have meant to New York in loss of commercial prestige, let alone human lives. The contention over that end of it was transferred to Albany, where the politicians took a hand. What is there they do not exploit? Years after, meeting one of them who knew my share in it, he asked me, with a wink and a confidential shove, "how much I got out of it." When I told him "nothing," I knew that upon my own statement he took me for either a liar or a fool, the last being considerably the worse of the two alternatives.

In all of this battlesome account I have said nothing about the biggest fight of all. I had that with my-self. In the years that had passed I had never for-gotten the sergeant in the Church Street police station, and my dog. It is the kind of thing you do not get over. Way back in my mind there was the secret thought, the day I went up to Mulberry Street, that my time was coming at last. And now it had come. I had a recognized place at Headquarters, and place in the police world means power, more or less. The backing of the *Tribune* had given me influence. More I had conquered myself in my fights with the police. Enough for revenge! At the thought I flushed with anger. It has power yet to make my blood boil, the thought of that night in the station-house.

It was then my great temptation came. No doubt the sergeant was still there. If not, I could find him. I knew the day and hour when it hap-pened. They were burned into my brain. I had only to turn to the department records to find out who made out the returns on that October morning while I was walking the weary length of the trestle-work bridge across Raritan Bay, to have him within reach. There were a hundred ways in which I could hound him then, out of place and pay, even as he had driven me forth from the last poor shelter and caused my only friend to be killed.

Speak not to me of the sweetness of revenge! Of all unhappy mortals the vengeful man must be the most wretched.   I suffered more in the anticipation of mine than ever I had when smarting under the injury, grievous as the memory of it is to me even now.   Day after day I went across the street to begin the search.   For hours I lingered about the record clerk's room where they kept the old station-house blotters, unable to tear myself away.   Once I even had the one from Church Street of October, 1870, in my hands; but I did not open it.   Even as I held it I saw another and a better way.   I would kill the abuse, not the man who was but the instrument and the victim of it.   For never was parody upon Christian charity more corrupting to human mind and soul than the frightful abomination of the police lodging-house, sole provision made by the municipality for its homeless wanderers.   Within a year I have seen the process in full operation in Chicago, have heard a sergeant in the Harrison Street Station there tell me, when my indignation found vent in angry words, that they " cared less for those men and women than for the cur dogs in the street."   Exactly so!   My sergeant was of the same stamp.   Those dens, daily association with them, had stamped him.   Then and there I resolved to wipe them out, bodily, if God gave me health and strength.   And I put the book away quick and

never saw it again. I do not know till this day
who the sergeant was, and I am glad I do not. It
is better so.

Of what I did to carry out my purpose, and how it
was done, I must tell hereafter. It was the source
and beginning of all the work which justifies the
writing of these pages; and among all the things
which I have been credited with doing since it is
one of the few in which I really bore a strong hand.
And yet it was not mine which finally wrought that
great work, but a stronger and better than mine,
Theodore Roosevelt's. Even while I was writing this
account we together drove in the last nail in the coffin of the bad old days, by persuading the Charter
Revision Commission to remove from the organic
law of the city the clause giving to the police the
care of vagrants, which was the cause of it all. It
had remained over in the Charter of the Greater
New York in spite of our protests. It was never
the proper business of the police to dispense charity.
They have their hands full with repressing crime.
It is the mixing of the two that confuses standards
and makes trouble without end for those who receive the "charity," and even more for those who
dispense it. You cannot pervert the first and finest
of human instincts without corrupting men : witness
my sergeant in Church Street and his Chicago
brother.

CHAPTER X

MY DOG IS AVENGED

THE lilacs blossom under my window, as I begin this chapter, and the bees are humming among them; the sweet smell of wild cherry comes up from the garden where the sunlight lies upon the young grass. Robin and oriole call to their mates in the trees. There upon the lawn is Elisabeth tending some linen laid out to dry. Her form is as lithe and her step as light as in the days I have written about, grandmother as she is. I can see, though her back is turned, the look of affectionate pride with which she surveys our home, for I know well enough what she is thinking of. And so it has been; a blessed, good home; how could it help being that with her in it? They say it is a sign one is growing old when one's thoughts dwell much on the past. Perhaps with me it is only a sign that the printers are on the war-path. Often when I hear her sing with the children my mind wanders back to the long winter evenings in those early years when she sat listening late for my step. She sang then to keep up her courage. My work in

Mulberry Street was at night, and she was much alone, even as I was, fighting my battles there. She had it out with the homesickness then, and I think hers was a good deal the harder fight. I had the enemy all in front where I could see to whack him. But so we found ourselves and each other, and it was worth all it cost.

Except in the short winter days it was always broad daylight when I came home from work. My route from the office lay through the Fourth and the Sixth wards, the worst in the city, and for years I walked every morning between two and four o'clock the whole length of Mulberry Street, through the Bend and across the Five Points down to Fulton Ferry. There were cars on the Bowery, but I liked to walk, for so I saw the slum when off its guard. The instinct to pose is as strong there as it is on Fifth Avenue. It is a human impulse, I suppose. We all like to be thought well of by our fellows. But at 3 A.M. the veneering is off and you see the true grain of a thing. So, also, I got a picture of the Bend upon my mind which so soon as I should be able to transfer it to that of the community would help settle with that pig-sty according to its deserts. It was not fit for Christian men and women, let alone innocent children, to live in, and therefore it had to go. So with the police lodging-rooms, some of the worst of which

were right there, at the Mulberry Street Station
and around the corner in Elizabeth Street. The
way of it never gave me any concern that I remember. That would open as soon as the truth was
told. The trouble was that people did not know
and had no means of finding out for themselves.
But I had. Accordingly I went poking about
among the foul alleys and fouler tenements of the
Bend when they slept in their filth, sometimes with
the policeman on the beat, more often alone, sound-
ing the misery and the depravity of it to their depth.
I think a notion of the purpose of it all crept into
the office, even while I was only half aware of it
myself, for when, after a year's service at the police
office, I was taken with a longing for the open, as
it were, and went to the city editor who had succeeded Mr. Shanks with the request that I be transferred to general work, he refused flatly. I had made
a good record as a police reporter, but it was not that.

"Go back and stay," he said. "Unless I am
much mistaken, you are finding something up there
that needs you. Wait and see."

And so for the second time I was turned back
to the task I wanted to shirk. Jonah was one of
us sure enough. Those who see only the whale
fail to catch the point in the most human story ever
told — a point, I am afraid, that has a special appli-
cation to most of us.

I have often been asked if such slumming is not full of peril.   No, not if you are there on business. Mere sightseeing at such unseasonable hours might easily be.   But the man who is sober and minds his own business — which presupposes that he has business to mind there — runs no risk anywhere in New York, by night or by day.   Such a man will take the other side of the street when he sees a gang ahead spoiling for a fight, and where he does go he will carry the quiet assumption of authority that comes with the consciousness of a right to be where he is.   That usually settles it.   There was perhaps another factor in my case that helped.   Whether it was my slouch hat and my spectacles, or the fact that I had been often called into requisition to help an ambulance surgeon patch up an injured man, the nickname " Doc " had somehow stuck to me, and I was supposed by many to be a physician con-nected with the Health Department.   Doctors are never molested in the slum.   It does not know but that its turn to need them is coming next.   No more was I.   I can think of only two occasions in more than twenty years of police reporting when I was in actual peril, though once I was very badly frightened.

One was when a cry of murder had lured me down Crosby Street into a saloon on the corner of Jersey Street, where the gang of the neighborhood had just stabbed the saloon-keeper in a drunken brawl. He was lying in a chair surrounded by shrieking women when I ran in. On the instant the doors were slammed and barred behind me, and I found myself on the battlefield with the battle raging unabated. Bottles were flying thick and fast, and the bar was going to smash. As I bent over the wounded man, I saw that he was done for. The knife was even then sticking in his neck, its point driven into the backbone. The instinct of the reporter came uppermost, and as I pulled it out and held it up in a pause of the fray, I asked incautiously : —

"Whose knife is this?"

A whiskey-bottle that shaved within an inch of my head, followed by an angry oath, at once recalled me to myself and showed me my rôle.

"You tend to your business, you infernal body-snatcher, and let us run ours," ran the message, and I understood. I called for bandages, a sponge, and a basin, and acted the surgeon as well as I could, trying to stanch the flow of blood, while the racket rose and the women shrieked louder with each passing moment. Through the turmoil I strained every nerve to catch the sound of policemen's tramp. It was hardly three minutes' run to the station-house, but time never dragged as it did then. Once I thought relief had come; but as I listened and caught the wail of men being beaten in the street, I smiled wickedly in the midst of my own troubles, for the voices told me that my opponents from headquarters, following on my track, had fallen among thieves: half the gang were then outside. At last, just as an empty keg knocked my patient from his chair, the doors fell in with a crash; the reserves had come. Their clubs soon cleared the air and relieved me of my involuntary task, with my patient yet alive.

Another time, turning a corner in the small hours of the morning, I came suddenly upon a gang of drunken roughs ripe for mischief. The leader had a long dirk-knife with which he playfully jabbed me in the ribs, insolently demanding what I thought of it. I seized him by the wrist with as calm a pretence of considering the knife as I could summon up, but really to prevent his cutting me. I felt the point pricking through my clothes.

"About two inches longer than the law allows," I said, sparring for time. "I think I will take that."

I knew even as I said it that I had cast the die; he held my life in his hand. It was a simple question of which was the stronger, and it was already decided. Despite my utmost effort to stay it, the point of the knife was piercing my skin. The gang stood by, watching the silent struggle. I knew

them — the Why-ōs, the worst cutthroats in the
city, charged with a dozen murders, and robberies
without end. A human life was to them, in the
mood they were in, worth as much as the dirt under
their feet, no more. At that instant, not six feet
behind their backs, Captain McCullagh — the same
who afterward became Chief — turned the corner
with his precinct detective. I gathered all my
strength and gave the ruffian's hand a mighty twist
that turned the knife aside. I held it out for
inspection.

" What do you think of it, Cap ? "

Four brawny fists scattered the gang to the winds
for an answer. The knife was left in my hand.

They gave me no time to get frightened. Once
when I really was scared, it was entirely my own
doing. And, furthermore, it served me right. It
was on a very hot July morning that, coming down
Mulberry Street, I saw a big gray cat sitting on a
beer-keg outside a corner saloon. It was fast asleep,
and snored so loudly that it aroused my anger. It
is bad enough to have a man snore, but a cat —!
It was not to be borne. I hauled off with my cane
and gave the beast a most cruel and undeserved
blow to teach it better manners. The snoring was
smothered in a yell, the cat came down from the
keg, and to my horror there rose from behind the
corner an angry Celt swearing a blue streak. He

seemed to my anguished gaze at least nine feet tall.
He had been asleep at his own door when my blow
aroused him, and it was his stocking feet, propped
up on the keg as he dozed in his chair around the
corner, I had mistaken for a gray cat. It was not a
time for explanations. I did the only thing there
was to be done; I ran. Far and fast did I run. It
was my good luck that his smarting feet kept him
from following, or I might not have lived to tell this
tale. As I said, it served me right. Perhaps it is
in the way of reparation that I now support twelve
cats upon my premises. Three of them are clawing
at my study door this minute demanding to be let
in. But I cannot even claim the poor merit of pro-
viding for them. It is my daughter who runs the
cats; I merely growl at and feed them.

The mention of Bowery night cars brings to my
mind an episode of that time which was thoroughly
characteristic of the "highway that never sleeps."
I was on the way down town in one, with a single
fellow-passenger who was asleep just inside the
door, his head nodding with every jolt as though
it were in danger of coming off. At Grand Street
a German boarded the car and proffered a bad half-
dollar in payment of his fare. The conductor bit it
and gave it back with a grunt of contempt. The
German fell into a state of excitement at once.

"Vat!" he shouted, "it vas pad?" and slapped

the coin down on the wooden seat with all his might, that we might hear the ring. It rebounded with a long slant and fell into the lap of the sleeping passenger, who instantly woke up, grabbed the half-dollar, and vanished through the door and into the darkness, without as much as looking around, followed by the desolate howl of the despoiled German : —

" Himmel! One United Shdades half-dollar clean gone!"

The time came at length when I exchanged night work for day work, and I was not sorry. A new life began for me, with greatly enlarged opportunities. I had been absorbing impressions up till then. I met men now in whose companionship they began to crystallize, to form into definite convictions; men of learning, of sympathy, and of power. My eggs hatched. From that time dates my friendship, priceless to me, with Dr. Roger S. Tracy, then a sanitary inspector in the Health Department, later its distinguished statistician, to whom I owe pretty much all the understanding I have ever had of the problems I have battled with; for he is very wise, while I am rather dull of wit. But directly I get talking things over with him, I brighten right up. I met Professor Charles F. Chandler, Major Willard Bullard, Dr. Edward H. Janes — men to whose practical wisdom and patient labors in the shaping

of the Health Department's work the metropolis
owes a greater debt than it is aware of; Dr. John
T. Nagle, whose friendly camera later on gave me
some invaluable lessons; and General Ely Parker,
Chief of the Six
Nations.

I suppose it was
the fact that he
was an Indian that
first attracted me
to him. As the
years passed we be-
came great friends,
and I loved noth-
ing better in an
idle hour than to
smoke a pipe with
the General in his
poky little office at
Police Headquar-

Dr. Roger S. Tracy.

ters. That was about all there was to it, too, for he
rarely opened his mouth except to grunt approval of
something I was saying. When, once in a while, it
would happen that some of his people came down
from the Reservation or from Canada, the powwow
that ensued was my dear delight. Three pipes and
about eleven grunts made up the whole of it, but
it was none the less entirely friendly and satisfactory.

We all have our own ways of doing things, and that was theirs. He was a noble old fellow. His title was no trumpery show, either. It was fairly earned on more than one bloody field with Grant's army. Parker was Grant's military secretary, and wrote the original draft of the surrender at Appomattox, which he kept to his death with great pride. It was not General Parker, however, but Donehogawa, Chief of the Senecas and of the remnant of the once powerful Six Nations, and guardian of the western door of the council lodge, that appealed to me, who in my boyhood had lived with Leather-stocking and with Uncas and Chingachgook. They had something to do with my coming here, and at last I had for a friend one of their kin. I think he felt the bond of sympathy between us and prized it, for he showed me in many silent ways that he was fond of me. There was about him an infinite pathos, penned up there in his old age among the tenements of Mulberry Street on the pay of a second-rate clerk, that never ceased to appeal to me. When he lay dead, stricken like the soldier he was at his post, some letters of his to Mrs. Harriet Converse, the adopted child of his tribe, went to my heart. They were addressed to her on her travels. He was of the " wolf " tribe, she a " snipe." " From the wolf to the wandering snipe," they ran. Even in Mulberry Street he was a true son of the forest.

Perhaps the General's sympathies **went out** to me as a fighter. The change of front from night to day brought no let-up on hostilities in our camp; rather the reverse. For this there was good cause: I had interfered with long-cherished privileges. I found the day men coming to work at all hours from ten to twelve or even one o'clock. I went on duty at eight, and the immediate result was to compel all the others to do the same. This was a sore grievance,

General Ely Parker,
Chief of the Six Nations.

and was held against me for a long time. The logical outcome of the war it provoked was to stretch the day farther into the small hours. Before I left Mulberry Street the circuit had been made. The watch now is kept up through the twenty-four hours without interruption. Like its neighbor the Bowery, Mulberry Street never sleeps.

There had been in 1879 an awakening of the public conscience on the tenement-house question which I had followed with interest, because it had started in the churches that have always seemed to me to be the right forum for such a discussion, on

every ground, and most for their own sake and the
cause they stand for.   But the awakening proved
more of a sleepy yawn than real — like a man
stretching himself in bed with half a mind to get
up.   Five years later, in 1884, came the Tenement-
House Commission which first brought home to us
the fact that the people living in the tenements
were "better than the houses."   That was a big
white milestone on a dreary road.   From that time
on we hear of "souls" in the slum.   The property
end of it had held the stage up till then, and in a
kind of self-defence, I suppose, we had had to forget that the people there had souls.   Because you
couldn't very well count souls as chattels yielding
so much income to the owner: it would not be
polite toward the Lord, say.   Sounds queer, but if
that was not the attitude I would like to know
what it was.   The Commission met at Police
Headquarters, and I sat through all its sessions as
a reporter, and heard every word of the testimony,
which was more than some of the Commissioners
did.   Mr. Ottendorfer and Mr. Drexel, the banker,
took many a quiet little nap when things were dull.
One man the landlords, who had their innings to
the full, never caught off his guard.   His clear,
incisive questions, that went through all subter-
fuges to the root of things, were sometimes like
flashes of lightning on a dark night discovering

the landscape far and near. He was Dr. Felix
Adler, whom I met there for the first time. The
passing years have given him a very warm place in
my heart. Adler was born a Jew. Often when I
think of the position the Christian Church took, or
rather did not take, on a matter so nearly concerning it as the murder of the home in a tenement
population of a million souls, — for that was what it
came to, — I am reminded of a talk we had once in
Dr. Adler's study. I was going to Boston to speak
to a body of clergymen at their monthly dinner
meeting. He had shortly before received an invitation to address the same body on " The Personality of Christ," but had it in his mind not to go.

" What will you tell them?" I asked.

The Doctor smiled a thoughtful little smile as he
said: "I shall tell them that the personality of Christ
is too sacred a subject for me to discuss at an
after-dinner meeting in a swell hotel."

Does that help you to understand that among the
strongest of moral forces in Christian New York
was and is Adler, the Jew or heretic, take it whichever way you please?

Four years later the finishing touch was put to
the course I took with the Adler Tenement-House
Commission, when, toward the end of a three days'
session in Chickering Hall of ministers of every
sect who were concerned about the losing fight the

Church was waging among the masses, a man stood in the meeting and cried out, "How are these men and women to understand the love of God you speak of, when they see only the greed of men?" He was a builder, Alfred T. White of Brooklyn, who had proved the faith that was in him by building real homes for the people, and had proved, too, that they were a paying investment. It was just a question whether a man would take seven per cent and save his soul, or twenty-five and lose it. And I might as well add here that it is the same story yet. All our hopes for betterment, all our battling with the tenement-house question, sum themselves up in the effort, since there are men yet who would take twenty-five per cent and run that risk, to compel them to take seven and save their souls for them. I wanted to jump up in my seat at that time and shout Amen! But I remembered that I was a reporter and kept still. It was that same winter, however, that I wrote the title of my book, "How the Other Half Lives," and copyrighted it. The book itself did not come until two years after, but it was as good as written then. I had my text.

It was at that Chickering Hall meeting that I heard the gospel preached to the poor in the only way that will ever reach them. It was the last word that was said, and I have always believed that it was not exactly in the plan. I saw some venerable brethren on the platform, bishops among them, wince when Dr. Charles H. Parkhurst, rending some eminently respectable platitudes to shreds and tatters, cried out for personal service, loving touch, as the key to it all : —

"What if, when the poor leper came to the Lord to be healed, he had said to Peter, or some other understrapper, 'Here, Peter, you go touch that fellow and I'll pay you for it'? Or what if the Lord, when he came on earth, had come a day at a time and brought his lunch with him, and had gone home to heaven overnight? Would the world ever have come to call him brother? We have got to give, not our old clothes, not our prayers. Those are cheap. You can kneel down on a carpet and pray where it is warm and comfortable. Not our soup — that is sometimes very cheap. Not our money — a stingy man will give money when he refuses to give himself. Just so soon as a man feels that you sit down alongside of him in loving sympathy with him, notwithstanding his poor, notwithstanding his sick and his debased, estate, just so soon you begin to worm your way into the very warmest spot in his life."

It was plain talk, but it was good. They whispered afterward in the corners about the "lack of discretion of that good man Parkhurst." A little of that lack would go a long way toward cleaning

up in New York—did go, not so many years after.
Worse shocks than that were coming from the same
quarter to rattle the dry bones.

Long before that the "something that needed
me" in Mulberry Street had come. I was in a
death-grapple with my two enemies, the police lodging-room and the Bend. The Adler Commission
had proposed to "break the back" of the latter by
cutting Leonard Street through the middle of it —
an expedient that had been suggested forty years
before, when the Five Points around the corner
challenged the angry resentment of the community.
But no expedient would ever cover that case. The
whole slum had to go. A bill was introduced in
the Legislature to wipe it out bodily, and in 1888,
after four years of pulling and hauling, we had
spunked up enough to file maps for the "Mulberry
Bend Park." Blessed promise! And it was kept,
if it did take a prodigious lot of effort, for right there
decency had to begin, or not at all. Go and look
at it to-day and see what it is like.

But that is another story. The other nuisance
came first. The first guns that I have any record
of were fired in my newspapers in 1883, and from
that time till Theodore Roosevelt shut up the vile
dens in 1895 the battle raged without intermission.
The guns I speak of were not the first that were
fired —they were the first I fired so far as I can

find. For quite a generation before that there had been protests and complaints from the police surgeons, the policemen themselves who hated to lodge under one roof with tramps, from citizen bodies that saw in the system an outrage upon Christian charity and all decency, but all without producing any other effect than spasmodic whitewashing and the ineffectual turning on of the hose. Nothing short of boiling water would have cleansed those dens. Nothing else came of it, because stronger even than the selfish motive that exploits public office for private gain is the deadly inertia in civic life which simply means that we are all as lazy as things will let us be. The older I get, the more patience I have with the sinner and the less with the lazy good-for-nothing who is at the bottom of more than half the share of the world's troubles. Give me the thief if need be, but take the tramp away and lock him up at hard labor until he is willing to fall in line and take up his end. The end he lets lie some one has got to carry who already has enough.

I ran to earth at last one of the citizens' bodies that were striving with the nuisance, and went and joined it. I will not say that I was received graciously. I was a reporter, and it was human nature to assume that I was merely after a sensation; and I did make a sensation of the campaign. That was the way to put life into it. Page after page I printed, now in this paper, now in that, and when the round was completed, went over the same road again. They winced a bit, my associates, but bore it, egged me on even. Anything for a change. Perchance it might help. It didn't then. But slowly something began to stir. The editors found something to be indignant about when there was nothing else. Ponderous leaders about our "duty toward the poor" appeared at intervals. The Grand Jury on its tours saw and protested. The City Hall felt the sting and squirmed. I remember when we went to argue with the Board of Estimate and Apportionment under Mayor Grant. It was my first meeting with Mrs. Josephine Shaw Lowell and John Finley, but not the last by a good many, thank God for that! I had gone to Boston to see the humane way in which they were dealing with their homeless there. They gave them a clean shirt and a decent bed and a bath — good way, that, to limit the supply of tramps — and something to eat in the morning, so they did not have to go out and beg the first thing. It seemed good to me, and it was good. But the Mayor did not think so.

"Boston! Boston!" he cried, impatiently, and waved us and the subject aside. "I am tired of hearing always how they do in Boston, and of the whole matter."

So were we, tired enough to keep it up. We

came back next time, though it didn't do any good,
and meanwhile the newspaper broadsides continued.
No chance was allowed to pass of telling the people
of New York what they were harboring. They
simply needed to know, I felt sure of that. And I
know now that I was right. But it takes a lot of
telling to make a city know when it is doing wrong.
However, that was what I was there for. When it
didn't seem to help, I would go and look at a stone-
cutter hammering away at his rock perhaps a hundred times without as much as a crack showing in
it. Yet at the hundred and first blow it would split
in two, and I knew it was not that blow that did it,
but all that had gone before together. When my
fellow-workers smiled, I used to remind them of the
Israelites that marched seven times around Jericho
and blew their horns before the walls fell.

"Well, you go ahead and blow yours," they said;
"you have the faith."

And I did, and the walls did fall, though it took
nearly twice seven years. But they came down, as
the walls of ignorance and indifference must every
time, if you blow hard enough and long enough,
with faith in your cause and in your fellow-man. It
is just a question of endurance. If you keep it up,
they can't.

They began to give, those grim walls, when typhus
fever broke out in the city in the winter of 1891–92.

The wonder was that it did not immediately centre in the police lodging-rooms. There they lay, young and old, hardened tramps and young castaways with minds and souls soft as wax for their foulness to be stamped upon,[1] on bare floors of stone or planks.

The Lodging-room at the Leonard Street Police Station.

Dirty as they came in from every vile contact, they went out in the morning to scatter from door to

[1] The old cry of sensation mongering was raised more than once when I was making my charges. People do not like to have their rest disturbed. Particularly did the critics object to the statement that there were young people in the dens; they were all old tramps, they said. For an answer I went in and photographed the boys and girls one night, and held their pictures up before the community. In the Oak Street Station alone, one of the vilest, there were six as likely young fellows as I ever saw, herded with forty tramps and thieves. Not one of them would come out unscathed.

door, where they begged their breakfast, the seeds
of festering disease. Turning the plank was "making the bed." Typhus is a filth-disease, of all the
most dreaded. If ever it got a foothold in those
dens, there was good cause for fear. I drew up at
once a remonstrance, had it signed by representa-
tives of the united charitable societies — some of
them shrugged their shoulders, but they signed —
and took it to the Health Board. They knew the
danger better than I. But the time had not yet
come. Perhaps they thought, with the reporters,
that I was just "making copy." For I made a
"beat" of the story. Of course I did. We were
fighting; and if I could brace the boys up to the
point of running their own campaigns for making
things better, so much was gained. But they did
not take the hint. They just denounced my
"treachery."

I warned them that there would be trouble with
the lodging-rooms, and within eleven months the
prophecy came true. The typhus broke out *there*.
The night after the news had come I took my camera and flashlight and made the round of the dens,
photographing them all with their crowds. Of the
negatives I had lantern-slides made, and with these
under my arm knocked at the doors of the Academy
of Medicine, demanding to be let in. That was the
place for that discussion, it seemed to me, for the

doctors knew the real extent of the peril we were then facing.   Typhus is no respecter of persons, and it is impossible to guard against it as against the smallpox.   They let me in, and that night's doings gave the cause of decency a big push.   I think that was the first time I told the real story of my dog. I had always got around it somehow; it choked me even then, twenty years after and more, anger boiled up in me so at the recollection.

We pleaded merely for the execution of a law that had been on the statute-books six years and over, permitting the city authorities to establish a decent lodging-house; but though the police, the health officials, the grand jury, the charitable socie- ties, and about everybody of any influence in the community fell in behind the medical profession in denouncing the evils that were, we pleaded in vain. The Tammany officials at the City Hall told us in- solently to go ahead and build lodging-houses our- selves; they had other things to use the city's money for than to care for the homeless poor; which, indeed, was true.   The Charity Organization Society that stood for all the rest gave up in dis- couragement and announced its intention to start a Wayfarer's Lodge itself, on the Boston plan, and did so.   "You see," was the good-by with which my colaborers left me, "we will never succeed." My campaign had collapsed.

But even then we were winning. Never was defeat in all that time that did not in the end turn out a step toward victory. This much the unceasing agitation had effected, though its humane purpose made no impression on the officials, that the accommodation for lodgers in the station-houses was sensibly shrunk. Where there had been forty that took them in, there were barely two dozen left. The demand for separate women's prisons with police matrons in charge, which was one of the phases the new demand for decency was assuming, bred a scarcity of house-room, and one by one the foul old dens were closed and not reopened. The nuisance was perishing of itself. Each time a piece of it sloughed off, I told the story again in print, "lest we forget." In another year reform came, and with it came Roosevelt. The Committee on Vagrancy, a volunteer body of the Charity Organization Society, of which Mrs. Lowell was the head and I a member, unlimbered its guns again and opened fire, and this time the walls came down. For Tammany was out.

We had been looking the police over by night, Roosevelt and I. We had inspected the lodging-rooms while I went over the long fight with him, and had come at last, at 2 A.M., to the Church Street Station. It was raining outside. The light flickered, cold and cheerless, in the green lamps as we went up the stone steps. Involuntarily I looked in the corner for my little dog; but it was not there, or any one who remembered it. The sergeant glanced over his blotter grimly; I had almost to pinch myself to make sure I was not shivering in a linen duster, wet to the skin. Down the cellar steps

The Church Street Station Lodging-room, in which I was robbed.

to the men's lodging-room I led the President of the Police Board. It was unchanged — just as it was the day I slept there. Three men lay stretched at full length on the dirty planks, two of them young lads from the country. Standing there, I told Mr. Roosevelt my own story. He turned alternately red and white with anger as he heard it.

"Did they do that to you?" he asked when I had

ended. For an answer I pointed to the young lads then asleep before him.

"I was like this one," I said.

He struck his clenched fists together. "I will smash them to-morrow."

He was as good as his word. The very next day the Police Board took the matter up. Provision was made for the homeless on a barge in the East River until plans could be perfected for sifting the tramps from the unfortunate; and within a week, on recommendation of the Chief of Police, orders were issued to close the doors of the police lodging-rooms on February 15, 1896, never again to be un-barred.

The battle was won. The murder of my dog was avenged, and forgiven, after twenty-five years. The yellow newspapers, with the true instinct that made them ever recognize in Roosevelt the implacable enemy of all they stood for, printed cartoons of homeless men shivering at a barred door "closed by order of T. Roosevelt"; but they did not, after all, understand the man they were attacking. That the thing was right was enough for him. Their shafts went wide of the mark, or fell harmless. The tramps for whom New York had been a paradise betook themselves to other towns not so discerning — went to Chicago, where the same wicked system was in operation until last spring, is yet for all I

know — and the honestly homeless got a chance.
A few tender-hearted and soft-headed citizens, of
the kind who ever obstruct progress by getting
some very excellent but vagrant impulses mixed
up with a lack of common sense, wasted their sympathy upon the departing hobo, but soon tired of it.
I remember the case of one tramp whose beat was
in the block in Thirty-fifth Street in which Dr.
Parkhurst lives.   He was arrested for insolence to
a housekeeper who refused him food.   The magis-
trate discharged him, with some tearful remarks
about the world's cruelty and the right of a man
to be poor without being accounted a criminal.
Thus encouraged, the tramp went right back and
broke the windows of the house that had repelled
him.   I presume he is now in the city by the
lake holding up people who offend him by being
more industrious and consequently more prosperous than he.

For the general results of the victory so labori-
ously achieved I must refer to [1] "A Ten Years'
War," in which I endeavored to sum up the situation as I saw it.   They are not worked out yet to
the full.   The most important link is missing.
That is to be a farm-school which shall sift the
young idler from the heap of chaff, and win him
back to habits of industry and to the world of men.
It will come when moral purpose has been reëstab-

[1] Now, "The Battle with the Slum."

lished at the City Hall. I have not set out here to
discuss reform and its merits, but merely to point
out that the way of it, the best way of bringing it
on — indeed, the only way that is always open — is
to make the facts of the wrong plain. And, having
said that, I have put the reporter where he belongs
and answered the
question why I have
never wanted execu-
tive office and never
will.

And now, in tak-
ing leave of this sub-
ject, of which I hope
I may never hear
again, for it has
plagued me enough
and had its full share
of my life, is there
not one ray of bright-

The Yellow Newspapers' Contribution.

ness that falls athwart its gloom? Were they all
bad, those dens I hated, yes, hated, with the shame
and the sorrow and hopeless surrender they stood
for? Was there not one glimpse of mercy that
dwells in the memory with redeeming touch? Yes,
one. Let it stand as testimony that on the brink
of hell itself human nature is not wholly lost. There
is still the spark of His image, however overlaid by

the slum.   And let it forever wipe out the score of my dog, and mine.   It was in one of the worst that I came upon a young girl, pretty, innocent — Heaven knows how she had landed there.   She hid her head in her apron and wept bitterly with the shame of the thing.   Around her half a dozen old hags, rum-sodden and foul, camped on the stone floor.   As in passing I stooped over the weeping girl, one of them, thinking I was one of the men about the place, and misunderstanding my purpose, sprang between us like a tigress and pushed me back.

"Not her!" she cried, and shook her fist at me; "not her!   It is all right with us.   We are old and tough.   But she is young, and don't you dare!"

I went out and stood under the stars, and thanked God that I was born.   Only tramps!   It had been dinned into my ears until I said it myself, God forgive me!   Aye, that was what we had made of them with our infernal machinery of rum-shop, tenement, dive, and — this place.   With Christian charity instead, what might they not have been?

CHAPTER XI

THE BEND IS LAID BY THE HEELS

IF there be any to whom the travail through which we have just come seems like a mighty tempest in a teapot, let him quit thinking so. It was not a small matter. To be sure, the wrong could have been undone in a day by the authorities, had they been so minded. That it was not undone was largely, and illogically, because no one had a word to say in its defence. When there are two sides to a thing, it is not difficult to get at the right of it in an argument, and to carry public opinion for the right. But when there is absolutely nothing to be said against a proposed reform, it seems to be human nature — American human nature, at all events — to expect it to carry itself through with the general good wishes but no particular lift from any one. It is a very charming expression of our faith in the power of the right to make its way, only it is all wrong: it will not make its way in the generation that sits by to see it move. It has got to be moved along, like everything else in this world, by men. That is how we take title to the name. That is what is the matter with half our dead-letter laws. The other half were just still-born. It is so, at this moment, with the children's playgrounds in New York. Probably all thinking people subscribe to-day to the statement that it is the business of the municipality to give its children a chance to play, just as much as to give them schools to go to. Everybody applauds it. The authorities do not question it; but still they do not provide playgrounds. Private charity has to keep a beggarly half-dozen going where there ought to be forty or fifty, as a matter of right, not of charity. Call it official conservatism, inertia, treachery, call it by soft names or hard; in the end it comes to this, I suppose, that it is the whetstone upon which our purpose is sharpened, and in that sense we have apparently got to be thankful for it. So a man may pummel his adversary and accept him as a means of grace at the same time. If there were no snags, there would be no wits to clear them away, or strong arms to wield the axe. It was the same story with the Mulberry Bend. Until the tramp lodging-houses were closed, until the Bend was gone, it seemed as if progress were flat down impossible. As I said, decency had to begin there, or not at all.

Before I tackle the Bend, perhaps I had better explain how I came to take up photographing as a — no, not exactly as a pastime. It was never that

The Mulberry Bend as it was.

with me. I had use for it, and beyond that I never went. I am downright sorry to confess here that I am no good at all as a photographer, for I would like to be. The thing is a constant marvel to me, and an unending delight. To watch the picture come out upon the plate that was blank before, and that saw with me for perhaps the merest fraction of a second, maybe months before, the thing it has never forgotten, is a new miracle every time. If I were a clergyman I would practise photography and preach about it. But I am jealous of the miracle. I do not want it explained to me in terms of HO_2

or such like formulas, learned, but so hopelessly unsatisfying. I do not want my butterfly stuck on a pin and put in a glass case. I want to see the sunlight on its wings as it flits from flower to flower, and I don't care a rap what its Latin name may be. Anyway, it is not its name. The sun and the flower and the butterfly know that. The man who sticks a pin in it does not, and never will, for he knows not its language. Only the poet does among men. So, you see, I am disqualified from being a photographer. Also, I am clumsy, and impatient of details. The axe was ever more to my liking than the graving-tool. I have lived to see the day of the axe and enjoy it, and now I rejoice in the coming of the men and women who know; the Jane Addamses, who to heart add knowledge and training, and with gentle hands bind up wounds which, alas! too often I struck. It is as it should be. I only wish they would see it and leave me out for my sins.

But there! I started out to tell about how I came to be a photographer, and here I am, off on the subject of philanthropy and social settlements. To be precise, then, I began taking pictures by proxy. It was upon my midnight trips with the sanitary police that the wish kept cropping up in me that there were some way of putting before the people what I saw there. A drawing might have done it, but I cannot draw, never could. There are certain

sketches of mine now on record that always arouse
the boisterous hilarity of the family. They were
made for the instruction of our first baby in wolf-
lore, and I know they were highly appreciated by
him at the time. Maybe the fashion in wolves has
changed since. But, anyway, a drawing would not
have been evidence of the kind I wanted. We used
to go in the small hours of the morning into the
worst tenements to count noses and see if the law
against overcrowding was violated, and the sights I
saw there gripped my heart until I felt that I must
tell of them, or burst, or turn anarchist, or something. "A man may be a man even in a palace"
in modern New York as in ancient Rome, but not
in a slum tenement. So it seemed to me, and in
anger I looked around for something to strike off
his fetters with. But there was nothing.

I wrote, but it seemed to make no impression.
One morning, scanning my newspaper at the breakfast table, I put it down with an outcry that startled
my wife, sitting opposite. There it was, the thing
I had been looking for all those years. A four-line
despatch from somewhere in Germany, if I remember right, had it all. A way had been discovered,
it ran, to take pictures by flashlight. The darkest
corner might be photographed that way. I went
to the office full of the idea, and lost no time in
looking up Dr. John T. Nagle, at the time in charge

of the Bureau of Vital Statistics in the Health Department, to tell him of it.   Dr. Nagle was an
amateur photographer of merit and a good fellow
besides, who entered into my plans with great readi-
ness.   The news had already excited much interest
among New York photographers, professional and
otherwise, and no time was lost in communicating
with the other side.   Within a fortnight a raiding
party composed of Dr. Henry G. Piffard and Richard Hoe Lawrence, two distinguished amateurs, Dr.
Nagle and myself, and sometimes a policeman or
two, invaded the East Side by night, bent on letting
in the light where it was so much needed.

At least that was my purpose.   To the photographers it was a voyage of discovery of the greatest interest; but the interest centred in the camera
and the flashlight.   The police went along from
curiosity; sometimes for protection.   For that they
were hardly needed.   It is not too much to say that
our party carried terror wherever it went.   The
flashlight of those days was contained in cartridges
fired from a revolver.   The spectacle of half a dozen
strange men invading a house in the midnight hour
armed with big pistols which they shot off recklessly
was hardly reassuring, however sugary our speech,
and it was not to be wondered at if the tenants
bolted through windows and down fire-escapes
wherever we went.   But as no one was murdered,

things calmed down after a while, though months
after I found the recollection of our visits hanging
over a Stanton Street block like a nightmare. We
got some good pictures; but very soon the slum and
the awkward hours palled upon the amateurs. I
found myself alone just when I needed help most.

"The tenants bolted through the windows."

I had made out by the flashlight possibilities my
companions little dreamed of.

I hired a professional photographer next whom I
found in dire straits. He was even less willing to
get up at 2 A.M. than my friends who had a good
excuse. He had none, for I paid him well. He
repaid me by trying to sell my photographs behind
my back. I had to replevin the negatives to get

them away from him.   He was a pious man, I take
it, for when I tried to have him photograph the
waifs in the baby nursery at the Five Points House
of Industry, as they were saying their " Now I lay
me down to sleep," and the plate came out blank
the second time, he owned up that it was his doing:
it went against his principles to take a picture of
any one at prayers.   So I had to get another man
with some trouble and expense.   But on the whole
I think the experience was worth what it cost.   The
spectacle of a man prevented by religious scruples
from photographing children at prayers, while plotting at the same time to rob his employer, has been
a kind of chart to me that has piloted me through
more than one quagmire of queer human nature.
Nothing could stump me after that.   The man was
just as sincere in the matter of his scruple as he
was rascally in his business dealings with me.

There was at last but one way out of it; namely,
for me to get a camera myself.   This I did, and
with a dozen plates took myself up the Sound to
the Potter's Field on its desert island to make my
first observations.   There at least I should be alone,
with no one to bother me.   And I wanted a picture
of the open trench.   I got it, too.   When I say
that with the sunlight of a January day on the
white snow I exposed that extra-quick instantaneous
plate first for six seconds, then for twelve, to make

sure I got the picture,[1] and then put the plate-holder
back among the rest so that I did not know which
was which, amateur photographers will understand
the situation.   I had to develop the whole twelve
to get one picture.   That was so dark, almost black,
from over-exposure as to be almost hopeless.   But
where there is life there is hope, if you can apply
that maxim to the Potter's Field, where there are
none but dead men.   The very blackness of my
picture proved later on, when I came to use it with
a magic lantern, the taking feature of it.   It added
a gloom to the show more realistic than any the
utmost art of professional skill might have attained.

So I became a photographer, after a fashion, and
thereafter took the pictures myself.   I substituted
a frying-pan for the revolver, and flashed the light
on that.   It seemed more homelike.   But, as I said,
I am clumsy.   Twice I set fire to the house with
the apparatus, and once to myself.   I blew the light
into my own eyes on that occasion, and only my spectacles saved me from being blinded for life.   For
more than an hour after I could see nothing and
was led about by my companion, helpless.   Photographing Joss in Chinatown nearly caused a riot

---

[1] Men are ever prone to doubt what they cannot understand.   With
all the accumulated information on the subject, even to this day, when
it comes to taking a snap-shot, at the last moment I weaken and take
it under protest, refusing to believe that it can be.   A little more faith
would make a much better photographer of me.

there. It seems that it was against *their* religious principles. Peace was made only upon express assurance being given the guardians of Joss that his picture would be hung in the "gallery at Police Headquarters." They took it as a compliment. The "gallery" at Headquarters is the rogues' gallery, not generally much desired. Those Chinese are a queer lot, but when I remembered my Christian friend of the nursery I did not find it in me to blame them. Once, when I was taking pictures about Hell's Kitchen, I was confronted by a wild-looking man with a club, who required me to subscribe to a general condemnation of reporters as "hardly fit to be flayed alive," before he would let me go; the which I did with a right good will, though with somewhat of a mental reservation in favor of my rivals in Mulberry Street, who just then stood in need of special correction.

What with one thing and another, and in spite of all obstacles, I got my pictures, and put some of them to practical use at once. I recall a midnight expedition to the Mulberry Bend with the sanitary police that had turned up a couple of characteristic cases of overcrowding. In one instance two rooms that should at most have held four or five sleepers were found to contain fifteen, a week-old baby among them. Most of them were lodgers and slept there for "five cents a spot." There was no pretence of beds. When the report was submitted to the Health Board the next day, it did not make much of an impression — these things rarely do, put in mere words — until my negatives, still dripping from

Lodgers at Five Cents a Spot.

the dark-room, came to reënforce them. From them there was no appeal. It was not the only instance of the kind by a good many. Neither the landlord's protests nor the tenant's plea "went" in face of the camera's evidence, and I was satisfied.

I had at last an ally in the fight with the Bend. It was needed, worse even than in the campaign against the police lodging-houses, for in that we were a company; in the Bend I was alone. From

T

the day — I think it was in the winter of 1886 —
when it was officially doomed to go by act of legislature until it did go, nine years later, I cannot
remember that a cat stirred to urge it on.   Whether
it was that it had been bad so long that people
thought it could not be otherwise, or because the
Five Points had taken all the reform the Sixth
Ward had coming to it, or because, by a sort of
tacit consent, the whole matter was left to me as
the recognized Mulberry Bend crank — whichever
it was, this last was the practical turn it took.   I
was left to fight it out by myself.   Which being so,
I laid in a stock of dry plates and buckled to.

The Bend was a much jollier adversary than the
police lodging-houses.   It kicked back.   It did not
have to be dragged into the discussion at intervals,
but crowded in unbidden.   In the twenty years of
my acquaintance with it as a reporter I do not
believe there was a week in which it was not heard
from in the police reports, generally in connection
with a crime of violence, a murder or a stabbing
affray.   It was usually on Sunday, when the Italians
who lived there were idle and quarrelled over their
cards.   Every fight was the signal for at least two
more, sometimes a dozen, for they clung to their
traditions and met all efforts of the police to get at
the facts with their stubborn "fix him myself."   And
when the detectives had given up in dismay and

the man who was cut had got out of the hospital, pretty soon there was news of another fight, and the feud had been sent on one step. By far the most cheering testimony that our Italian is becoming one of us came to me a year or two ago in the evidence that on two occasions Mulberry Street had refused to hide a murderer even in his own village.[1] That was conclusive. It was not so in those days. So, between the vendetta, the mafia, the ordinary neighborhood feuds, and the Bend itself, always picturesque if outrageously dirty, it was not hard to keep it in the foreground. My scrap-book from the year 1883 to 1896 is one running comment on the Bend and upon the official indolence that delayed its demolition nearly a decade after it had been decreed. But it all availed nothing to hurry up things, until, in a swaggering moment, after four years of that sort of thing, one of the City Hall officials condescended to inform me of the real cause of the delay. It was simply that "no one down there had been taking any interest in the thing."

I could not have laid it out for him to suit my case better than he did. It was in the silly season,

---

[1] The Italians here live usually grouped by "villages," that is, those from the same community with the same patron saint keep close together. The saint's name-day is their local holiday. If the police want to find an Italian scamp, they find out first from what village he hails, then it is a simple matter, usually, to find where he is located in the city.

Bandits' Roost—a Mulberry Bend Alley.

and the newspapers fell greedily upon the sensation
I made.   The Bend, moreover, smelled rather worse
than usual that August.   They made " the people's
cause " their own, and shouted treason until the
commission charged with condemning the Bend

actually did meet and greased its wheels. But at
the next turn they were down in a rut again, and the
team had to be prodded some more. It had taken
two years to get a map of the proposed park filed
under the law that authorized the laying out of it.
The commission consumed nearly six years in condemning the forty-one lots of property, and charged
the city $45,498.60 for it. The Bend itself cost a
million, and an assessment of half a million was laid
upon surrounding property for the supposed benefit
of making it over from a pig-sty into a park. Those
property-owners knew better. They hired a lawyer
who in less than six weeks persuaded the Legislature that it was an injury, not a benefit. The town
had to foot the whole bill. But at last it owned the
Bend.

Instead of destroying it neck and crop, it settled
down complacently to collect the rents; that is to
say, such rents as it could collect. A good many
of the tenants refused to pay, and lived rent free
for a year. It was a rare chance for the reporter,
and I did not miss it. The city as landlord in the
Bend was fair game. The old houses came down
at last, and for a twelvemonth, while a reform government sat at the City Hall, the three-acre lot lay,
a veritable slough of despond filled with unutter-
able nastiness, festering in the sight of men. No
amount of prodding seemed able to get it out of

that, and all the while money given for the relief
of the people was going to waste at the rate of a
million dollars a year. The Small Parks Act of
1887 appropriated that amount, and it was to be
had for the asking. But no one who had the
authority asked, and as the appropriation was not
cumulative, each passing year saw the loss of just
so much to the cause of decency that was waiting
without. Eight millions had been thrown away
when they finally came to ask a million and a half
to pay for the Mulberry Bend park, and then they
had to get a special law and a special appropriation
because the amount was more than "a million in
one year." This in spite of the fact that we were
then in the Christmas holidays with one year just
closing and the other opening, each with its un-
claimed appropriation. I suggested that to the
powers that were, but they threw up their hands:
that would have been irregular and quite without
precedent. Oh, for irregularity enough to throttle
precedent finally and for good! It has made more
mischief in the world, I verily believe, than all the
other lawbreakers together. At the very outset it
had wrecked my hopes of getting the first school
playground in New York planted in the Bend by
simply joining park and school together. There
was a public school in the block that went with the
rest. The Small Parks Law expressly provided for

the construction of " such and so many " buildings
for the comfort, health, and " instruction " of the
people, as might be necessary.   But a school in a
park!   The thing had never been heard of.   It
would lead to conflict between two departments!
And to this day there is no playground in the Mulberry Bend, though the school is right opposite.

Bottle Alley, Mulberry Bend.   Headquarters of the Whyo Gang.

It was, nevertheless, that sort of thing that lent
the inspiration which in the end made the old Bend
go.   It was when, in the midst of the discussion,
they showed me a check for three cents, hung up
and framed in the Comptroller's office as a kind of

red-tape joss for the clerks to kow-tow to, I suppose.
They were part of the system it glorified. The
three cents had miscarried in the purchase of a
school site, and, when the error was found, were
checked out with all the fuss and flourish of a
transaction in millions and at a cost, I was told, of
fifty dollars' worth of time and trouble. Therefore
it was hung up to be forever admired as the ripe
fruit of an infallible system. No doubt it will be
there when another Tweed has cleaned out the
city's treasury to the last cent. However, it suggested a way out to me. Two could play at that
game. There is a familiar principle of sanitary
law, expressed in more than one ordinance, that
no citizen has a right to maintain a nuisance on his
premises because he is lazy or it suits his conven-
ience in other ways. The city is merely the aggre-
gate of citizens in a corporation, and must be
subject to the same rules. I drew up a complaint
in proper official phrase, charging that the state of
Mulberry Bend was "detrimental to health and
dangerous to life," and formally arraigned the municipality before the Health Board for maintaining a
nuisance upon its premises.

I have still a copy of that complaint, and, as the
parting shot to the worst slum that ever was, and,
let us hope, ever will be, I quote it here in part: —

"The Bend is a mass of wreck, a dumping-ground

for all manner of filth from the surrounding tenements.   The Street-cleaning Department has no
jurisdiction over it, and the Park Department, in
charge of which it is, exercises none.

"The numerous old cellars are a source of danger
to the children that swarm over the block.   Water
stagnating in the holes will shortly add the peril of
epidemic disease.   Such a condition as that now
prevailing in this block, with its dense surrounding
population, would not be tolerated by your department for a single day if on private property.   It
has lasted here many months.

"The property is owned by the city, having been
taken for the purposes of a park and left in this
condition after the demolition of the old buildings.
The undersigned respectfully represents that the
city, in the proposed Mulberry Bend park, is at
present maintaining a nuisance, and that it is the
duty of your honorable Board to see to it that it is
forthwith abolished, to which end he prays that you
will proceed at once with the enforcement of the
rules of your department prohibiting the maintaining of nuisances within the city's limits."

If my complaint caused a smile in official quarters, it was short-lived, except in the Sanitary
Bureau, where I fancy it lurked.   For the Bend
was under its windows.   One whiff of it was
enough to determine the kind of report the health

inspectors would have to make when forced to act.
That night, before they got around, some boys
playing with a truck in the lots ran it down into
one of the cellar holes spoken of and were crushed
under it, and so put a point upon the matter that
took the laughter out of it for good.   They went
ahead with the park then.

When they had laid the sod, and I came and
walked on it in defiance of the sign to "keep off
the grass," I was whacked by a policeman for doing
it, as I told in the "Ten Years' War."[1] But that
was all right.   We had the park.   And I had been
"moved on" before when I sat and shivered in
reeking hallways in that very spot, alone and forlorn in the long ago; so that I did not mind.   The
children who were dancing there in the sunlight
were to have a better time, please God! We had
given them their lost chance. Looking at them
in their delight now, it is not hard to understand
what happened: the place that had been redolent
of crime and murder became the most orderly in
the city.   When the last house was torn down in
the Bend, I counted seventeen murders in the
block all the details of which I remembered.   No
doubt I had forgotten several times that number.
In the four years after that during which I remained in Mulberry Street I was called only once
to record a deed of violence in the neighborhood,

---

[1] Now, "The Battle with the Slum."

and that was when a stranger came in and killed
himself.   Nor had the Bend simply sloughed off
its wickedness, for it to lodge and take root in some
other place.   That would have been something;
but it was not that.   The Bend had become decent
and orderly because the sunlight was let in, and

The Mulberry Bend as it is.

shone upon children who had at last the right to
play, even if the sign "keep off the grass" was still
there.   That was what the Mulberry Bend park
meant.   It was the story it had to tell.   And as
for the sign, we shall see the last of that yet.
The park has notice served upon it that its time
is up.

So the Bend went, and mighty glad am I that I had a hand in making it go. The newspapers puzzled over the fact that I was not invited to the formal opening. I was Secretary of the Small Parks Committee at the time, and presumably even officially entitled to be bidden to the show; though, come to think of it, our committee was a citizens' affair and not on the pay-rolls! The Tammany Mayor who came in the year after said that we had as much authority as "a committee of bootblacks" about the City Hall, no more. So that it seems as if there is a something that governs those things which survives the accidents of politics, and which mere citizens are not supposed to understand or meddle with. Anyway, it was best so. Colonel Waring, splendid fellow that he was, when he grew tired of the much talk, made a little speech of ten words that was not on the programme, and after that the politicians went home, leaving the park to the children. There it was in the right hands. What mattered the rest, then?

And now let me go back from the slum to my Brooklyn home for just a look. I did every night, or I do not think I could have stood it. I never lived in New York since I had a home, except for the briefest spell of a couple of months once when my family were away, and that nearly stifled me. I have to be where there are trees and birds and green hills, and where the sky is blue above. So we built our nest in Brooklyn, on the outskirts of the great park, while the fledglings grew, and the nest was full when the last of our little pile had gone to make it snug. Rent was getting higher all the time, and the deeper I burrowed in the slum, the more my thoughts turned, by a sort of defensive instinct, to the country. My wife laughed, and said I should have thought of that while we yet had some money to buy or build with, but I borrowed no trouble on that score. I was never a good business man, as I have said before, and yet — no! I will take that back. It is going back on the record. I trusted my accounts with the Great Paymaster, who has all the money there is, and he never gave notice that I had overdrawn my account. I had the feeling, and have it still, that if you are trying to do the things which are right, and which you were put here to do, you can and ought to leave ways and means to Him who drew the plans, after you have done your own level best to provide. Always that, of course. If then things don't come out right, it is the best proof in the world, to my mind, that you have got it wrong, and you have only to hammer away waiting for things to shape themselves, as they are bound to do, and let in the light. For nothing in all this world is without a purpose, and least of all what you and I are doing, though we may not be able to make it out. I got that faith from my mother, and it never put her to shame, so she has often told me.

Neither did it me. It was in the winter when all our children had the scarlet fever that one Sunday, when I was taking a long walk out on Long Island where I could do no one any harm, I came upon Richmond Hill, and thought it was the most beautiful spot I had ever seen. I went home and told my wife that I had found the place where we were going to live, and that sick-room was filled with the scent of spring flowers and of balsam and pine as the children listened and cheered with their feeble little voices. The very next week I picked out the lots I wanted. There was a tangle of trees growing on them that are shading my study window now as I write. I did not have any money, but right then an insurance company was in need of some one to revise its Danish policies, and my old friend General C. T. Christensen thought I would do. And I did it, and earned $200; whereupon Edward Wells, who was then a prosperous druggist, offered to lend me what more I needed to buy the lots, and the manager of our Press Bureau built me a house and took a mortgage for all it cost. So before the next winter's snows we were snug in the house that has been ours ever

My Little Ones gathering Daisies for "the Poors."

since, with a ridge of wooded hills, the "backbone of Long Island," between New York and us. The very lights of the city were shut out. So was the slum, and I could sleep.

Fifteen summers have passed since. The house lies yonder, white and peaceful under the trees. Long since, the last dollar of the mortgage was paid and our home freed from debt.[1]   The flag flies from it on Sundays in token thereof. Joy and sorrow have come to us under its roof. Children have been born, and one we carried over the hill to the churchyard with tears for the baby we had lost. But He to whom we gave it back has turned our grief to joy. Of all our babies, the one we lost is the only one we have kept. The others grew out of our arms; I hardly remember them in their little white slips. But he is our baby forever. Fifteen happy years of peace have they been, for love held the course.

It was when the daisies bloomed in the spring that the children brought in armfuls from the fields, and bade me take them to " the poors " in the city. I did as they bade me, but I never got more than half a block from the ferry with my burden. The street children went wild over the "posies." They

---

[1] I have had my study built on the back lawn so that I may always have it before me, and have a quiet place at the same time, where "papa is not to be disturbed." But, though I put it as far back as I could, I notice that they come right in.

pleaded and fought to get near me, and when I had no flowers left to give them sat in the gutter and wept with grief.   The sight of it went to my heart, and I wrote this letter to the papers.   It is dated in my scrap-book June 23, 1888 : —

" The trains that carry a hundred thousand people to New York's stores and offices from their homes in the country rush over fields, these bright June mornings, glorious with daisies and clover blossoms.   There are too many sad little eyes in the crowded tenements, where the summer sunshine means disease and death, not play or vacation, that will close without ever having looked upon a field of daisies.

" If we cannot give them the fields, why not the flowers?   If every man, woman, or child coming in should, on the way to the depot, gather an armful of wild flowers to distribute in the tenements, a mission work would be set on foot with which all the alms-giving of this wealthy city could not be compared.

" Then why not do it?   Ask your readers to try. The pleasure of giving the flowers to the urchins who will dog their steps in the street, crying with hungry voices and hungry hearts for a 'posy,' will more than pay for the trouble.   It will brighten the office, the store, or the schoolroom all through the day.   Let them have no fear that their gift will not be appreciated because it costs nothing.   Not alms, but the golden rule, is what is needed in the tenements of the poor.

"If those who have not the time or opportunity themselves will send their flowers to 303 Mulberry Street, opposite Police Headquarters, it will be done for them. The summer doctors employed by the Health Department to canvass the tenements in July and August will gladly coöperate. Let us have the flowers."

If I could have foreseen the result, I hardly think that last paragraph would have been printed. I meant to give people a chance to discover for themselves how much pleasure they could get out of a little thing like taking an armful of flowers to town, but they voted unanimously, so it seemed, to let me have it all. Flowers came pouring in from every corner of the compass. They came in boxes, in barrels, and in bunches, from field and garden, from town and country. Express-wagons carrying flowers jammed Mulberry Street, and the police came out to marvel at the row. The office was fairly smothered in fragrance. A howling mob of children besieged it. The reporters forgot their rivalries and lent a hand with enthusiasm in giving out the flowers. The Superintendent of Police detailed five stout patrolmen to help carry the abundance to points of convenient distribution. Wherever we went, fretful babies stopped crying and smiled as the messengers of love were laid against their wan cheeks.   Slovenly women courtesied and made way.

" The good Lord bless you," I heard as I passed through a dark hall, " but you are a good man.   No such has come this way before." Oh! the heartache of it, and yet the joy!   The Italians in the Barracks stopped quarrelling to help keep order.   The worst street became suddenly good and neighborly.   A year or two after, Father John Tabb, priest and poet, wrote, upon reading my statement that I had seen an armful of daisies keep the peace of a block better than the policeman's club: —

> Peacemakers ye, the daisies, from the soil
>   Upbreathing wordless messages of love,
> Soothing of earth-born brethren the toil
>   And lifting e'en the lowliest above.

Ay, they did.   The poet knew it; the children knew it; the slum knew it.   It lost its grip where the flowers went with their message.   I saw it.

I saw, too, that I had put my hand to a task that was too great for me, yet which I might not give over, once I had taken it up.   Every day the slum showed me that more clearly.   The hunger for the beautiful that gnawed at its heart was a constant revelation.   Those little ones at home were wiser than I.   At most I had made out its stomach.   This was like cutting windows for souls that were being shrunk and dwarfed in their mean setting. Shut them up once the sunlight had poured in — never! I could only drive ahead, then, until a way opened. Somewhere beyond it was sure to do that.

And it did. Among the boxes from somewhere out in Jersey came one with the letters I. H. N. on. I paid little attention to it then, but when more came so marked, I noticed that they were not all from one place, and made inquiries as to what the letters meant. So I was led to the King's Daughters' headquarters, where I learned that they stood for " In His Name." I liked the sentiment; I took to it at once. And I liked the silver cross upon which it was inscribed. I sometimes wish I had lived — no! I do not. That's dream- ing. I have lived in the best of all times, when you do not have to dream things good, but can help make them so. All the same, when I put on the old crusader's cross which King Christian sent me a year ago from Denmark, and think of the valiant knights who wore it, I feel glad and proud that, however far behind, I may ride in their train.

So I put on the silver cross, and in the Broadway Tabernacle spoke to the members of the order, asking them to make this work theirs. They did it at once. A committee was formed, and in the summer of

1890 it opened an office in the basement of the Mariners' Temple, down in the Fourth Ward. The Health Department's summer doctors were enlisted, and the work took a practical turn from the start. There were fifty of the doctors, whose duty it was to canvass the thirty thousand tenements during the hot season and prescribe for the sick poor. They had two months to do it in, and with the utmost effort, if they were to cover their ground, could only get around once to each family. In a great many cases that was as good as nothing. They might as well have stayed away, for what was wanted was advice, instruction, a friendly lift out of a hopeless rut, more than medicine. We hired a nurse, and where they pointed there she went, following their track and bringing the things the doctor could not give. It worked well. At the end of the year, when we would have shut up shop, we found ourselves with three hundred families on our hands, to leave whom would have been rank treachery. So we took a couple of rooms in a tenement, and held on. And from this small beginning has grown the King's Daughters' settlement, which to-day occupies two houses at 48 and 50 Henry Street, doing exactly the same kind of work as when they began in the next block. The flowers were and are the open sesame to every home. They were laughed at by some at the start; but that was because they did not know.

They are not needed now to open doors; the little cross is known for a friend wherever it goes.

We sometimes hear it said, and it is true, that the poor are more charitable among themselves than the outside world is to them. It is because they know the want; and it only goes to prove that human nature is at bottom good, not bad. In real straits it comes out strongest. So, if you can only make the others see, will they do. The trouble is, they do not know, and some of us seem to have cotton in our ears: we are a little hard of hearing. Yet, whenever we put it to the test, up-town rang true. I remember the widow with three or four little ones who had to be wheeled if she were to be able to get about as the doctor insisted. There was no nursery within reach. And I remember the procession of baby-carriages that answered our appeal. It strung clear across the street into Chatham Square. Whatever we needed we got. We saw the great heart of our city, and it was good to see.

Personally I had little to do with it, except to form the link with the official end of it, the summer doctors, etc., and to make trouble occasionally. As, for instance, when I surreptitiously supplied an old couple we had charge of with plug tobacco. The ladies took it ill, but, then, they had never smoked. I had, and I know what it is to do without tobacco, for the doctor cut my supply off a long while ago.

Those two were old, very old, and they wanted their pipe, and they got it.   I suppose it was irregular, but I might as well say it here that I would do the same thing again, without doubt.   I feel it in my bones. So little have I profited.   But, good land! a pipe is not a deadly sin.   For the rest, I was mighty glad to see things managed with system. It was a new experience to me.   On the *Tribune* I had a kind of license to appeal now and again for some poor family I had come across, and sometimes a good deal of money came in.   It was hateful to find that it did not always do the good it ought to. I bring to mind the aged bookkeeper and his wife whom I found in a Greene Street attic in a state of horrid want.   He had seen much better days, and it was altogether a very pitiful case.   My appeal brought in over $300, which, in my delight, I brought him in a lump.   The next morning, when going home at three o'clock, whom should I see in a vile Chatham Street dive, gloriously drunk, and in the clutches of a gang of Sixth Ward cutthroats, but my protégé, the bookkeeper, squandering money right and left.   I caught sight of him through the open door, and in hot indignation went in and yanked him out, giving him a good talking to. The gang followed, and began hostilities at once. But for the providential coming of two policemen, we should probably have both fared ill.   I had the old man locked up in the Oak Street Station. For a wonder, he had most of the money yet, and thereafter I spent it for him.

On another occasion we were deliberately victimized — the reporters in Mulberry Street, I mean — by a man with a pitiful story of hardship, which we took as truth and printed. When I got around there the next morning to see about it, I found that some neighborhood roughs had established a tollgate in the alley, charging the pitying visitors who came in shoals a quarter for admission to the show in the garret. The man was a fraud. That was right around the corner from a place where, years before, I used to drop a nickel in a beggar woman's hand night after night as I went past, because she had a baby cradled on her wheezy little hand-organ, until one night the baby rolled into the gutter, and I saw that it was a rag baby, and that the woman was drunk. It was on such evidence as this, both as to them and myself, that I early pinned my faith to organized charity as just orderly charity, and I have found good reasons since to confirm me in the choice. If any doubt had lingered in my mind, my experience in helping distribute the relief fund to the tornado sufferers at Woodhaven a dozen years ago would have dispelled it. It does seem as if the chance of getting something for nothing is, on the whole, the greatest temptation one can hold out to frail human nature, whether in the slum, in Wall Street, or out where the daisies grow.

Everything takes money. Our work takes a good deal. It happened more than once, when the bills came in, that there was nothing to pay them with. Now these were times to put to the test my faith, as recorded above. My associates in the Board will bear me out that it was justified. It is true that the strain was heavy once or twice. I recall one afternoon, as do they, when we sat with bills amounting to $150 before us and not a cent in the bank, so the treasurer reported. Even as she did, the mail-carrier brought two letters, both from the same town, as it happened — Morristown, N.J. Each of them contained a check for $75, one from a happy mother "in gratitude and joy," the other from "one stricken by a great sorrow" that had darkened her life. Together they made the sum needed. We sat and looked at each other dumbly. To me it was not strange: that was my mother's faith. But I do not think we, any of us, doubted after that; and we had what we needed, as we needed it.

CHAPTER XII

I BECOME AN AUTHOR AND RESUME MY INTERRUPTED
CAREER AS A LECTURER

FOR more than a year I had knocked at the doors
of the various magazine editors with my pictures, pro-
posing to tell them how the other half lived, but no
one wanted to know. One of the Harpers, indeed,
took to the idea, but the editor to whom he sent me
treated me very cavalierly. Hearing that I had
taken the pictures myself, he proposed to buy them
at regular photographer's rates and "find a man
who could write" to tell the story. We did not
part with mutual expressions of esteem. I gave up
writing for a time then, and tried the church doors.
That which was bottled up within me was, perhaps,
getting a trifle too hot for pen and ink. In the
church one might, at all events, tell the truth un-
hindered. So I thought; but there were cautious
souls there, too, who held the doors against Mulberry Street and the police reporter. It was fair,
of course, that they should know who I was, but I
thought it sufficient introduction that I was a
deacon in my own church out on Long Island.

They did not, it seemed.   My stock of patience, never very large, was showing signs of giving out, and I retorted hotly that then, if they wanted to know, I was a reporter, and perhaps Mulberry Street had as much sanctity in it as a church that would not listen to its wrongs.   They only shut the doors a little tighter at that.   It did not mend matters that about that time I tried a little truth-telling in my own fold and came to grief.   It did not prove to be any more popular on Long Island than in New York.   I resigned the diaconate and was thinking of hiring a hall — a theatre could be had on Sunday — wherein to preach my lay sermon, when I came across Dr. Schauffler, the manager of the City Mission Society, and Dr. Josiah Strong, the author of " Our Country."   They happened to be together, and saw at once the bearing of my pictures.   Remembering my early experience with the magic lantern, I had had slides made from my negatives, and on February 28, 1888, I told their story in the Broadway Tabernacle.   Thereafter things mended somewhat.   Plymouth Church and Dr. Parkhurst's opened their doors to me and the others fell slowly into line.

I had my say and felt better.   I found a note from Dr. Schauffler among my papers the other day that was written on the morning after that first speech. He was pleased with it and with the collection of

$143.50 for the mission cause. I remember it made me smile a little grimly. The fifty cents would have come handy for lunch that day. It just happened that I did not have any. It happened quite often. I was, as I said, ever a bad manager. I mention it here because of two letters that came while I have been writing this, and which I may as well answer now. One asks me to lift the mortgage from the writer's home. I get a good many of that kind. The writers seem to think I have much money and might want to help them. I should like nothing better. To go around, if one were rich, and pay off mortgages on little homes, so that the owners when they had got the interest together by pinching and scraping should find it all gone and paid up without knowing how, seems to me must be the very finest fun in all the world. But I shall never be able to do it, for I haven't any other money than what I earn with my pen and by lecturing, and never had. So their appeals only make me poorer by a two-cent stamp for an answer to tell them that, and make them no richer. The other letter asks why I and other young men who have had to battle with the world did not go to the Young Men's Christian Association, or to the missionaries, for help. I do not know about the others, but I did not want anybody to help me. There were plenty that were worse off and needed help more. The

only time I tried was when Pater Breton, the good
French priest in Buffalo, tried to get me across to
France to fight for his country, and happily did not
succeed.   As to battling with the world, that is good
for a young man, much better than to hang on to
somebody for support.   A little starvation once in
a while even is not out of the way.   We eat too
much anyhow, and when you have fought your way
through a tight place, you are the better for it.   I
am afraid that is not always the case when you have
been shoved through.

And then again, as I have just told, when I did
go to the ministers with a fair proposition, they did
not exactly jump at it.   No, it was better the way
it was.

The thing I had sought vainly so long came in
the end by another road than I planned.   One of
the editors of *Scribner's Magazine* saw my pictures
and heard their story in his church, and came to
talk the matter over with me.   As a result of that
talk I wrote an article that appeared in the Christmas *Scribner's*, 1889, under the title " How the
Other Half Lives," and made an instant impression.   That was the beginning of better days.

Before I let the old depart I must set down an
incident of my reporter's experience that crowds in
with a good hearty laugh, though it was not the
slum that sent me to the Church of the Holy Com-

munion over on Sixth Avenue. And though the door was shut in my face, it was not by the rector, or with malice prepense. A despatch from the Tenderloin police station had it that the wife of the Rev. Dr. Henry Mottet was locked up there, out of her mind. We had no means of knowing that Dr. Mottet was at that time a confirmed bachelor. So I went over to condole with him, and incidentally to ask what was the matter with his wife, any way. The servant who came to the door did not know whether the doctor was in; she would go and see. But even as she said it the wind blew the door shut behind her. It had a snap-lock.

"Oh!" she said, "I am shut out. If the doctor isn't in the house, I can't get in."

We rang, but no one came. There was only one way: to try the windows. The poor girl could not be left in the street. So we went around the rectory and found one unlatched. She gave me a leg up, and I raised the sash and crawled in.

Halfway in the room, with one leg over the sill, I became dimly conscious of a shape there. Tall and expectant, it stood between the door-curtains.

"Well, sir! and who are you?" it spoke sternly.

I climbed over the sill and put the question myself: "And who are you, sir?"

"I am Dr. Mottet, and live in this house." He had been in after all and had come down to hear what the ringing was about. " And now may I ask, sir — ? "

" Certainly, you may. I am a reporter from Police Headquarters, come up to tell you that your wife is locked up in the Thirtieth Street police station."

The doctor looked fixedly at me for a full minute. Then he slowly telescoped his tall frame into an armchair, and sank down, a look of comic despair settling upon his face.

" O Lord ! " he sighed heavily. " A strange man climbs through my parlor window to tell me, a bachelor, that my wife is locked up in the police station. What will happen next ? "

And then we laughed together and made friends. The woman was just an ordinary lunatic.

I was late home from the office one evening the week my Christmas article was printed. My wife was waiting for me at the door, looking down the street. I saw that she had something on her mind, but the children were all right, she said; nothing was amiss. Supper over, she drew a chair to the fire and brought out a letter.

" I read it," she nodded. It was our way. The commonest business letter is to me a human document when she has read it. Besides, she knows so much more than I. Her heart can find a way where my head bucks blindly against stone walls.

The letter was from Jeanette Gilder, of the
Critic, asking if I had thought of making my
article into a book. If so, she knew a publisher.
My chance had come. I was at last to have my say.

I should have thought I would have shouted and
carried on. I didn't. We sat looking into the fire
together, she and I. Neither of us spoke. Then
we went up to the children. They slept sweetly in
their cribs. I saw a tear in her eye as she bent
over the baby's cradle, and caught her to me,
questioning.

"Shall we lose you now?" she whispered, and
hid her head on my shoulder. I do not know what
jealous thought of authors being wedded to their
work had come into her mind; or, rather, I do. I
felt it, and in my heart, while I held her close, I
registered a vow which I have kept. It was the
last tear she shed for me. Our daughter pouts at
her father now and then; says I am "fierce." But
She comes with her sewing to sit where I write, and
when she comes the sun shines.

Necessarily, for a while, my new work held me
very close. "How the Other Half Lives" was
written at night while the house slept, for I had my
office work to attend to in the day. Then it was
my habit to light the lamps in all the rooms of the
lower story and roam through them with my pipe,
for I do most of my writing on my feet. I began

the book with the new year. In November it was published, and on the day it came out I joined the staff of the *Evening Sun*. I merely moved up one flight of stairs. Mulberry Street was not done with me yet, nor I with it.

I had had a falling out with the manager of the Associated Press Bureau, — the *Tribune* had retired from the copartnership some years before, — and during one brief summer ran an opposition shop of my own. I sold police news to all the papers, and they fell away from the Bureau with such hearty unanimity that the manager came around and offered to farm out the department to me entirely if I would join forces. But independence was ever sweet to me, and in this instance it proved profitable even. I made at least three times as much money as before, but I did it at such cost of energy and effort that I soon found it could not last, even with the phenomenal streak of good luck I had struck. It seemed as if I had only to reach out to turn up news. I hear people saying once in a while that there is no such thing as luck. They are wrong. There is; I know it. It runs in streaks, like accidents and fires. The thing is to get in the way of it and keep there till it comes along, then hitch on, and away you go. It is the old story of the early bird. I got up at five o'clock, three hours before any of my competitors, and some·

times they came down to the office to find my news
hawked about the street in extras of their own papers.

One way or another, a fight there was always on
hand. That seemed foreordained. If it was not
"the opposition" it was the police. When Mulberry Street took a rest the publisher's "reader"
began it, and the proof-reader. This last is an
enemy of human kind anyhow. Not only that he
makes you say things you never dreamed of, but
his being so cocksure that he knows better every
time, is a direct challenge to a fight. The "reader"
is tarred with the same stick. He is the one who
passes on the manuscript, and he has an ingrown
hatred of opinion. If a man has that, he is his
enemy before he ever sets eye on him. He passed
on my manuscript with a blue pencil that laid waste
whole pages, once a whole chapter, with a stroke.
It was like sacking a conquered city. But he did
not die in his sins. I joined battle at the first sight
of that blue pencil. The publishers said their reader
was a very capable man. So he was, and a fine fellow to boot; had forgotten more than I ever knew,
except as to the other half, of which he did not
know anything. I suggested to the firm that if
they did not think so, they had better let him write
a book to suit, or else print mine as I wrote it. It
was fair, and they took my view of it. So did he.
The blue pencil went out of commission.

How deadly tired I was in those days I do not think I myself knew until I went to Boston one evening to help discuss sweating at the Institute of Technology. I had an hour to spare, and went around into Beacon Street to call upon a friend. I walked mechanically up the stoop and rang the bell. My friend was not in, said the servant who came to the door. Who should she say called? I stood and looked at her like a fool: I had forgotten my name. I was not asleep; I was rummaging in an agony of dread and excitement through every corner and crevice of my brain for my own name, but I did not find it. As slowly as I could, to gain time, I reached for my card-case and fumbled for a card, hoping to remember. But no ray came. Until I actually read my name on my card it was as utterly gone as if I had never heard it. If the people of Boston got anything out of my speech that day they did better than I. All the time I spoke something kept saying over within me: "You are a nice fellow to make a speech at the Institute of Technology; you don't even know your own name."

After that I was haunted by a feeling that I would lose myself altogether, and got into the habit of leaving private directions in the office where I would probably be found, should question arise. It arose at last in a Brooklyn church where I was making a speech with my magic-lantern pictures. While I spoke a feeling kept growing upon me that I ought to be down in the audience looking at the pictures. It all seemed a long way off and in no way related to me. Before I knew it, or any one had time to notice, I had gone down and taken a front seat. I sat there for as much as five minutes perhaps, while the man with the lantern fidgeted and the audience wondered, I suppose, what was coming next. Then it was the pictures that did not change which fretted me; with a cold chill I knew I had been lost, and went back and finished the speech. No one was any the wiser, apparently. But I was glad when, the following week, I wrote the last page in my book. That night, my wife insists, I deliberately turned a somerset on the parlor carpet while the big children cheered and the baby looked on, wide-eyed, from her high chair.

I preserve among my cherished treasures two letters of that period from James Russell Lowell. In one of them he gives me permission to use the verses with which I prefaced the book. They were the text from which I preached my sermon. He writes that he is "glad they have so much life left in them after forty years." But those verses will never die. They tell in a few lines all I tried to tell on three hundred pages. The other letter was written when he had read the book. I reproduce it here.

ELMWOOD,
CAMBRIDGE, MASS.

21th Nov: 1890.

Dear Sir,

I have read your book with deep & painful interest. I felt as Dante much when he looked over the edge of the abyss at the bottom of which Geryon lay in ambush. I had but a vague idea of these horrors before. You brought them so feelingly home to me. I cannot conceive how such a book should fail of doing great good, if it move other people as it has moved me. I found it hard to get asleep the night after I had been reading it.

Faithfully yours

J. R. Lowell

J. A. Riis, Esq.

Mr. Lowell's Letter.

For myself I have never been able to satisfactorily explain the great run " How the Other Half Lives " had. It is a curiously popular book even to-day. Perhaps it was that I had had it in me so long that it burst out at last with a rush that caught on. The title had a deal to do with it. Mr. Howells asked me once where I got it. I did not get it. It came of itself. Like Topsy, it growed. It had run in my mind ever since I thought of the things I tried to describe. Then there was the piece of real good luck that Booth's " In Darkest England " was published just then. People naturally asked, " how about New York ? " That winter Ward McAllister wrote his book about society as he had found it, and the circuit was made. Ministers preached about the contrast. " How the Other Half Lives " ran from edition to edition. There was speedily a demand for more " copy," and I wrote " The Children of the Poor," following the same track. Critics said there were more " bones " in it, but it was never popular like the " Other Half."

By " bones " I suppose they meant facts to tie to. They were scarce enough at that stage of the inquiry. I have in my desk a table giving the ages at which children get their teeth that bears witness to that. I had been struggling with the problem of child-labor in some East Side factories, and was not making any headway. The children had certificates, one and all, declaring them to be "fourteen,' and therefore fit to be employed. It was perfectly evident that they were not ten in scores of cases, but the employer shrugged his shoulders and pointed to the certificate. The father, usually a tailor, would not listen at all, but went right on ironing. There was no birth registry to fall back on; that end of it was neglected. There seemed to be no way of proving the fact, yet the fact was there and must be proven. My own children were teething at the time, and it gave me an idea. I got Dr. Tracy to write out that table for me, showing at what age the dog-teeth should appear, when the molars, etc. Armed with that I went into the factories and pried open the little workers' mouths. The girls objected: their teeth were quite generally bad; but I saw enough to enable me to speak positively. Even allowing for the backwardness of the slum, it was clear that a child that had not yet grown its dog-teeth was not "fourteen," for they should have been cut at twelve at the latest. Three years later the Reinhardt Committee reported to the Legislature that the net result of the Factory Law was a mass of perjury and child-labor, and day began to dawn for the little ones, too.

Rough ways and rough work? Yes, but you must use the tools that come to hand, and be glad for them, if you want to get things done. Bludg eons were needed just then, and, after all, you can get a good deal of fun out of one when it is needed. I know I did. By that time the whole battle with the slum had evolved itself out of the effort to clean one pig-sty, and, as for my own share in it, to settle for one dead dog. It was raging all along the line with demands for tenement-house reform and the destruction of the old rookeries; for parks for the people who were penned up in the slum; for playgrounds for their children; for decent teaching and decent schools. There were too many dark spots in New York where we had neither. So dense was the ignorance of the ruling powers of the needs and real condition of the public schools, which, on parade days, they spoke of sententiously as the "corner-stone of our liberties," while the people cheered the sentiment, that it was related how a Tammany Mayor had appointed to the office of school trustee in the Third Ward a man who had been dead a whole year, and how, when the world marvelled, it had been laughed off at the City Hall with the comment that what did it matter: there were no schools in the ward; it was the wholesale grocery district. I do not know how true it was, but there was no reason why it might not be. It was exactly on a par with the rest of it. I do not mean to say that there were no good schools in New York. There were some as good as anywhere; for there were high-souled teachers who redeemed even the slough we were in from utter despair. But they were there in spite of it and they were far from being the rule. Let us hope for the day when that shall have been reversed as a statement of fact. No one will hail it more gladly than I. There is an easy way of putting it to the test; we did it once before. Broach a measure of school reform and see what the question is that will be asked by the teachers. If it is, "How is it going to benefit the children?" hoist the flag; the day of deliverance is at hand. In the battle I refer to that question was not asked once. The teachers stood shoulder to shoulder for *their* rights, let the children fare as they might.

However, that is an old grievance. We had it out over it once, and I have no mind to rip it up again unless it is needed. My own father was a teacher; perhaps that is one reason why I revere the calling so that I would keep its skirts clear of politics at any hazard. Another is that I most heartily subscribe to the statement that the public school is the corner-stone of our liberties, and to the sentiment that would keep the flag flying over it always. Only I want as much respect for the flag: a clean school under an unsoiled flag! So we shall pull through; not otherwise. The thing requires no argument.

My own effort in that fight was mainly for decent

schoolhouses, for playgrounds, and for a truant school to keep the boys out of jail. If I was not competent to argue over the curriculum with a professor of pedagogy, I could tell, at least, if a schoolroom was so jammed that to let me pass into the next room the children in the front seat had

The Boys' "Playground" in an Old-time School.

to rise and stand; or if there was light enough for them to see their slates or the blackboard. Nor did it take the wisdom of a Solomon to decide that a dark basement room, thirty by fifty feet, full of rats, was not a proper place for a thousand children to call their only "playground." Play, in the kindergarten scheme, is the "normal occupation of the child through which he first begins to perceive moral relations." Nice kind of morals burrowed there for him! There was, in the whole of Manhattan, but a single outdoor playground attached to a public school, and that was an old burial-ground in First Street that had been wrested from the dead with immense toil. When I had fed fat my grudge upon these things, I could still go where the public school children came, and learn, by a little judicious pumping, how my friend, the professor, had stored their minds. That is, if they did not come to me. Many hundreds of them did, when under Roosevelt we needed two thousand new policemen, and it was from some of them we learned that among the thirteen States which formed the Union were " England, Ireland, Wales, Belfast, and Cork "; that Abraham Lincoln was " murdered by Ballington Booth," and that the Fire Department was in charge of the city government when the Mayor was away. Don't I wish it were, and that they would turn the hose on a while! What a lot of trouble it would save us in November.

As for a truant school, the lack of one was the worst outrage of all, for it compelled the sending of boys, who had done no worse harm than to play hooky on a sunny spring day, to a jail with iron bars in the windows. For the boy who did this wicked thing — let me be plain about it and say that if he had not; if he had patiently preferred

some of the schools I knew to a day of freedom out
in the sunshine, I should have thought him a miserable little lunkhead quite beyond hope! As for
those who locked him up, almost nothing I can
think of would be bad enough for them. The
whole effort of society should be, and is getting to
be more and more, thank goodness and common
sense, to keep the boy out of jail. To run to it
with him the moment the sap begins to boil up in
him and he does any one of the thousand things we
have all done or wanted to do if we dared, why, it
is sinful folly. I am not saying that there are not
boys who ought to be in jail, though to my mind
it is the poorest use you can put them to; but to
put truants there, to learn all the tricks the jail has
to teach, with them in the frame of mind in which
it receives them, — for boys are not fools, whatever
those who are set over them may be, and they
know when they are ill-used, — I know of nothing
so wickedly wasteful. That was our way; is still
in fact, to a large extent, though the principle has
been disavowed as both foul and foolish. But in
those days the defenders of the system — Heaven
save the mark! — fought for it yet, and it was give
and take right along, every day and all day.

Before this, in time to bear a strong hand in it
all, there had come into the field a new force that
was destined to give both energy and direction

to our scattered efforts for reform. Up till then we had been a band of guerillas, the incentive proceeding usually from Dr. Felix Adler, Mrs. Josephine Shaw Lowell, or some one of their stamp; and the rest of us joining in to push *that* cart up the hill, then taking time to breathe until another came along that needed a lift. The social settlements, starting as neighborhood guilds to reassert the lost brotherhood, became almost from the first the fulcrum, as it were, whence the lever for reform was applied, because the whole idea of that reform was to better the lot of those whom the prosperous up-town knew vaguely only as " the poor." If parks were wanted, if schools needed bettering, there were at the College Settlement, the University Settlement, the Nurses' Settlement, and at a score of other such places, young enthusiasts to collect the facts and to urge them, with the prestige of their non-political organization to back them. The Hull House out in Chicago set the pace, and it was kept up bravely at this end of the line. For one, I attached myself as a kind of volunteer " auxiliary " to the College Settlement — that was what the girls there called me — and to any one that would have me, and so in a few years' time slid easily into the day when my ruder methods were quite out of date and ready to be shelved.

How it came about that, almost before I knew it,

my tongue was enlisted in the fight as well as my
pen I do not know myself. It could not be because
I had a "silver-tongue," for I read in the local newspaper one day when I had been lecturing in the
western part of the state that "a voluble German
with a voice like a squeaky cellar-door" had been
in town. It seems that I had fallen into another
newspaper row, all unsuspecting, and was in the
opposition editor's camp. But, truly, I lay no claim
to eloquence. So it must have been the facts, again.
There is nothing like them. Whatever it was, it
made me smile sometimes in the middle of a speech
to think of the prophecies when I was a schoolboy
that "my tongue would be my undoing," for here it
was helping right wrongs instead. In fact, that was
what it had tried to do in the old days when the teachers were tyrannical. It entered the lists here when
Will Craig, a clerk in the Health Department, with
whom I had struck up a friendship, helped me turn
my photographs into magic-lantern slides by paying
the bills, and grew from that, until now my winters
are spent on the lecture platform altogether. I
always liked the work. It tires less than the office
routine, and you feel the touch with your fellows
more than when you sit and write your message.
Also, if you wish to learn about a thing, the best
way is always to go and try to teach some one else
that thing. I never make a speech on a subject I

am familiar with but that I come away knowing more about it than I did at the start, though no one else may have said a word.

Then there is the chairman. You never can tell what sort of surprise is in store for you. In a Massachusetts town last winter I was hailed on the stage by one of his tribe, a gaunt, funereal sort of man, who wanted to know what he should say about me.

"Oh," said I, in a spirit of levity, "say anything you like. Say I am the most distinguished citizen in the country. They generally do."

Whereupon my funereal friend marched upon the stage and calmly announced to the audience that he did not know this man Riis, whom he was charged with introducing, never heard of him.

" He tells me," he went on with never a wink, "that he is the most distinguished citizen in the country. You can judge for yourselves when you have heard him."

I thought at first it was some bad kind of joke; but no! He was not that kind of man. I do not suppose he had smiled since he was born. Maybe he was an undertaker. Assuredly, he ought to be. But he had bowels after all. Instead of going off the stage and leaving me blue with rage, he stayed to exhort the audience in a fifteen minutes' speech to vote right, or something of that sort. The single remark, when at last he turned his back, that it was a relief to have him "extinguished," made us men and brothers, that audience and me. I think of him with almost as much pleasure as I do of that city editor chap out in Illinois who came blowing upon the platform at the last minute and handed me a typewritten speech with the question if that would do. I read it over. It began with the statement that it was the general impression that all newspaper-men were liars, and went on by easy stages to point out that there were exceptions, myself for instance. The rest was a lot of praise to which I had no claim. I said so, and that I wished he would leave it out.

"Oh, well," he said, with a happy smile, "don't you see it gives you your cue. Then you can turn around and say that anyway I am a liar."

With tongue or pen, the argument shaped itself finally into the fundamental one for the rescue of the home imperilled by the slum. There all roads met. Good citizenship hung upon that issue. Say what you will, a man cannot live like a pig and vote like a man. The dullest of us saw it. The tene-ment had given to New York the name of "the homeless city." But with that gone which made life worth living, what were liberty worth? With no home to cherish, how long before love of country would be an empty sound? Life, liberty, pursuit of happiness? Wind! says the slum, and the slum is right if we let it be. We cannot get rid of the tenements that shelter two million souls in New York to-day, but we set about making them at least as nearly fit to harbor human souls as might be. That will take a long time yet. But a beginning was made. With reform looming upon the heels of the Lexow disclosures came the Gilder Tenement-House Commission in the autumn of 1894.

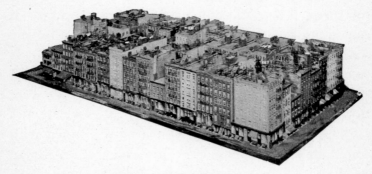

Typical East Side Tenement Block.
Five hundred babies in it, not one bathtub.

Greater work was never done for New York than by that faithful body of men. The measure of it is not to be found in what was actually accomplished, though the volume of that was great, but in what it made possible. Upon the foundations they laid down we may build for all time and be the better for it. Light and air acquired a legal claim, and where the sun shines into the slum, the slum is doomed. The worst tenements were destroyed; parks were opened, schools built, playgrounds made. The children's rights were won back for them. The slum denied them even the chance to live, for it was shown that the worst rear tenements murdered the babies at the rate of one in five. The Commission made it clear that the legislation that was needed was "the kind that would root out every old ramshackle disease-breeding tenement in the city." That was the way to begin it. As to the rest of them, it laid the foundation deeper yet, for it made us see that life in them "conduces to the corruption of the young." That told it all. It meant that a mortgage was put on the civic life of the morrow, which was not to be borne. We were forewarned.

The corruption of the young! We move with rapid strides in our time. That which was a threat, scoffed at by many, has become a present and dreadful peril in half a dozen brief years. We took a short cut to make it that when we tried to drain the pool of police blackmail of which the Lexow disclosures had shown us the hideous depths. We drained it into the tenements, and for the police infamy got a real-estate blackmail that is worse. The chairman of the Committee of Fifteen tells us that of more than a hundred tenements, full of growing children, which his committee has can-

v

vassed, not one had escaped the contamination that piles up the landlord's profits. Twelve dollars for an honest flat, thirty for the other kind and no questions asked! I find in my scrap-book this warning, sounded by me in the Christmas holidays, 1893, when the country was ringing with Dr. Park-hurst's name: —

" I would not, whatever else might happen, by any hasty or ill-advised system of wholesale raids crowd these women into the tenements and flats of our city. That is what will surely happen, is happening now. It is a danger infinitely greater than any flowing from their presence where they are, and as they are. Each centre of moral conta-gion by this scattering process becomes ten or twenty, planted where they will do the most pos-sible harm. Think of the children brought in daily, hourly contact with this vice! Think of the thou-sands of young women looking vainly for work this hard winter! Be there ever so little money for woman's honest work, there is always enough to buy her virtue. Have tenement houses moral re-sources that can be trusted to keep her safe from this temptation?

" This is a wicked villany that must not be per-mitted, come whatever else may. We hear of dan-ger to 'our young men,' from present conditions. What sort of young men must they be who would risk the sacrifice of their poorer sisters for their own 'safety'? And it is being risked wherever houses of this kind are being shut up and the women turned into the streets, there to shift for themselves. The jail does not keep them. Christian families will not receive them. They cannot be killed. No door opens to them: yet they have to go somewhere. And they go where they think they can hide from the police and still ply the trade that gives them the only living society is willing they shall have, though it says it is not."

And they did go there. Dr. Parkhurst was not to blame. He was fighting Tammany that dealt the cards and took all the tricks, and for that fight New York owes him a debt it hardly yet knows of. Besides, though those raids hastened the process, it was already well underway. The police extortion of itself would have finished it in time. A blackmailer in the long run always kills the goose that lays his golden egg. His greed gets the better of his sense. The interview I quoted was not a plea for legalizing wrong. That will get us no farther. It was rather a summons to our people to cease skulking behind lying phrases and look the matter squarely in the face. With a tenement-house law, passed this winter, which sends the woman to jail and fines the landlord and his house $1000, we shall be in the way shortly of doing so.

Until we do that justice first, I do not see how we can. Poverty's back is burdened enough without our loading upon it the sins we are afraid to face. Meanwhile we shall be getting up courage to talk plainly about it, which is half the battle. Think of the shock it would have given our grandmothers to hear of a meeting of women in a public hall " to protest against protected vice." On a Sunday, too. Come to think of it, I do not know but that wholesome, plain speech on this subject is nearer the whole than half the battle. I rather guess it is.

CHAPTER XIII

ROOSEVELT COMES — MULBERRY STREET'S GOLDEN
AGE

SEE now how things fall out. Hardly had I sent the chapter to the printer in which I posted proof-readers as enemies of mankind when here comes the proof of the previous one with a cordial note of thanks from this particular enemy "for the inspiration" he found in it. So then I was mistaken, as I have been often before, and owe him the confession. Good land! what are we that we should think ourselves always right, or, lest we do wrong, sit idle all our lives waiting for light? The light comes as we work toward it. Roosevelt was right when he said that the only one who never makes mistakes is the one who never does anything. Preserve us from him; from the man who eternally wants to hold the scales even and so never gets done weighing — never hands anything over the counter. Take him away and put red blood into his veins. And let the rest of us go ahead and make our mistakes — as few as we can, as many as we must: only let us go ahead.

All of which has reference to other things I have in mind, not to the proof-reader, against whom I have no grudge to-day. As for him, perhaps, he is just a sign that the world moves.

Move it did at last in the year (1894) that gave us the Lexow Investigating Committee, the Citizens' Seventy, and reform. Tammany went out, speeded on its way by Dr. Parkhurst, and an administration came in that was pledged to all we had been longing and laboring for. For three years we had free hands and we used them. Mayor Strong's administration was not the millennium, but it brought New York much nearer to it than it had ever been, and it set up some standards toward which we may keep on striving with profit to ourselves. The Mayor himself was not a saint. He was an honest gentleman of sturdy purpose to do the right, and, normally, of singular practical wisdom in choosing the men to help him do it, but with an intermittent delusion that he was a shrewd politician. When it came uppermost he made bargains and appointed men to office who did their worst to undo what good the Warings, the Roosevelts, and their kind had wrought. In the struggle that ensued Mayor Strong was always on the side of right, but when he wanted most to help he could not. It is the way of the world. Nevertheless, as I said, it moved.

How far we came is history, plain to read in our streets that will never again be as dirty as they were, though they may not be as clean as Waring left them; in the threescore splendid new school-houses that stand as monuments of those busy years; in the open spots that let the sunlight into the slum where it was darkest and most foul; in the death rate that came down from 26.32 per thousand of the living in 1887 to 19.53 in 1897. That was the "Ten Years' War"[1] I wrote about and have here before referred to. The three years of the Strong administration saw all the big battles in which we beat the slum. I am not going to rehearse them, for I am trying to tell my own story, and now I am soon done with it. I carried a gun as a volunteer in that war, and that was all; not even in the ranks at that. I was ever an irregular, given to sniping on my own hook. Roosevelt, indeed, wanted me to have a seat among Mayor Strong's official advisers; but we had it out over that when he told me of it, and the compact we made that he should never ask that service of me he has kept. So he spared the Mayor much embarrassment; for, as I said, I am not good in the ranks, more is the pity: and me he saved for such use as I could be of, which was well. For shortly it all centred in Mulberry Street, where he was.

We were not strangers. It could not have been

---

[1] Now, "The Battle with the Slum."

long after I wrote "How the Other Half Lives" that he came to the *Evening Sun* office one day looking for me. I was out, and he left his card, merely writing on the back of it that he had read my book and had "come to help." That was all, and it tells the whole story of the man. I loved him from the day I first saw him; nor ever in all the years that have passed has he failed of the promise made then. No one ever helped as he did. For two years we were brothers in Mulberry Street. When he left I had seen its golden age. I knew too well the evil day that was coming back to have any heart in it after that.

Not that we were carried heavenward "on flowery beds of ease" while it lasted. There is very little ease where Theodore Roosevelt leads, as we all of us found out. The lawbreaker found it out who predicted scornfully that he would "knuckle down to politics the way they all did," and lived to respect him, though he swore at him, as the one of them all who was stronger than pull. The peace-loving citizen who hastened to Police Headquarters with anxious entreaties to "use discretion" in the enforcement of unpopular laws found it out and went away with a new and breathless notion welling up in him of an official's sworn duty. That was it; that was what made the age golden, that for the first time a moral purpose came into the

President Theodore Roosevelt, of the Police Board.

street. In the light of it everything was trans-formed.

Not all at once. It took us weary months to understand that the shouting about the "enforce-ment of the dead Excise Law" was lying treachery or rank ignorance, one as bad as the other. The Excise Law was not dead. It was never so much alive as under Tammany, but it was enforced only against those saloon-keepers who needed discipline. It was a Tammany club, used to drive them into camp with; and it was used so vigorously that no less than eight thousand arrests were made under it in the year before Roosevelt made them all close up. Pretty lively corpse, that! But we understood at last, most of us; understood that the tap-root of the police blackmail was there, and that it had to be pulled up if we were ever to get farther. We under-stood that we were the victims of our own sham-ming, and we grew to be better citizens for it. The police force became an army of heroes — for a sea-son. All the good in it came out; and there is a lot of it in the worst of times. Roosevelt had the true philosopher's stone that turns dross to gold, in his own sturdy faith in his fellow-man. Men be-came good because he thought them so.

By which I am not to be understood as meaning that he just voted them good — the police, for instance — and sat by waiting to see the wings

grow.   No, but he helped them sprout.   It is long
since I have enjoyed anything so much as I did
those patrol trips of ours on the "last tour" between
midnight and sunrise, which earned for him the
name of Haroun al Roosevelt.   I had at last found
one who was willing to get up when other people
slept — including, too often, the police — and see
what the town looked like then.   He was more
than willing.   I laid out the route, covering ten or a
dozen patrol-posts, and we met at 2 A.M. on the steps
of the Union League Club, objects of suspicion on
the part of two or three attendants and a watchman
who shadowed us as night-prowlers till we were out
of their bailiwick.   I shall never forget that first
morning when we travelled for three hours along
First and Second and Third avenues, from Forty-
second Street to Bellevue, and found of ten patrolmen just one doing his work faithfully.   Two or
three were chatting on saloon corners and guyed
the President of the Board when he asked them if
that was what they were there for.   One was sitting
asleep on a butter-tub in the middle of the sidewalk,
snoring so that you could hear him across the street,
and was inclined to be "sassy" when aroused and
told to go about his duty.   Mr. Roosevelt was a
most energetic roundsman and a fair one to boot.
It was that quality which speedily won him the
affection of the force.   He hunted high and low

before he gave up his man, giving him every chance. We had been over one man's beat three times, searching every nook and cranny of it, and were reluctantly compelled to own that he was not there, when the "boss" of an all-night restaurant on Third Avenue came out with a club as we passed and gave the regulation signal raps on the sidewalk. There was some trouble in his place. Three times he repeated the signal calling for the patrolman on the beat before he turned to Roosevelt, who stood by, with the angry exclamation:—

"One was sitting asleep on a butter-tub."

"Where in thunder does that copper sleep? He orter'd tole me when he giv' up the barber-shop, so's a fellow could find him."

We didn't find him then, but he found the President of the Board later on when summoned to Police Headquarters to explain why he had changed his sleeping quarters.   The whole force woke up as a result of that night's work, and it kept awake those two years, for, as it learned by experience, Mr. Roosevelt's spectacles might come gleaming around the corner at any hour.   He had not been gone a year before the Chief found it necessary to transfer half the force in an up-town precinct to keep it awake.   The firemen complained that fires at night gained too much headway while the police slept. There was no Roosevelt to wake them up.

Looking after his patrolmen was not the only errand that took him abroad at night.   As Police President, Mr. Roosevelt was a member of the Health Board, and sometimes it was the tenements we went inspecting when the tenants slept.   He was after facts, and learned speedily to get them as he could.   When, as Governor, he wanted to know just how the Factory Law was being executed, he came down from Albany and spent a whole day with me personally investigating tenements in which sweating was carried on.   I had not found a Governor before, or a Police President either, who would do it; but so he learned exactly what he wanted to know, and what he ought to do, and did it.

I never saw Theodore Roosevelt to better advantage than when he confronted the labor men at their meeting-place, Clarendon Hall.   The police were all the time having trouble with strikers and their " pickets." Roosevelt saw that it was because neither party understood fully the position of the other and, with his usual directness, sent word to the labor organizations that he would like to talk it over with them. At his request I went with him to the meeting. It developed almost immediately that the labor men had taken a wrong measure of the man. They met him as a politician playing for points, and hinted at trouble unless their demands were met. Mr. Roosevelt broke them off short : —

" Gentlemen ! " he said, with that snap of the jaws that always made people listen, " I asked to meet you, hoping that we might come to understand one another. Remember, please, before we go farther, that the worst injury any one of you can do to the cause of labor is to counsel violence. It will also be worse for himself. Understand distinctly that order will be kept. The police will keep it. Now we can proceed."

I was never so proud and pleased as when they applauded him to the echo. He reddened with pleasure, for he saw that the best in them had come out on top, as he expected it would.

It was of this incident that a handle was first made by Mr. Roosevelt's enemies in and out of the Police Board — and he had many — to attack him. It happened that there was a music hall in the building in which the labor men met. The yellow newspapers circulated the lie that he went there on purpose to see the show, and the ridiculous story was repeated until the liars nearly persuaded themselves that it was so. They would not have been able to understand the kind of man they had to do with, had they tried. Accordingly they fell into their own trap. It is a tradition of Mulberry Street that the notorious Seeley dinner raid was planned by his enemies in the department of which he was the head, in the belief that they would catch Mr. Roosevelt there. The diners were supposed to be his "set."

Some time after that I was in his office one day when a police official of superior rank came in and requested private audience with him. They stepped aside and the policeman spoke in an undertone, urging something strongly. Mr. Roosevelt listened. Suddenly I saw him straighten up as a man recoils from something unclean and dismiss the other with a sharp: "No, sir! I don't fight that way." The policeman went out crestfallen. Roosevelt took two or three turns about the floor, struggling evidently with strong disgust. He told me afterward that the man had come to him with what he said was certain knowledge that his enemy could that night be found in a known evil house up-town, which it was his alleged habit to visit. His proposition was to raid it then and so "get square." To the policeman it must have seemed like throwing a good chance away. But it was not Roosevelt's way; he struck no blow below the belt. In the Governor's chair afterward he gave the politicians whom he fought, and who fought him, the same terms. They tried their best to upset him, for they had nothing to expect from him. But they knew and owned that he fought fair. Their backs were secure. He never tricked them to gain an advantage. A promise given by him was always kept to the letter.

Failing to trap him only added to the malignity of his enemies. Roosevelt was warned that he was "shadowed" night and day, but he laughed their scheming to scorn. It is an article of faith with him that an honest man has nothing to fear from plotters, and he walked unharmed among their snares. The whole country remembers the year-long fight in the Police Board and Mayor Strong's vain attempt to remove the obstructionist who, under an ill-conceived law, was able to hold up the scheme of reform. Most of the time I was compelled to stand idly by, unable to help. Once I eased my feelings by telling Commissioner Parker in his own office what I thought of him. I went in and shut the door, and then told it all to him. Nor did I mince matters; I might not get so good a chance again. Mr. Parker sat quite still, poking

the fire. When I ceased at last, angry and exas-
perated, he looked up and said calmly: —

" Well, Mr. Riis, what you tell me has at least the
merit of frankness."

You see how it was. I should never have been
able to help in the Board. Out of it, my chance
came at last when it was deemed necessary to give
the adversary "a character." Mr. Roosevelt had
been speaking to the Methodist ministers, and as
usual had carried all before him. The community
was getting up a temper that would shortly put an
end to the deadlock in the Police Board and set the
wheels of reform moving again. Then one day we
heard that Commissioner Parker had been invited
by the Christian Endeavorers of an up-town church
to address them on " Christian Citizenship." That
was not consecrated common sense. I went to the
convention of Endeavorers the next week and told
them so. I asked them to send a despatch to Governor Black then and there endorsing Roosevelt and
Mayor Strong, and urging him to end the deadlock
that made public scandal by removing Commissioner
Parker; and they did. I regret to say that I felt
compelled to take a like course with the Methodist
ministers, for so I grieved a most good-natured
gentleman, Colonel Grant, who was Mr. Parker's
ally in the Board. Grant was what was described
as "a great Methodist." But I feel sure that

Brother Simmons would have approved of me. I was following the course he laid down. The one loyal friend Mr. Roosevelt had in the Board was Avery D. Andrews, a strong, sensible, and clean young man, who stood by his chief to the last, and left with him a good mark on the force.

The yellow newspapers fomented most industriously the trouble in the Board, never failing to take the wrong side of any question. One of them set about doling out free soup that winter, when work was slack, as a means, of course, of advertising its own "charity." Of all forms of indiscriminate almsgiving, that is the most offensive and most worthless, and they knew it, or they would not have sent me a wheedling invitation to come and inspect their "relief work," offering to have a carriage take me around. I sent word back that I should certainly look into the soup, but that I should go on foot to it. Roosevelt and I made the inspection together. We questioned the tramps in line, and learned from their own lips that they had come from out of town to take it easy in a city where a man did not have to work to live. We followed the pails that were carried away from the "relief station" by children, their contents sometimes to figure afterwards as "free lunch" in the saloon where they had been exchanged for beer; and, knowing the facts, we denounced the thing as

z

a nuisance. The paper printed testimonials from Commissioners Parker and Grant, who certified from Mulberry Street, which they had not left, that the soup was a noble Christian charity, and so thought it evened things up, I suppose. I noticed, however, that the soup ran out soon after, and I hope we have seen the last of it. We can afford to leave that to Philadelphia, where common sense appears to be drowned in it.

I had it out with them at last all together. When I have told of it let the whole wretched thing depart and be gone for good. It was after Roosevelt had gone away. That he was not there was no bar to almost daily attacks on him, under which I chafed, sitting at the meetings as a reporter. I knew right well they were intended to provoke me to an explosion that might have given grounds for annoying me, and I kept my temper until one day, when, the subject of dives being mentioned, Commissioner Parker drawled, with the reporter from the soup journal whispering in his ear : —

"Was not — er-r — that the place where — er-r — Mr. Roosevelt went to see a show with his friend?"

He was careful not to look in my direction, but the reporter did, and I leaped at the challenge. I waited until the Board had formally adjourned, then halted it as Mr. Parker was trying to escape. I do not now remember what I said. It would not make calm reading, I suspect. It was the truth, anyhow, and came pretty near being the whole truth. Mr. Parker fled, putting his head back through the half-closed door to explain that he "only knew what that reporter told" him. In the security of his room it must have occurred to him, however, that he had another string to his bow; for at the next session Commissioner Grant moved my expulsion because I had "disturbed the Board meeting." But President Moss reminded him curtly that I had done nothing of the kind, and that ended it.

One of the early and sensational results of reform in Mulberry Street was the retirement of Superintendent Byrnes. There was not one of us all who had known him long who did not regret it, though I, for one, had to own the necessity of it; for Byrnes stood for the old days that were bad. But, chained as he was in the meanness and smallness of it all, he was yet cast in a different mould. Compared with his successor, he was a giant every way. Byrnes was a "big policeman." We shall not soon have another like him, and that may be both good and bad. He was unscrupulous, he was for Byrnes — he was a policeman, in short, with all the failings of the trade. But he made the detective service great. He chased the thieves to Europe, or gave them license to live in New York on condition that they did not rob there.   He was a Czar, with all an autocrat's irresponsible powers, and he exercised them as he saw fit.   If they were not his, he took them anyhow; police service looks to results first. There was that in Byrnes which made me stand up for him in spite of it all.   Twice I held Dr. Park-

hurst from his throat, but in the end I had to admit that the Doctor was right. I believed that, untrammelled, Byrnes might have been a mighty engine for good, and it was with sorrow I saw him go. He left no one behind him fit to wear his shoes.

Byrnes was a born policeman. Those who hated him said he was also a born tyrant. He did ride

Chief of Police Thomas Byrnes.

a high horse when the fit was on him and he thought it served his purpose.   So we came into collision in the early days when he was captain in Mercer Street.   They had a prisoner over there with a story which I had cause to believe my rivals had obtained.   I went to Byrnes and was thundered out of the station-house.   There he was boss and it suited him to let me see it.   We had not met

before. But we met again that night. I went to
the Superintendent of Police, who was a Republican, and, applying all the pressure of the *Tribune*, which I served, got from him an order on
Captain Byrnes to let me interview his prisoner.
Old Mr. Walling tore his hair; said the thing had
never been done before, and it had not. But I got
the order and got the interview, though Byrnes,
black with rage, commanded a policeman to stand
on either side of the prisoner while I talked to him.
He himself stood by, glaring at me. It was not a
good way to get an interview, and, in fact, the man
had nothing to tell. But I had my way and I made
the most of it. After that Captain Byrnes and I
got along. We got to think a lot of each other
after a while.

Perhaps he was a tyrant because he was set over
crooks, and crooks are cowards in the presence of
authority. His famous "third degree" was chiefly
what he no doubt considered a little wholesome
"slugging." He would beat a thief into telling
him what he wanted to know. Thieves have no
rights a policeman thinks himself bound to respect.
But when he had to do with men with minds he
had other resources. He tortured his prisoner into
confession in the Unger murder case by locking
him up out of reach of a human voice, or sight of
a human face, in the basement of Police Headquar-

ters, and keeping him there four days, fed by invisible hands. On the fifth he had him brought up through a tortuous way, where the tools he had used in murdering his partner were displayed on the walls as if by accident. Led into the Inspector's presence by the jailer, he was made to stand while Byrnes finished a letter. Then he turned his piercing glance upon him with a gesture to sit. The murderer sank trembling upon a lounge, the only piece of furniture in the room, and sprang to his feet with a shriek the next instant: it was the one upon which he had slaughtered his friend, all blood-bespattered as then. He sprawled upon the floor, a gibbering, horror-stricken wretch, and confessed his sin.

As in this instance, so in the McGloin murder case, the moral certainty of guilt was absolute, but the legal evidence was lacking. McGloin was a young ruffian who had murdered a saloon-keeper at a midnight raid on his place. He was the fellow who the night before he was hanged invited the Chief of Detectives to "come over to the wake; they'll have a devil of a time." For six months Byrnes had tried everything to bring the crime home to him, but in vain. At last he sent out and had McGloin and his two "pals" arrested, but so that none of them knew of the plight of the others. McGloin was taken to Mulberry Street, and orders were given to bring the others in at a certain hour fifteen or twenty minutes apart. Byrnes put McGloin at the window in his office while he questioned him. Nothing could be got out of him. As he sat there a door was banged below. Looking out he saw one of his friends led across the yard in charge of policemen. Byrnes, watching him narrowly, saw his cheek blanch; but still his nerve held. Fifteen minutes passed; another door banged. The murderer, looking out, saw his other pal led in a prisoner. He looked at Byrnes. The Chief nodded : —

"Squealed, both."

It was a lie, and it cost the man his life. "The jig is up then," he said, and told the story that brought him to the gallows.

I could not let Byrnes go without a word, for he filled a large space in my life. It is the reporter, I suppose, who sticks out there. The boys called him a great faker, but they were hardly just to him in that. I should rather call him a great actor, and without being that no man can be a great detective. He made life in a mean street picturesque while he was there, and for that something is due him. He was the very opposite of Roosevelt — quite without moral purpose or the comprehension of it, yet with a streak of kindness in him that sometimes put preaching to shame. Mulberry

Street swears by him to-day, even as it does, under its breath, by Roosevelt. Decide from that for yourself whether his presence there was for the good or the bad.

In writing " How the Other Half Lives " I had been at great pains not to overstate my case. I knew that it would be questioned, and was anxious that no flaws should be picked in it, for, if there were, harm might easily come of it instead of good. I saw now that in that I had been wise. The Gilder Tenement-House Commission more than confirmed all that I had said about the tenements and the schools. The Reinhardt Committee was even more emphatic on the topic of child labor. I was asked to serve on the Seventy's sub-committee on Small Parks. In the spring of 1896, the Council of Confederated Good Government Clubs appointed me its general agent, and I held the position for a year, giving all my spare time to the planning and carrying out of such work as it seemed to me ought to make a record for a reform administration. We wanted it to last. That was a great year. They wanted a positive programme, and my notions of good government were nothing if not positive. They began and ended with the people's life. We tore down unfit tenements, forced the opening of parks and playgrounds, the establishment of a truant school and the remodelling of the

whole school system, the demolition of the overcrowded old Tombs and the erection on its site
of a decent new prison. We overhauled the civil
courts and made them over new in the charter of
the Greater New York. We lighted dark halls;
closed the "cruller" bakeries in tenement-house
cellars that had caused the loss of no end of lives,
for the crullers were boiled in fat in the early
morning hours while the tenants slept, and when
the fat was spilled in the fire their peril was awful.
We fought the cable-car managers at home and
the opponents of a truant school at Albany. We
backed up Roosevelt in his fight in the Police
Board, and — well, I shall never get time to tell it all.
But it was a great year. That it did not keep the
Good Government clubs alive was no fault of my
programme. It was mine, I guess. I failed to
inspire them with the faith that was in me. I had
been going it alone so long that I did not know
how to use the new tool that had come to hand.
There is nothing like an organization if you know
how to use it. I did not. Perhaps, also, politics
had something to do with it. They were in for
playing the game. I never understood it.

But if I did not make the most of it, I had a
good time that year. There were first the two
small parks to be laid out over on the East Side,
where the Gilder Commission had pointed to the

smothering crowds. I had myself made a member
of the Citizens' Committee that was appointed to
locate them. It did not take us any nine years or
six, or three. We did the business in three weeks,
and having chosen the right spots, we went to the
Legislature with a bill authorizing the city to seize
the property at once, ahead of condemnation, and it
was passed. We were afraid that Tammany might
come back, and the event proved that we were wise.
You bring up the people slowly to a reform programme, particularly when it costs money. They will
pay for corruption with a growl, but seem to think
that virtue ought always to be had for nothing. It
makes the politicians' game easy. They steal the
money for improvements, and predict that reform
will raise the tax-rate. When the prophecy comes
true, they take the people back in their sheltering
embrace with an "I told you so!" and the people
nestle there repentant. There was a housing con-
ference at which that part of the work was parcelled
out: the building of model tenements to the capi-
talists who formed the City and Suburban Homes
Company; the erection of model lodging-houses
to D. O. Mills, the banker philanthropist, who was
anxious to help that way. I chose for the Good
Government clubs the demolition of the old tenements. It was my chance. I hated them. A
law had been made the year before empowering

the Health Board to seize and destroy tenement-house property that was a threat to the city's health, but it had remained a dead letter. The authorities hesitated to attack property rights, vested rights. Charles G. Wilson, the President of the Board, was a splendid executive, but he was a hold-over Tammany appointee, and needed backing.

Now that Theodore Roosevelt sat in the Health Board, fresh from his war on the police lodging-rooms of which I told, they hesitated no longer. I put before the Board a list of the sixteen worst rear tenements in the city outside of the Bend, and while the landlords held their breath in aston-ishment, they were seized, condemned, and their tenants driven out. The Mott Street Barracks were among them. In 1888 the infant death-rate among the 350 Italians they harbored had been 325 per thousand — that is to say, one-third of all the babies died that year. That was the kind of evi-dence upon which those rear tenements were ar-raigned. Ninety-four of them, all told, were seized that year, and in them there had been in four years 956 deaths — a rate of 62.9 when the general city death-rate was 24.63. I shall have once more, and for the last time, to refer to " A Ten Years' War " for the full story of that campaign. As I said, it was great.

Conceive, if you can, the state of mind of a man

to whom a dark, overcrowded tenement had ever
been as a personal affront, now suddenly finding
himself commissioned with letters of marque and

The Mott Street Barracks.

reprisal, as it were, to seize and destroy the enemy
wherever found, not one at a time, but by blocks and
battalions in the laying out of parks. I fed fat my
ancient grudge and grew good humor enough to
last me for a dozen years in those two. They were

the years when, in spite of hard work, I began to grow stout, and honestly, I think it was tearing down tenements that did it. Directly or indirectly, I had a hand in destroying seven whole blocks of them as I count it up. I wish it had been seventy.

The landlords sued, but the courts sided with the Health Board. When at last we stopped to take breath we had fairly broken the back of the slum and made precedents of our own that would last a while. Mr. Roosevelt was personally sued twice, I think, but that was all the good it did them. We were having our innings that time, and there were a lot of arrears to collect. The city paid for the property that was taken, of course, and more than it ought to have paid, to my way of thinking. The law gave the owner of a tenement that was altogether unfit just the value of the brick and timbers that were in it. It was enough, for "unfit" meant murderous, and why should a man have a better right to kill his neighbor with a house than with an axe in the street? But the lawyers who counselled compromise bought Gotham Court, one of the most hopeless slums in the Fourth Ward, for nearly $20,000. It was not worth so many cents. The Barracks with their awful baby death-rate were found to be mortgaged to a cemetery corporation. The Board of Health gave them the price of opening one grave for their share, and tore down the rear tenements. A year or two later I travelled to Europe on an ocean steamer with the treasurer of that graveyard concern. We were ten days on the way, and I am afraid he did not have altogether a good time of it. The ghost of the Barracks would keep rising out of the deep before us, sitting there in our steamer chairs, from whichever quarter the wind blew. I suppose he took it as a victory when the Court of Appeals decided upon a technicality that the Barracks should not have been destroyed; but so did I, for they were down by that time. The city could afford to pay. We were paying for our own neglect, and it was a good lesson.

I have said more than once in these pages that I am not good at figuring, and I am not; a child could do better. For that very reason I am going to claim full credit for every time I do a sum right. It may not happen again. Twice during that spell, curiously enough, did I downright distinguish myself in that line. I shall never be able to tell you how; I only know that I did it. Once was when I went before the Board of Estimate and Apportionment to oppose an increase in the appropriation for the Tombs which the Commissioner of Correction had asked for. His plea was that there had been a large increase in the census of the prison, and he marched up a column of figures to prove it. To the amazement of the Board, and really, if the truth be told,

of myself, I demonstrated clearly from his own figures that not only had there been no increase, but
that there could not be without criminally over-

Gotham Court.

crowding the wretched old prison, in which already
every cell had two inmates, and some three. The
exhibit was so striking that the Commissioner and his
bookkeeper retired in confusion. It was just the

power of the facts again.   I wanted to have the hor·
rid old pile torn down, and had been sitting up nights
acquainting myself with all that concerned it.   Now
it is gone, and a good riddance to it.

The other computation was vastly more involved.
It concerned the schools, about which no one knew
anything for certain.   The annual reports of the
Department of Education were models of how to say
a thing so that no one by any chance could understand what it was about.   It was possible to prove
from them that, while there was notoriously a dearth
of school accommodation, while children knocked
vainly for admission and the Superintendent clamored for more schools, yet there were ten or twenty
thousand seats to spare.   But it was not possible to
get the least notion from them of what the real need
was.   I tried for many months, and then set about
finding out for myself how many children who ought
to be in school were drifting about the streets.   The
truant officers, professionally discreet, thought about
800.   The Superintendent of Schools guessed at
8000.   The officers of the Association for the
Improvement of the Condition of the Poor, with
an eye on the tenements, made it 150,000.   I can-
vassed a couple of wards from the truant officers'
reports, and Dr. Tracy compared the showing with
the statistics of population.   From the result I
reasoned that there must be about 50,000.   They

scorned me at the City Hall for it.   It was all guess-
work they said, and so it was.   We had first to
have a school census, and we got one, so that we
might know where we were at.   But when we had
the result of that first census before us, behold! it
showed that of 339,756 children of school age in the
city, 251,235 were accounted for on the roster of
public or private schools, 28,452 were employed, and
50,069 on the street or at home.   So that, if I am
not smart at figuring, I may reasonably claim to be
a good guesser.

The showing that a lack of schools which threw
an army of children upon the street went hand in
hand with overcrowded jails made us get up and
demand that something be done.   From the school
executive came the helpless suggestion that the thing
might be mended by increasing the classes in neigh-
borhoods where there were not enough schools
from sixty to seventy-five.   Forty or forty-five pupils
is held to be the safe limit anywhere.   But the time
had passed for such pottering.   New York pulled
itself together and spent millions in building new
schools while "the system" was overhauled; we
dragged in a truant school by threatening the city
authorities with the power of the State unless they
ceased to send truants to institutions that received
child criminals.   But a man convinced against his
will is of the same opinion still; we shall have to

do that all over again next.　My pet scheme was to have trained oculists attached to the public schools, partly as a means of overcoming stupidity — half of what passes for that in the children is really the teacher's; the little ones are near-sighted; they cannot see the blackboard — partly also that they might have an eye on the school buildings and help us get rid of some where they had to burn gas all day. That was upset by the doctors, who were afraid that "private practice would be interfered with." We had not quite got to the millennium yet.　It was so with our bill to establish a farm school to win back young vagrants to a useful life.　It was killed at Albany with the challenge that we "had had enough of reform in New York."　And so we had, as the events showed.　Tammany came back.

But not to stay.　We had secured a hold during those three years which I think they little know of. They talk at the Wigwam of the "school vote," and mean the men friends and kin of the teachers on whom the machine has a grip, or thinks it has; but there is another school vote that is yet to be heard from, when the generation that has had its right to play restored to it comes to the polls. That was the great gain of that time.　It was the thing I had in mind back of and beyond all the rest.　I was bound to kill the Bend, because it was bad.　I wanted the sunlight in there, but so that it might shine on the children at play. That is a child's right, and it is not to be cheated of it. And

when it is cheated of it, it is not the child but the community that is robbed of that beside which all its wealth is but tinsel and trash. For men, not money, make a country great, and joyless children do not make good men.

So when the Legislature, urged by the Tenement House Commission, made it law that no public school should ever again be built in New York without an outdoor playground, it touched

A Tenement House Air-shaft.

the quick. Thereafter it was easy to rescue the small parks from the landscape gardener by laying them

under the same rule. It was well we did it, too,
for he is a dangerous customer, hard to get around.
Twice he has tried to steal one of the little parks
we laid out, the one that is called Seward Park,
from the children, and he "points with pride" almost to the playground in the other, which he laid
out so badly that it was a failure from the start.
However, we shall convert him yet; everything in
its season.

The Board of Education puzzled over its end of
it for a while. The law did not say how big the
playground should be, and there was no precedent.
No, there was not. I found the key to that puzzle,
at least one that fitted, when I was Secretary of the
Small Parks Committee.   It was my last act as
agent of the Good Government clubs to persuade
Major Strong to appoint that committee. It made
short work of its task. We sent for the police to
tell us where they had trouble with the boys, and
why. It was always the same story: they had no
other place to play in than the street, and there
they broke windows. So began the trouble. It
ended in the police-station and the jail. The city
was building new schools by the score. We got a
list of the sites, and as we expected, they were
where the trouble was worst. Naturally so; that
was where the children were. There, then, was our
field as a playground committee. Why not kill

two birds with one stone, and save money by making them one? By hitching the school and the
boys' play together we should speedily get rid of
the truant. He was just there as a protest against
the school without play.

We asked the Board of Education to make their
school playgrounds the neighborhood recreation
centres. So they would not need to worry over
how big they should be, but just make them as
big as they could, whether on the roof or on the
ground. They listened, but found difficulties in
" the property." Odd, isn't it, this disposition of
the world to forever make of the means the end,
to glorify the establishment! It was the same story
when I asked them to open the schools at night
and let in the boys to have their clubs there. The
saloon was bidding for them, and bidding high, but
the School Board hesitated because a window might
be broken or a janitor want extra pay for cleaning
up. Before a reluctant consent was given I had to
make a kind of promise that I would not appear
before the Board again to argue for throwing the
doors wider still. But it isn't going to keep me
from putting in the heaviest licks I can, in the
campaign that is coming, for turning the schools
over to the people bodily, and making of them the
neighborhood centre in all things that make for
good, including trades-union meetings and political

discussions. Only so shall we make of our schools real corner-stones of our liberties. So, also, we shall through neighborhood pride restore some of the neighborhood feeling, the *home* feeling that is now lacking in our cities to our grievous loss. Half the tenement-house population is always moving, and to the children the word "home" has no meaning. Anything that will help change that will be a great gain. And that old Board is gone long since, anyhow.

The club prevailed in the end. At least one school let it in, and though tne boys did break a window-pane that winter with a ball, they paid for it like men, and that ghost was laid. The school playground holds aloof yet from the neighborhood except in the long vacation. But that last is something, and the rest is coming. It could not be coming by any better road than the vacation schools, which are paving the way for common sense everywhere. "Everything takes ten years," said Abram S. Hewitt, when he took his seat as the chairman of the Small Parks Committee. Ten years before, when he was Mayor, he had put through the law under which the Mulberry Bend had been at last wiped out. We held our meetings at the City Hall, where I had been spurned so often. All things come to those who wait — and fight for them. Yes, fight! I say it advisedly. I have come to the time of life when a man does not lay about him with a club unless he has to. But — eternal vigilance is the price of liberty! To be vigilant is to sit up with a club. We, as a people, have provided in the republic a means of fighting for our rights and getting them, and it is our business to do it. We shall never get them in any other way. Colonel Waring was a wise man as well as a great man. His declaration that he cleaned the streets of New York, all prophecies to the contrary notwithstanding, by "putting a man instead of a voter behind every broom," deserves to be put on the monument we shall build by and by to that courageous man, for it is the whole gospel of municipal righteousness in a nutshell. But he never said anything better than when he advised his fellow-citizens to fight, not to plead, for their rights. So we grow the kind of citizenship that sets the world, or anyhow our day, ahead. We will all hail the day when we shall be able to lay down the club. But until it comes I do not see that we have any choice but to keep a firm grip on it.

CHAPTER XIV

I TRY TO GO TO THE WAR FOR THE THIRD AND LAST TIME

THAT which I have described as "sitting up with a club" in a city like New York is bound to win your fight if you sit up long enough, for it is to be remembered that the politicians who oppose good government are not primarily concerned about keeping you out of your rights. They want the things that make for their advantage; first of all the offices through which they can maintain their grip. After that they will concede as many of the things you want as they have to, and if you are not yourself out for the offices, more than otherwise, though never more than you wring out of them. They really do not care if you do have clean streets, good schools, parks, playgrounds, and all the things which make for good citizenship because they give the best part of the man a chance, though they grudge them as a sad waste of money that might be turned to use in "strengthening the organization," which is the sum of all their self-seeking, being their means of ever getting more and more.

Hence it is that a mere handful of men and women who rarely or never had other authority than their own unselfish purpose, have in all times, even the worst, been able to put their stamp upon the community for good. I am thinking of the Felix Adlers, the Dr. Rainsfords, the Josephine Shaw Lowells, the Robert Ross McBurneys, the R. Fulton Cuttings, the Father Doyles, the Jacob H. Schiffs, the Robert W. de Forests, the Arthur von Briesens, the F. Norton Goddards, the Richard Watson Gilders, and their kind; and thinking of them brings to mind an opportunity I had a year or two ago to tell a club of workmen what I thought of them. It was at the Chicago Commons. I had looked in on a Sunday evening upon a group of men engaged in what seemed to me a singularly unprofitable discussion of human motives. They were of the school which professes to believe that everything proceeds from the love of self, and they spoke learnedly of the ego and all that; but as I listened the conviction grew, along with the feeling of exasperation that sort of nonsense always arouses in me, that they were just vaporing, and I told them so. I pointed to these men and women I have spoken of, some of them of great wealth — the thing against which they seemed to have a special grudge — and told them how they had given their lives and their means in the cause of humanity

without asking other reward than that of seeing
the world grow better, and the hard lot of some of
their fellow-men eased; wherein they had succeeded
because they thought less of themselves than of
their neighbors, and were in the field, anyway, to
be of such use as they could. I told them how
distressed I was that upon their own admission
they should have been engaged in this discussion
four years without getting any farther, and I closed
with a remorseful feeling of having said more than
I intended and perhaps having made them feel bad.
But not they. They had listened to me throughout
with undisturbed serenity. When I had done, the
chairman said courteously that they were greatly
indebted to me for my frank opinion. Every man
was entitled to his own. And he could quite sym-
pathize with me in my inability to catch their point
of view.

"Because here," he added, "I have been reading
for ten years or more the things Mr. Riis writes in
his newspaper and in the magazines, and by which
he makes a living, and for the life of me I never
was able to understand how any one could be found
to pay for such stuff."

So there you have my measure as a reformer.
The meeting nodded gravely. I was apparently
the only one there who took it as a joke.

I spoke of the women's share in the progress we

made. A good big one it was. We should have been floundering yet in the educational mud-puddle we were in, had it not been for the women of New York who went to Albany and literally held up the Legislature, compelling it to pass our reform bill. And not once but a dozen times, during Mayor Strong's administration, when they had wearied of me at the City Hall — I was not always *persona grata* there with the reform administration — did I find it the part of wisdom to send committees of women instead to plead with the Mayor over his five o'clock tea. They could worm a playground or a small park out of him when I should have met with a curt refusal and a virtual invitation to be gone. In his political doldrums the Mayor did not have a kindly eye to reformers; but he was not always able to make them out in petticoats.

The women prevailed at Albany by the power of fact. They knew, and the legislators did not. They received them up there with an indulgent smile, but it became speedily apparent that they came bristling with information about the schools to which the empty old Tammany boast that New York "had the best schools in the world" was not an effective answer. In fact they came nearer being the worst. I had myself had an experience of that kind, when I pointed out in print that an East Side school was so overrun with rats that it

The School of the New Day.

was difficult to hear oneself think for their squeaking in the dark "playground," when the children were upstairs in their classes. The Board of Estimate and Apportionment, which comprises the important officials of the city Government with the Mayor as presiding officer, took umbrage at the statement, and said in plain words that I lied and that there were no rats. That was a piece of unthinking ignorance, for an old schoolhouse without rats in it would be a rare thing anywhere; but it was impertinence, too, of a kind of which I had had so much from the City Hall that I decided the time had come for a demonstration. I got me a

rat trap, and prepared to catch one and have it sent
in to the Board, duly authenticated by affidavit as
hailing from Allen Street; but before I could carry
out my purpose the bottom fell out of the Tammany conspiracy of ignorance and fraud and left
us the way clear for three years. So I saved my
rat for another time.

This "fact," which was naturally my own weapon,
the contribution I was able to make from my own
profession and training, was in reality a tremendously effective club before which nothing could or
can stand in the long run. If I can leave that conviction as a legacy to my brother reporters, I shall
feel that I have really performed a service. I
believe they do not half understand it, or they
would waste no printer's ink idly. The school
war was an illustration of it, all through. I was
at Police Headquarters, where I saw the East Side,
that had been orderly, becoming thievish and immoral. Going to the schools, I found them overcrowded, ill ventilated, dark, without playgrounds,
repellent. Following up the boys, who escaped
from them in disgust — if indeed they were not
barred out; the street swarmed with children for
whom there was not room — I saw them herded
at the prison to which Protestant truants were sent,
with burglars, vagrants, thieves, and " bad boys "
of every kind. They classified them according to

size: four feet, four feet seven, and over four feet seven! No other way was attempted. At the Catholic prison they did not even do that. They kept them on a "footing of social equality" by mixing them all up together; and when in amazement I asked if that was doing right by the truant who might be reasonably supposed to be in special danger from such contact, the answer I got was "would it be fair to the burglar to set him apart with the stamp on him?" I went back to the office and took from the Rogues' Gallery a handful of photographs of boy thieves and murderers and printed them in the *Century Magazine* with a statement of the facts, under the heading, "The Making of Thieves in New York." I quote the concluding sentence of that article because it seemed to me then, and it seems to me now, that there was no getting away from its awful arraignment:—

"While we are asking at this end of the line if it would be quite fair to the burglar to shut him off from social intercourse with his betters, the State Reformatory, where the final product of our schools of crime is garnered, supplies the answer year after year, unheeded. Of the thousands who land there, barely one per cent kept good company before coming. All the rest were the victims of evil association, of corrupt environment. They were not thieves by heredity; they were made.

And the manufacture goes on every day. The street and the jail are the factories."

Upon the lay mind the argument took hold; that of the official educator resisted it stubbornly for a season. Two years later, when one of the School Commissioners spoke indulgently of the burglars and highway robbers in the two prisons as probably guilty merely of "the theft of a top, or a marble, or maybe a banana," in extenuation of the continued policy of his department in sending truants there in flat defiance of the State law that forbade the mingling of thieves and truants, the police office had once more to be invoked with its testimony. I had been keeping records of the child crimes that came up in the course of my work that year. They began before the kindergarten age with burglary and till-tapping. "Highwaymen" at six sounds rather formidable, but there was no other name for it. Two lads of that age had held up a third and robbed him in the street; at seven and eight there were seven housebreakers and two common thieves; at ten I had a burglar, one boy and four girl thieves, two charged with assault and one with forgery; at eleven four burglars, two thieves with a record, two charged with assault, a highway robber, an habitual liar, and a suicide; at twelve five burglars, three thieves, two "drunks," three incendiaries, three arrested for assault, and two suicides; at thirteen five burglars, one with a record, five thieves, five charged with assault, one "drunk," one forger; at fourteen four burglars, seven thieves, one drunk enough to fight a policeman, six highway robbers, and ten charged with assault. And so on. The street had borne its perfect crop, and they were behind the bars every one, locked in with the boys who had done nothing worse than play hooky.

It was a knock-out blow. Classification by measurement had ceased at the first broadside; the last gave us the truant school which the law demanded. To make the most of it, we shall apparently have to have a new deal. I tried to persuade the Children's Aid Society to turn its old machinery to this new work. Perhaps the George Junior Republic would do better still. When there is room for every boy on the school bench, and room to toss a ball when he is off it, there will not be much left of that problem to wrestle with; but little or much, the peril of the prison is too great to be endured for a moment.

It must have been about that time that I received a letter from an old friend who was in high glee over a statement in some magazine that I had evolved a "scientific theory" as to why boys go to the bad in cities. It was plain that he was as much surprised as he was pleased, and so was I when I heard what it was all about. That which

they had pitched upon as science and theory was
the baldest recital of the facts as seen from Mulberry Street.   Beyond putting two and two together, there was very little reasoning about it.

That such conditions as
were all about us should
result in making "toughs"
of the boys was not
strange. Rather, it would
have been strange had
anything else come of it.
With the home cor-
rupted by the tenement;
the school doors closed
against them where the
swarms were densest, and
the children thrown upon
the street, there to take

The Way to prevent the Manufacture of "Toughs."

their chance; with honest play interdicted, every
natural right of the child turned into a means of
oppression, a game of ball become a crime for
which children were thrust into jail, indeed, shot
down like dangerous criminals when running away
from the policeman who pursued them;[1] with dead-
letter laws on every hand breeding blackmail and
bringing the police and authority into disrepute;

[1] Such a case occurred on Thanksgiving Day, 1897.   A great public
clamor arose and the policeman was sent to Sing Sing.

2 B

with the lawlessness of the street added to want of rule at home, where the immigrant father looked on helpless, himself dependent in the strange surroundings upon the boy and no longer his master —it seemed as if we had set out to deliberately make the trouble under which we groaned. And we were not alone in it. The shoe fits every large city more or less snugly. I know, for I have had a good deal to do with fitting it on the last two or three years; and often, when looking my audience over in lecturing about Tony and his hardships, I am thinking about Mulberry Street and the old days when problems, civic or otherwise, were farthest from my mind in digging out the facts that lay ready to the hand of the police reporter.

In him as a reporter there may be no special virtue; but there is that in his work, in the haste and the directness of it, which compels him always to take the short cut and keeps it clear of crankery of every kind. The "isms" have no place in a newspaper office, certainly not in Mulberry Street. I confess I was rather glad of it. I had no stomach for abstract discussions of social wrongs; I wanted to right those of them that I could reach. I wanted to tear down the Mulberry Bend and let in the light so that we might the more readily make them out; the others could do the rest then. I used to say that to a very destructive crank who would have nothing

less, upon any account, than the whole loaf. My
" remedies " were an abomination to him. The landlords should be boiled in oil to a man ; hanging was
too good for them. Now he is a Tammany office-
holder in a position where propping up landlord
greed is his daily practice and privilege, and he
thrives upon it. But I ought not to blame him. It
is precisely because of his kind that Tammany is
defenceless against real reform. It never can make
it out. That every man has his price is the language
of Fourteenth Street. They have no dictionary there
to enable them to understand any other ; and as a
short cut out of it they deny that there is any other.

It helped me vastly that my associations in the
office were most congenial. I have not often been
in accord with the editorial page of my own paper,
the *Sun*. It seemed as if it were impossible for anybody to get farther apart in their views of most things
on the earth and off it than were my paper and I.
It hated and persecuted Beecher and Cleveland ;
they were my heroes. It converted me to Grant
by its opposition to him. The sign " Keep off the
grass ! " arouses in its editorial breast no desire to
lock up the man who planted it ; it does in mine.
Ten years and more I have striven in its columns to
make the tenement out a chief device of the devil,
and it must be that I have brought some over to my
belief ; but I have not converted the *Sun*. So that

on the principle which I laid down before that I must be always fighting with my friends, I ought to have had a mighty good time of it there. And so in fact I did. They let me have in pretty nearly everything my own way, though it led us so far apart. As time passed and the duties that came to me took more and more of my time from my office work, I found that end of it insensibly lightened to allow me to pursue the things I believed in, though they did not. No doubt the old friendship that existed between my immediate chief on the *Evening Sun*, William McCloy, and myself, bore a hand in this. Yet it could not have gone on without the assent and virtual sympathy of the Danas, father and son; for we came now and then to a point where opposite views clashed and proved irreconcilable. Then I found these men, whom some deemed cynical, most ready to see the facts as they were, and to see justice done.

I like to think of my last meeting with Charles A. Dana, the " Old Chief," as he was always called in the office. In all the years I was on the *Sun* I do not think I had spoken with him a half dozen times. When he wanted anything of me personally, his orders were very brief and to the point. It was generally something — a report to be digested or the story of some social experiment — which showed me that in his heart he was faithful to his early love;

he had been in his youth, as everybody knows, an enthusiastic reformer, a member of the Brook Farm Community. But if he thought I saw, he let no sign escape him. He hated shams; perhaps I was on trial all the time. If so, I believe that he meant to tell me in that last hand-shake that he had not found me wanting. It was on the stairs in the *Sun* office that we met. I was going up; he was coming down — going home to die. He knew it. In me there was no suspicion of the truth when I came upon him at the turn of the stairs, stumbling along in a way very unlike the usual springy step of the Old Chief. I hardly knew him when he passed, but as he turned and held out his hand I saw that it was Mr. Dana, looking somehow older than I had ever seen him, and changed. I took off my hat and we shook hands.

"Well," he said, "have you reformed everything to suit you, straightened out every kink in town?"

"Pretty nearly," I said, falling into his tone of banter; "all except the *Sun* office. That is left yet, and as bad as ever."

"Ha!" he laughed, "you come on! We are ready for you. Come right along!" And with another hearty hand-shake he was gone. He never saw the *Sun* office again.

It was the only time he had ever held out his hand to me, after that first meeting of ours when

I was a lonely lad, nearly thirty years before. That time there was a dollar in it and I spurned it. This time I like to believe his heart was in it. And I took it gladly and gratefully.

The police helped — sometimes. More frequently we were at odds, and few enough in the rank and file understood that I was fighting for them in fighting the department. A friend came into my office, laughing, one day, and told me that he had just overheard the doorman at Police Headquarters say, as he saw me pass: —

" Ugh! the hypocrite! See him take off his hat and then lay us out cold in his paper when he gets the chance."

He referred to my old-country habit of raising the hat in salutation instead of merely nodding or touching the brim. No doubt he expressed a feeling that was quite general at the time. But after Mulberry Street had taken notice of Roosevelt's friendship for me there was a change, and then it went to the other extreme. It never quite got over the fact that he did not "ring me in" on President McKinley and the Government, or at least make me his private secretary and deputy boss of the Empire State while he was Governor. The Mulberry Street idea of friendship includes the loaves and fishes first and last, and "pull" is the Joss it worships. In fact I had several times to explain that Mr. Roosevelt had not "gone back on me" to save his political reputation. When at a public meeting he once spoke of me as his friend, a dozen policemen brought me copies of the paper containing "the notice," with a frankly expressed wish to be remembered when I came into my own. About that time, being in the neighborhood, I strayed into the Bend one day to enjoy the sunlight there and the children sporting in it. At the curb stood a big policeman leisurely peeling an orange, to which he had helped himself from a cringing Italian's cart. I asked him how were things in the Bend since the park had come. He eyed me very coldly, and said, " Bad, very bad." At that I expressed my astonishment, saying that I was a reporter at Police Headquarters and had understood differently.

"What paper?" he grunted insolently. I told him. He bestowed a look of mingled pity and contempt upon me.

"Nix! mine friend," he said, spreading his feet farther apart and tossing the peel at the Italian, who grinned with delight at such condescension. I regarded him expectantly. He was a very aggravating chap.

"Did you say you were at Police Headquarters — for the *Sun?*" he observed at length.

"Yes!" He shook his head.

"Nixie! not guilty!" he said tauntingly.

"Why, what do you mean?"

"Haven't you heard of Mr. Riis, Jacob Riis?"
I said I had.

"The Governor's friend?"

"Yes; what of it?"

"Well, ain't he at Headquarters for the *Sun*?"
I said that was so.

"Well?"

I took out my card and handed it to him. "I
am that man," I said.

For a fraction of a second the policeman's jaw
dropped; but he was a thoroughbred. His heels
came together before, as it seemed, he could have
read my name; he straightened up. The half-peeled
orange fell from his hand and rolled into the gutter,
covertly speeded by a dextrous little kick. The
unhappy Italian, believing it a mishap, made haste
to select the biggest and juiciest fruit on his stand,
and held it out with a propitiatory bow, but he
spurned him haughtily away.

"These dagoes," he said, elaborately placing my
card in the sweat-band of his hat, "ain't got no manners. It's a hard place for a good man down here.
It's time I was a roundsman. You can do it.
You've got de 'pull.'"

When Roosevelt had gone to Washington to
help fit out the navy for the war with Spain, I spent

a part of the winter there with him, and Mulberry
Street took it for granted that I had at last been
"placed" as I should have been long before.   There
was great amazement when I came back to take my
old place.   The truth was that I had gone partly to
observe what went on at the capital for my paper,
and partly to speed on the war, in which I was a
hearty believer from the first.   It was to me a
means, first and last, of ending the murder in Cuba.
One of the very earliest things I had to do with as
a reporter was the *Virginius* massacre, and ever
since it had been bloodshed right along.   It was
time to stop it, and the only way seemed to wrest
the grip of Spain from the throat of the island.   I
think I never quite got over the contempt I con-
ceived for Spain and Spanish ways when I read as
a boy, in Hans Christian Andersen's account of his
travels in the country of the Dons, that the shep-
herds brought butter from the mountains in sheep's
intestines and measured them off in lengths demanded by the customers by tying knots upon
them.   What was to be expected from a country
that sold butter by the yard ?   As the event showed,
it ran its navies after the same fashion and was
justly punished.   I made friends that winter with
Dr. Leonard Wood, whom we all came to know and
admire afterwards as General and Governor Wood;
and a fine fellow he was.   He was Roosevelt's

friend and physician, and we spent many strenuous hours together, being in that mood.

For the third time in my life, and the last, I wanted to go to the war, when they went, and oh! so badly. Not to fight, — I had had all I needed of that at home, — but to tell the truth about what was going on in Cuba. The *Outlook* offered me that post, and the *Sun* agreed heartily; but once more the door was barred against me. Two of my children had scarlet fever, my oldest son had gone to Washington trying to enlist with the Rough Riders, and the one next in line was engineering to get into the navy on his own hook. My wife raised no objection to my going, if it was duty; but her tears fell silently — and I stayed. It was "three times and out." I shall never go to the war now unless in defence of my own home, which may God forbid. Within a year I knew that, had I gone then, I should most likely not have returned. I had received notice that to my dreams of campaigning in that way there was an end. Thankful that I had been spared, I yet took leave of them with a sigh; most illogically, for I hate the sight of human suffering and of brutal passions aroused. But deep down in my heart there is the horror of my Viking forefathers of dying in bed, unable to strike back, as it were. I know it is wicked and foolish, but all my life I have so wished to get on a horse with a sword, and slam in just

once, like another Sheridan.   I, who cannot sit on a
horse !   Even the one Roosevelt got me at Montauk
that was warranted " not to bite or scratch " ran
away with me.   So it is foolishness, plain to see.
Yet, so I might have found out which way I would
really have run when the call came.   I do hope the
right way, but I never have felt quite sure.

The casualties of war are not all on the battlefield.   The Cuban campaign wrecked a promising
career as a foreign correspondent which I had been
building up for some ten or fifteen years with toilsome
effort.   It was for a Danish newspaper I wrote with
much approval, but when the war came, they did not
take the same view of things that I did, and fell to
suppressing or mutilating my letters, whereupon our
connection ceased abruptly.   My letters were, explained the editor to me a year or two later when I
saw him in Copenhagen, so — er-r — ultra-patriotic,
so — er-r — youthful in their enthusiasm, that —
huh !   I interrupted him with the remark that I was
glad we were young enough yet in my country to
get up and shout for the flag in a fight, and left him
to think it over.   They must have aged suddenly
over there, for they were not that way when I was a
boy.   The real fact was that somehow they could
not get it into their heads that a European bully
could be whipped in one round by "the States."
They insisted on printing ridiculous despatches

about Spanish victories. I think there was some·
thing about codfish, too, something commercial
about corks and codfish — Iceland keeping Spain
on a fish diet in Lent, in return for which she corked
the Danish beer — I have forgotten the particulars.
The bottom fact was a distrust of the United States
that was based upon a curiously stubborn ignorance,
entirely without excuse in a people of high intel-
ligence like the Danes. I tried hard as a correspondent to draw a reasonable, human picture of
American affairs, but it seemed to make no impression. They would jump at the Munchausen
stories that are always afloat, as if America were
some sort of menagerie and not a Christian country.
I think nothing ever aggravated me as did an instance
of that kind the year Ben Butler ran for the Presi-
dency. I had been trying in my letters to present
the political situation and issues fairly, and was
beginning to feel that they *must* understand, when
I received a copy of my paper from Copenhagen and
read there a "life" of General Butler, which con-
densed ran something like this: —

"Mr. Butler was an ambitious young lawyer,
shrewd and full of bold schemes for enriching himself. When the war with the South broke out, he
raised all the money he could and fitted out a fleet
of privateers. With this he sailed for New Orleans,
captured the city, and, collecting all the silver spoons

it contained, freighted his vessels with them, and returned to the North. Thus he laid the foundation for his great fortune, but achieved lasting unpopularity in the South, which will prevent his election to the Presidency."

I am not joking. That was how the story of the silver spoons looked in Danish a quarter of a century after the war. Really, now, what would you have done? I laughed and — well! made remarks by turns, and in the end concluded that there was nothing else that could be done except buckle to and try again; which I did.

If I could not go to the war, I could at least go electioneering with Roosevelt when he came back and try to help him out the best I knew how in matters that touched the poor and their life, once he sat in Cleveland's chair in Albany. I do not think he felt that as an added dignity, but I did and I told him so, whereat he used to laugh a little. But there was nothing to laugh at. They are men of the same stamp, not saints any more than the rest of us, but men with minds and honest wills, if they have different ways of doing things. I wish some Cleveland would come along again soon and give me another chance to vote the ticket which Tammany obstructs with its impudent claim that it is the Democratic party. As for Roosevelt, few were nearer to him, I fancy, than I, even at Albany. No doubt he made his mistakes like the rest of us, and when he did there were not wanting critics to make the most of it. I wish they had been half as ready to lend him a hand. We might have been farther on the road then. I saw how faithfully he labored. I was his umpire with the tailors, with the drug clerks, in the enforcement of the Factory Law against sweaters, and I know that early and late he had no other thought than how best to serve the people who trusted him. I want no better Governor than that, and I guess we shall want him a long time before we get one as good.

I found out upon our electioneering tours that I was not a good stump-speaker, especially on the wing with five-minute stops of the train. It used to pull out with me inwardly raging, all the good things I meant to say unsaid. The politicians knew that trick better, and I left the field to them speedily. Thereafter I went along just for company. Only two or three times did I rise to the occasion. Once when I spoke in the square at Jamestown, N.Y., where I had worked as a young lad and trapped muskrats in the creek for a living. The old days came back to me as I looked upon that mighty throng, and the cheers that arose from it told me that I had "caught on." I was wondering whether by any chance the old ship captain who finished me as a lecturer once was in it, but he was not; he was dead. Another time was in Flushing, Long Island. There was not room in the hall, and they sent me out to talk to the crowd in the street. The sight of it, with the flickering torchlight upon the sea of upturned faces, took me somehow as nothing ever had, and the speech I made from the steps, propped up by two policemen, took the crowd, too; it cheered so that Roosevelt within stopped and thought some enemy had captured the meeting. When he was gone, with the spirit still upon me I talked to the meeting in the hall till it rose and shouted. My political pet enemy from Richmond Hill was on the platform and came over to embrace me. We have been friends since. The memory of that evening lingers yet in Flushing, I am told.

A picture from that day's trip through Long Island will ever abide on my mind. The train was about to pull out from the station in Greenport, when the public school children came swarming down to see "Teddy." He leaned out from the rear platform, grasping as many of the little hands as he could, while the train hands did their best to keep the track clear. Way back in the jostling, cheering crowd I made out the slim figure of a pale, freckled little girl in a worn garment, struggling eagerly but hopelessly to get near him. The stronger children pushed her farther back, and her mournful face was nearly the last of them all when Roosevelt saw her. Going down the steps even as the train started, he made a quick dash, clearing a path through the surging tide to the little girl, and taking her hand, gave it the heartiest shake of all, then sprinted for the departing car and caught it. The last I saw of Greenport was the poor little girl holding tight the hand her hero had shaken, with her face all one sunbeam of joy.

I know just how she felt, for I have had the same experience. One of the things I remember with a pleasure which the years have no power to dim is my meeting with Cardinal Gibbons some years ago. They had asked me to come to Baltimore to speak for the Fresh Air Fund, and to my great delight I found that the Cardinal was to preside. I had always admired him at a distance, but during the fifteen minutes' talk we had before the lecture he won my heart entirely. He asked me to forgive him if he had to go away before I finished my speech, for he had had a very exhausting service the day before, "and I am an old man, on the sunny side of sixty," he added as if in apology.

"On the shady side, you mean," amended the Presbyterian clergyman who was on the committee. The Cardinal shook his head, smiling.

"No, doctor! The sunny side — nearer heaven."

The meeting was of a kind to inspire even the

dullest speaker. When I finished my plea for the
children and turned around, there sat the Cardinal
yet behind me, though it was an hour past his bed-
time. He came forward and gave me his blessing
then and there. I was never so much touched and
moved. Even my mother, stanch old Lutheran that
she is, was satisfied when I told her of it, though, in
the nature of things, the idea of her son consorting
in that way with principalities and powers in the
enemy's camp must have been a shock to her.

Speaking of which, reminds me of the one brief
glimpse into the mysteries of the universe I had
while in Galesburg, Ill., the same year. I had been
lecturing at Knox College, of which my friend John
Finley was the President. It rained before the
meeting, but when we came out, the stars shone
brightly, and I was fired with a sudden desire to see
them through the observatory telescope. The professor of astronomy took me into the dark dome
and pointed the glass at Saturn, which I knew as a
scintillating point of light, said to be a big round
ball like our earth, and had taken on trust as a matter of course. But to see it hanging there, white
and big as an apple, suspended within its broad and
shining ring, was a revelation before which I stood
awe-stricken and dumb. I gazed and gazed; between the star and its ring I caught the infinite
depth of black space beyond; I seemed to see

2 C

almost the whirl, the motion; to hear the morning stars sing together — and then like a flash it was gone. Crane my neck on my ladder as I might I could not get sight of it.

"But where did she go?" I said, half to myself. Far down in the darkness came the old professor's deep voice: —

"That time you saw the earth move."

And so I did. The clockwork that made the dome keep up with the motion of the stars — of our world rather — had run down, and when Saturn passed out of my sight, as I thought, it was the earth instead which I literally saw move.

And now that I am on my travels let me cross the ocean long enough to say that my digging among the London slums one summer only served to convince me that their problem is the same as ours, and is to be solved along the same lines. They have their ways, and we have ours, and each has something to learn from the other. We copied our law that enabled us to tear down slum tenements from the English statute under which they cleared large areas over yonder long before we got to work. And yet in their poor streets — in "Christian Street" of all places — I found families living in apartments entirely below the sidewalk grade. I found children poisoned by factory fumes in a charitable fold, and people huddled in sleeping-rooms as I had never seen it in New York. And when I asked why the police did not interfere, they looked at me, uncomprehending, and retorted that they were on their own premises — the factory, too — and where did the police come in? I told them that in New York they came in when and where they saw fit, and systematically in the middle of the night so that they might get at the exact facts. As for our cave-dwellers, we had got rid of them a long time since by the simple process of dragging out those who wouldn't go and shutting the cellar doors against them. It had to be done and it was done, and it settled the matter.

"I thought yours was a free country," said my policeman conductor.

"So it is," I told him, "freedom to poison yourself and your neighbor excepted." He shook his head, and we went on.

But these were mere divergences of practice. The principle is not affected. It was clear enough that in London, as in New York, it was less a question of transforming human nature in the tenant than of reforming it in the landlord. At St. Giles I found side by side with the work-house a church, a big bath and wash-house, and a school. It was the same at Seven Dials. At every step it recalled the Five Points. To the one as to the other, steeped in poverty and crime, had come the road-builder, the missionary, the school-teacher, and let light in together. And in their track was following, rather faster there than here as yet, the housing reformer with his atoning scheme of philanthropy and five per cent. That holds the key. In the last analysis it is a question of how we rate the brotherhood, what per cent we will take. My neighbor at table in my London boarding-house meant that, though he put it in a way all his own. He was a benevolent enough crank, but no friend of preaching. Being a crank, he condemned preachers with one fell swoop: —

" The parsons!" he said; "my 'evings, what hare they? In hall me life hi've known only two that were fit to be in the pulpit."

. Returning to my own country, I found the ·conviction deepening wherever the slum had got a grip, that it was the problem not only of government but of humanity. In Chicago they are setting limits to it with parks and playgrounds and the home restored. In Cincinnati, in Cleveland, in Boston, they are bestirring themselves. Indeed, in Boston they have torn down more foul tenements than did we in the metropolis, and with less surrender to the slum landlord. In New York a citizens' movement paved the way for the last Tenement-House Commission, which has just finished its great work, and the movement is warrant that the fruits of that work will not be lost.   Listen to the arraignment of the tenement by that Commission, appointed by the State: —

"All the conditions which surround childhood, youth, and womanhood in New York's crowded tenement quarters make for unrighteousness.   They also make for disease. . . .   From the tenements there comes a stream of sick, helpless people to our hospitals and dispensaries . . . from them also comes a host of paupers and charity seekers.   Most terrible of all . . . the fact that, mingled with the drunken, the dissolute, the improvident, the diseased, dwell the great mass of the respectable workingmen of the city with their families."

This after all the work of twenty years!   Yet the work was not wasted, for at last we see the truth.   Seeing, it is impossible that the monstrous wrong should go unrighted and government of the people endure, as endure it will, I know.   We have only begun to find out what it can do for mankind in the day when we shall all think enough about the common good, the *res publica*, to forget about ourselves.

In that day, too, the boss shall have ceased from troubling.   However gross he wax in our sight, he has no real substance.   He is but an ugly dream of political distemper.   Sometimes when I hear him spoken of with bated breath, I think of the

Irish teamster who went to the priest in a fright; he had seen a ghost on the church wall as he passed it in the night.

"And what was it like?" asked the priest.

"It was like nothing so much as a big ass," said Patrick, wide-eyed.

"Go home, Pat! and be easy. You've seen your own shadow."

But I am tired now and want to go home to mother and rest awhile.

CHAPTER XV

WHEN I WENT HOME TO MOTHER

THERE was a heavy step on the stairs, a rap that sounded much as if an elephant had knocked against the jamb in passing, and there in the door stood a six-foot giant, calmly surveying me, as if I were a specimen bug stuck on a pin for inspection, instead of an ordinary man-person with no more than two legs.

"Well?" I said, groping helplessly among the memories of the past for a clew to the apparition. Somewhere and sometime I had seen it before; that much I knew and no more.

The shape took a step into the room. "I am Jess," it said simply, "Jess Jepsen from Lustrup."

"Lustrup!" I pushed back papers and pen and strode toward the giant to pull him up to the light. Lustrup! Talk about seven league boots! that stride of mine was four thousand miles long, if it was a foot. It spanned the stormy Atlantic and the cold North Sea and set me down in sight of the little village of straw-thatched farm-houses where I played in the long ago, right by the dam

in the lazy brook where buttercups and forget-me-
nots nodded ever over the pool, and the pewit built
its nest in spring. Just beyond, the brook issued
forth from the meadows to make a detour around
the sunken walls of the old manse and lose itself
in the moor that stretched toward the western hills.
Lustrup! Oh, yes! I pushed my giant into a
chair so that I might have a look at him.

Ribe, in my Childhood.

Seen from Elisabeth's garden.

He was just like the landscape of his native
plain; big and calm and honest. Nothing there
to hide; couldn't if it tried. And, like his village,
he smelled of the barn-yard. He was a driver, he
told me, earning wages. But he had his evenings
to himself; and so he had come to find, through
me, a school where he might go and learn English.

Just so! It was Lustrup all over. I remembered as though it were yesterday the time I went up to have a look at the dam I hadn't seen for thirty years, and the sun-fish and the pewit so anxiously solicitous for her young, and found the brook turned aside and the western earth-wall of the manse, which it skirted, all gone; and the story the big farmer, Jess Jepsen's father, told me with such quiet pride, standing there, of how because of trouble made by the Germans at the "line" a mile away the cattle business had run down and down until the farm didn't pay; how he and "the boy" unaided, working patiently year by year with spade and shovel, had dug down the nine acres of dry upland, moved the wall into the bottoms and turned the brook, making green meadow of the sandy barren, and saving the farm. The toil of twenty years had broken the old man's body, but his spirit was undaunted as ever. There was a gleam of triumph in his eye as he shook his fist at the "line" post on the causeway. "We beat them," he said; "we did."

They did. I had heard it told many times how this brave little people, driven out of the German market, had conquered the English and held it against the world, three times in one man's lifetime making a new front to changed industrial conditions; turning from grain-raising to cattle on the hoof, again to slaughtered meat, and once more to dairy-farming, and holding always their own. How, robbed of one-third of their country by a faithless foe, they had set about with indomitable energy to reclaim the arid moor, and in one generation laid under the plough or planted as woodland as great an area as that which had been stolen from them. Ay, it was a brave record, a story to make one proud of being of such a people. I, too, heard the pewit's plaint in my childhood and caught the sun-fish in the brook. I was a boy when they planted the black post at the line and watered it with the blood of my countrymen. Gray-haired and with old-time roots in a foreign soil, I dream with them yet of the day that shall see it pulled up and hurled over the river where my fathers beat back the southern tide a thousand years.

Jess? He went away satisfied. He will be there, when needed. His calm eyes warranted that. And I— I went back to the old home, to Denmark and to my mother; because I just couldn't stay away any longer.

We had wandered through Holland, counting the windmills, studying the " explications " set forth in painfully elaborate English on its old church walls with the information for travellers that further particulars were to be obtained of the sexton, who might be found with the key " in the neighborhood

No. 5." We had argued with the keeper of the Prinzenhof in Delft that William the Silent could not possibly have been murdered as he said he was — that he must have come down the stairs and not gone across the hall when the assassin shot him, as any New York police reporter could tell from the bullet-hole that is yet in the wall — and thereby wounding his patriotic pride so deeply that an extra fee was required to soothe it. I caught him looking after us as we went down the street and shaking his head at those "wild Americans" who accounted nothing holy, not even the official record of murder done while their ancestors were yet savages roaming the plains. We had laughed at the coal-heavers on the frontier carrying coal in baskets up a ladder to the waiting engine and emptying it into the fender. And now, after parting company with my fellow-traveller at Hamburg, I was nearing the land where once more I should see old Dannebrog, the flag that fell from heaven with victory to the hard-pressed Danes. Literally out of the sky it fell in their sight, the historic fact being apparently that the Christian bishops had put up a job with the Pope to wean the newly converted Danes away from their heathen pirate flag and found their opportunity in one of the crusades the Danes undertook on their own hook into what is now Prussia. The Pope had sent a silken banner with the device of a white cross in red, and at the right moment, when the other was taken, the priest threw it down from a cliff into the thick of the battle and turned its tide. Ever after, it was the flag of the Danes, and their German foes had reason to hate it. Here in Slesvig, through which I was travelling, to display it was good cause for banishment. But over yonder, behind the black post, it was waiting, and my heart leaped to meet it. Have I not felt the thrill, when wandering abroad, at the sight of the stars and stripes suddenly unfolding, the flag of my home, of my manhood's years and of my pride? Happy he who has a flag to love. Twice blest he who has two, and such two.

We have yet a mile to the frontier and, with the panorama of green meadows, of placid rivers, and of long-legged storks gravely patrolling the marshes in search of frogs and lizards, passing by our car-window, I can stop to tell you how this filial pride in the flag of my fathers once betrayed me into the hands of the Philistines. It was in London, during the wedding of the Duke of York. The king and queen of Denmark were in town, and wherever one went was the Danish flag hung out in their honor. Riding under one on top of a Holborn bus, I asked a cockney in the seat next to mine what flag it was. I wanted to hear him praise it, that was why I pretended not to know. He sur-

veyed it with the calm assurance of his kind, and
made reply: —

"That, ah, yes! It is the sign of St. John's ham-
bulance corps, the haccident flag, don't you know,"
and he pointed to an ambulance officer just passing
with the cross device on his arm. The Dannebrog
the "haccident flag"! What did I do? What
would you have done? I just fumed and suppressed
as well as I could a desire to pitch that cockney into
the crowds below, with his pipe and his miserable
ignorance. But I had to go down to do it.

But there is the hoary tower of the old Domkirke
in which I was baptized and confirmed and married,
rising out of the broad fields, and all the familiar
landmarks rushing by, and now the train is slow-
ing up for the station, and a chorus of voices shout
out the name of the wanderer. There is mother in
the throng with the glad tears streaming down her
dear old face, and half the town come out to see
her bring home her boy, every one of them sharing
her joy, to the very letter-carrier who brought her
his letters these many years and has grown fairly to
be a member of the family in the doing of it. At
last the waiting is over, and her faith justified. Dear
old mother! Gray-haired I return, sadly scotched
in many a conflict with the world, yet ever thy boy,
thy home mine. Ah me! Heaven is nearer to us
than we often dream on earth.

At Home in the Old Town.
The last time we were all together.

How shall I tell you of the old town by the North Sea that was the home of the Danish kings in the days when kings led their armies afield and held their crowns by the strength of their grip? Shall I paint to you the queer, crooked streets with their cobblestone pavements and tile-roofed houses where the swallow builds in the hall and the stork on the ridge-pole, witness both that peace dwells within? For it is well known that the stork will not abide with a divided house; and as for the swallow, a plague of boils awaits the graceless hand that disturbs its nest. When the Saviour hung upon the cross, did it not perch upon the beam and pour forth its song of love and pity to His dying ear, "Soothe Him! soothe Him"?   The stork from the meadow cried, "Strength Him! strength Him!" but the wicked pewit, beholding the soldiers with their spears, cried, "Pierce Him! pierce Him!"   Hence stork and swallow are the friends of man, while the pewit dwells in exile, fleeing ever from his presence with its lonesome cry.

Will you wander with me through the fields where the blue-fringed gentian blooms with the pink bell-heather, and the bridal torch nods from the brook-side, bending its stately head to the west wind that sweeps ever in from the sea with touch as soft as of a woman's hand?   Flat and uninteresting?   Yes, if you will.   If one sees only the fields.   My children saw them and longed back to the hills of Long Island; and in their cold looks I felt the tugging of the chain which he must bear through life who exiled himself from the land of his birth, however near to his heart that of his choice and his adoption. I played in these fields when I was a boy.   I fished in these streams and built fires on their banks in spring to roast potatoes in, the like of which I have never tasted since.   Here I lay dreaming of the great and beautiful world without, watching the sky-lark soar ever higher with its song of triumph and joy, and here I learned the sweet lesson of love that has echoed its jubilant note through all the years, and will until we reach the golden gate, she and I, to which love holds the key.

Uninteresting! Say you so? But linger here with me, casting for pickerel among the water-lilies until the sun sets red and big over the sea yonder, and you shall see a light upon these meadows where the grass is as fine silk, that is almost as if it were not of earth. And as we walk home through the long Northern twilight, listening to the curlew's distant call; with the browsing sheep looming large against the horizon upon the green hill where stood the old kings' castle, and the gray Dom rearing its lofty head over their graves, teeming with memories of centuries gone and past, you shall learn to know the poetry of this Danish summer that holds the hearts of its children with such hoops of steel.

At the south gate the "gossip benches" are filled. The old men smoke their pipes and doff their caps to "the American" with the cheery welcome of friends who knew and spanked him with hearty good will when as "a kid" he absconded with their boats for a surreptitious expedition up to the lake. Those boats! heavy, flat-bottomed, propelled with a pole that stuck in the mud and pulled them back half the time farther than they had gone. But what fun it was! In after years a steam whistle woke the echoes of these quiet waters. It was the first one, and the last. The railroad, indeed, came to town, long after I had grown to be a man, and a cotton-mill interjected its bustle into the drowsy hum of the waterwheels that had monopolized the industry of the town before, disturbing its harmony for a season. But the steamboat had no successors.

"The 'gossip benches' are filled."

The river that had once borne large ships gradually sanded up at the mouth, and nothing heavier than a one-masted lighter has come up, in the memory of man, to the quay where grass grows high among the cobblestones and the lone customs official smokes his pipe all day long in unbroken peace. The steamer was a launch of the smallest.

It had been brought across country on a wagon. Some one had bought it at an auction for a lark; and a huge lark was its year on the waters of the Nibs River. The whole town took a sail in it by turns, always with one aft whose business it was to disentangle the rudder from the mass of seaweed which with brief intervals suspended progress, and all hands ready to get out and lift the steamer off when it ran on a bank.

There came a day when a more than commonly ambitious excursion was undertaken, even to the islands in the sea, some six or seven miles from the town. The town council set out upon the journey, with the rector of the Latin School and the burgo-master, bargaining for dinner on their return at dusk. But it was destined that those islands should remain undiscovered by steam and the dinner un-eaten. Barely outside, the tide left it high and dry upon the sands. It was then those Danes showed what stuff there was in them. The water would not be back to lift them off for six hours and more. They indulged in no lamentations, but sturdily produced the schnapps and sandwiches without which no Dane is easily to be tempted out of sight of his home: the rector evolved a pack of cards from the depths of his coat pocket, and upon the sandbank the party camped, playing a cheerful game of whist until the tide came back and bore them home.

The night comes on.   The people are returning
from their evening constitutional, walking in the
middle of the street and taking off their hats to
their neighbors as they pass.   It is their custom,
and the American habit of nodding to friends is
held to be evidence of backwoods' manners excus-
able only in a people so new.   In the deep recesses
of the Domkirke dark shadows are gathering.   The
tower clock peals forth.   At the last stroke the
watchman lifts up his chant in a voice that comes
quavering down from bygone ages: —

Ho, watchman! heard ye the clock strike ten? This
hour is worth the know-ing Ye house-holds high and
low, The time is here and go-ing When ye to bed should
go; Ask God to guard, and say A-men! Be
quick and bright, Watch fire and light, Our clock just now struck ten.

I shall take his advice. But first I must go to the shoe-store to get a box of polish for my russet shoes. Unexpectedly I found it for sale there. I strike the storekeeper in an ungracious mood. He objects to being bothered about business just when he is shutting up shop.

"There," he says, handing me the desired box. "Only one more left; I shall presently have to send for more. Twice already have I been put to that trouble. I don't know what has come over the town." And he slams down the shutter with a fretful jerk. I grope my way home in Egyptian darkness, thanking in my heart the town council for its forethought in painting the lamp-posts white. It was when a dispute sprang up about the price of gas, or something. Danish disputes are like the law the world over, slow of gait; and it was in no spirit of mockery that a resolution was passed to paint the lamp-posts white, pending the controversy, so that the good people in the town might avoid running against them in the dark and getting hurt, if by any mischance they strayed from the middle of the road.

Bright and early the next morning I found women at work sprinkling white sand in the street in front of my door, and strewing it with wintergreen and twigs of hemlock. Some one was dead, and the funeral was to pass that way. Indeed they all did. The cemetery was at the other end of the street. It was one of the inducements held out to my mother she told me, when father died, to move from the old home into that street. Now that she was quite alone, it was so "nice and lively; all the funerals passed by." The one buried that day I had known, or she had known me in my boyhood, and it was expected that I would attend. My mother sent the wreath that belongs, — there is both sense and sentiment in flowers at a funeral when they are wreathed by the hands of those who loved the dead, as is still the custom here; none where they are bought at a florist's and paid for with a growl, — and we stood around the coffin and

The Extinct Chimney-sweep.

sang the old hymns, then walked behind it, two by two, men and women, to the grave, singing as we passed through the gate.

"Earth to earth, ashes to ashes, dust to dust." The clods rang upon the coffin with almost cheerful sound, for she whose mortal body lay within was full of years and very tired. The minister paused.

From among the mourners came forth the nearest relative and stood by the grave, hat in hand. Ours were all off. "From my heart I thank you, neighbors all," he said, and it was over. We waited to shake hands, to speculate on the weather, safe topic even at funerals; then went each to his own.

I went down by the cloister walk and sat upon a bench and thought of it all. The stork had built its nest there on the stump of a broken tree, and was hatching its young. The big bird stood on one leg and looked down upon me out of its grave, unblinking eye as it did forty years ago when we children sang to it in the street the song about the Pyramids and Pharaoh's land. The town lay slumbering in the sunlight and the blossoming elders. The far tinkle of a bell came sleepily over the hedges. Once upon a time it called the monks to prayers. Ashes to ashes! They are gone and buried with the dead past. To-day it summons the Latin School boys to recitations. I shuddered at the thought. They had at the school, when the bell called me with the rest, a wretched tradition that some king had once expressed wonder at the many learned men who came from the Latin School. And the rector told him why.

"We have near here," he said, "a little birch forest. It helps, your Majesty, it helps." Faith·

fully did it play its part in my day, though I cannot bear witness that it helped. But its day passed, too, and is gone. The world moves and all the while forward. Not always with the speed of the wind; but it moves. The letter-carrier on his collecting rounds with his cart has stopped at the bleaching yard where his wife and little boy are hanging out washing. He lights his pipe and, after a

The Ancient Bellwoman.

brief rest to take breath, turns to helping the gude-wife hang the things on the line. Then he packs the dry clothes in his cart, puts the boy in with them and, puffing leisurely at his pipe, lounges soberly homeward. There is no hurry with the mail.

There is not. It was only yesterday that, crossing the meadows on a "local," I found the train pulling up some distance from the village to let an old woman, coming puffing and blowing from a farm-house with a basket on her arm, catch up.

"Well, mother, can she hurry a bit?" spake the

conductor when she came within hearing. They address one another in the third person out of a sort of neighborly regard, it appears.

" Now, sonny," responded the old woman, as she lumbered on board, "don't I run as fast as I can?"

" And has she got her fare, now?" queried the conductor.

" Why, no, sonny; how should I have that till I've been in to sell my eggs?" and she held up the basket in token of good faith.

" Well, well," growled the other, "see to it that she doesn't forget to pay it when she comes back." And the train went on.

Time to wait! The deckhand on the ferry-boat lifts his hat and bids you God speed, as you pass. The train waits for the conductor to hear the station-master's account of that last baby and his assurance that the mother is doing well. The laborer goes on strike when his right is questioned to stop work to take his glass of beer between meals; the tele-graph messenger, meeting the man for whom he has a message, goes back home with him "to hear the news." It would not be proper to break it in the street. I remember once coming down the chain of lakes in the Jutland peninsula on a steamer that stopped at an out-of-the-way landing where no pas-sengers were in waiting. One, a woman, was made out, though, hastening down a path that lost itself

in the woods a long way off.   The captain waited.
As she stepped aboard another woman appeared in
the dim distance, running, too.   He blew his whistle
to tell her he was waiting, but said nothing.   When
she was quite near the steamer, a third woman turned
into the path, bound, too, for the landing.   I looked
on in some fear lest the steamboat man should lose
his temper at length.   But not he.   It was only
when a fourth and last woman appeared like a
whirling speck in the distance, with the three aboard
making frantic signals to her
to hurry, that he showed signs
of   impatience.   " Couldn't
she,"   he   said,   with   some
asperity,   as   she   flounced
aboard,   " couldn't   she   get
here sooner? "

" No," she said, " I couldn't.
Didn't   you   see   me   run? "
And he rang the bell to start
the boat.

Time   to   wait!   In   New
York   I   have   seen   men,   in
the   days   before   the   iron

The Village Express.

gates were put on the ferry-boats, jump when the
boat was yet a yard from the landing and run as if
their lives depended on it ; then, meeting an acquaintance in the street, stop and chat ten minutes

with him about nothing. How much farther did they get than these? When all Denmark was torn up last summer by a strike that involved three-fourths of the working population and extended through many months, to the complete blocking of all industries, not a blow was struck or an ill word spoken during all the time, determined as both sides were. No troops or extra police were needed. The strikers used the time to attend university extension lectures, visit museums and learn something useful. The people, including many of the employers, contributed liberally to keep them from starving. It was a war of principles, and it was fought out on that line, though in the end each gave in to something. Yes, it is good, sometimes, to take time to think, even if you cannot wait for the tide to float you off a sandbank. Though what else they could have done, I cannot imagine.

That night there was a great to-do in the old town. The target company had its annual shoot, and the target company included all of the solid citizens of the town. The "king," who had made the best score, was escorted with a band to the hotel on the square opposite the Dom, and made a speech from a window, adorned with the green sash of his office, and flanked by ten tallow-dips by way of illumination. And the people cheered. Yes! it was petty and provincial and all that. But it was pleasant and neighborly, and oh! how good for a tired man.

When I was rested, I journeyed through the islands to find old friends, and found them. The heartiness of the welcome that met me everywhere! No need of their telling me they were glad to see me. It shone out of their faces and all over them. I shall always remember that journey: the people in the cars that were forever lunching and urging me to join in, though we had never met before. Were we not fellow-travellers? How, then, could we be strangers? And when they learned I was from New York, the inquiries after Hans or Fritz, somewhere in Nebraska or Dakota. Had I ever met them? and, if I did, would I tell them I had seen father, mother, or brother, and that they were well? And would I come and stay with them a day or two? It was with very genuine regret that I had mostly to refuse. My vacation could not last forever. As it was, I packed it full enough to last me for many summers. Of all sorts of things, too. Shall I ever forget that ride on the stage up the shore-road from Elsinore, which I made outside with the driver, a slow-going farmer who had conscientious scruples, so it seemed, against passing any vehicle on the road and preferred to take the dust of them all, until we looked like a pair of dusty millers up there on the box. To my protests he turned an incredulous ear, remarking only that there was always some one ahead, which was a fact. When at last we drew near our destination he found himself a passenger short. After some puzzled inquiry of the rest he came back and, mounting to his seat beside me, said quietly: " One of them fell out on his head, they say, down the road. I had him to deliver at the inn, but it can't be blamed on me, can it ? "

He was not the only philosopher in that company. Inside rode two passengers, one apparently an official, sheriff, or something, the other a doctor, who debated all the way the propriety of uniforming the physician in attendance upon executions. The sheriff evidently considered such a step an invasion of his official privilege. "Why," cried the doctor, "it is almost impossible now to tell the difference between the doctor and the delinquent." " Ah, well," sighed the other, placidly settling back in his seat. "Just let them once take the wrong man, then we shall see."

Through forest and field, over hill and vale, by the still waters where far islands lay shimmering upon the summer sea like floating fairy-lands, into the deep, gloomy moor went my way. The moor was ever most to my liking. I was born on the edge of it, and once its majesty has sunk into a human soul, that soul is forever after attuned to it.

How little we have the making of ourselves. And how much greater the need that we should make of that little the most. All my days I have been preaching against heredity as the arch-enemy of hope and effort, and here is mine, holding me fast. When I see, rising out of the dark moor, the lonely cairn that sheltered the bones of my fathers before the White Christ preached peace to their land, a great yearning comes over me. There I want to lay mine. There I want to sleep, under the heather where the bees hum drowsily in the purple broom at noonday and white shadows walk in the night. Mist from the marshes they are, but the people think them wraiths. Half heathen yet, am I? Yes, if to yearn for the soil whence you sprang is to be a heathen, heathen am I, not half, but whole, and will be all my days.

But not so. He is the heathen who loves not his native land. Thor long since lost his grip on the sons of the vikings. Over the battlefield he drives his chariot yet, and his hammer strikes fire as of old. The British remember it from Nelson's raid on Copenhagen; the Germans felt it in 1849, and again when in the fight for very life the little country held its own a whole winter against two great powers on rapine bent; felt it at Helgoland where its sailors scattered their navies and drove them from the sea, beaten. Yet never did the

White Christ work greater transformation in a people, once so fierce, now so gentle unless when fighting for its firesides.   Forest and field teem with
legends that tell of it; tell of the battle between the
old and the new, and the victory of peace.   Every
hilltop bears witness to it.

Holy Andrew's Cross.

Here by the wayside stands a wooden cross.   All
the country-side knows the story of " Holy Andrew," the priest whose piety wrought miracles far
and near.   Once upon a time, runs the legend, he
went on a pilgrimage to the Holy Land, and was
left behind by his companions because he would
not sail, be wind and tide ever so fair, without first

going to mass to pray for a safe journey. When, his devotions ended, he went to the dock, he saw only the sail of the departing craft sinking below the horizon. Overcome by grief and loneliness, he stood watching it, thinking of friends at home whom he might never again see, when a horseman reined in his steed and bade him mount with him; he would see him on his way. Andrew did, and fell asleep in the stranger's arms. When he awoke he lay on this hill, where the cross has stood ever since, heard the cattle low and saw the spire of his church in the village where the vesper bells were ringing. Many months went by before his fellow-pilgrims reached home. Holy Andrew lived six hundred years ago. A masterful man was he, beside a holy one, who bluntly told the king the truth when he needed it, and knew how to ward the faith and the church committed to his keeping. By such were the old rovers weaned from their wild life. What a mark he left upon his day is shown yet by the tradition that disaster impends if the cross is allowed to fall into decay. Once when it was neglected, the cattle-plague broke out in the parish and ceased, says the story, not until it was restored, when right away there was an end.

Holy Andrew's church still stands over yonder. Not that one with the twin towers. That has another story to tell, one that was believed to be

half or wholly legend, too, until a recent restoration
of it brought to light under the whitewash of the
reformation mural paintings which furnished the
lacking proof that it was all true. It was in
the days of Holy Andrew that the pious knight,
Sir Asker Ryg, going to the war, told the lady
Inge to build a new church. The folk-song tells
what was the matter with the old one " with wall
of clay, straw-thatched and grim " : —

> The wall it was mouldy and foul and green,
> And rent with a crack full deep;
> Time gnaweth ever with sharper tooth,
> Leaves little to mend, I ween.

Nothing was left to mend in the church of
Fjenneslev, so she must build a new. "It is not
fitting," says the knight in the song, "to pray to
God in such a broken wrack. The wind blows in
and the rain drips " : —

> Christ has gone to His heavenly home;
> No more a manger beseems Him.

"And," he whispers to her at the leave-taking,
"an' thou bearest to our house a boy, build a
tower upon the church; if a daughter come, build
but a spire. A man must fight his way, but
humility becomes a woman."

Then the fight, and the return with victory; the
impatient ride that left all the rest behind as they

neared home, the unspoken prayer of the knight
as he bent his head over the saddle-bow, riding up
the hill over the edge of which the church must
presently appear, that it might be a tower; and his
"sly laugh" when it comes into view with two
towers for one.   Well might he laugh.   Those
twin brothers be-
came the makers
of Danish history
in its heroic age;
the one a mighty
captain, the other
a great bishop,
King Valdemar's
friend and coun-
sellor, who fought
when there was
need "as well with
sword as with
book." Absalon
left the country
Christian to the

Sir Asker Ryg's Church at Fjennesloevlille.

core. It was his clerk, Saxo, surnamed Grammaticus
because of his learning, who gave to the world the
collection of chronicles and traditionary lore to
which we owe our Hamlet.

The church stands there with its two towers.
They made haste to restore them when they read

2 E

in the long-hidden paintings the story of Sir Asker's return and gratitude, just as tradition had handed it down from the twelfth century. It is not the first time the loyal faith of the people has proved a better guide than carping critics, and likely it will not be the last.

I rediscovered on that trip the ancient bellwoman, sole advertising medium before the advent of the printing-press, the extinct chimney-sweep, the ornamental policeman who for professional excitement reads detective novels at home, and the sacrificial rites of — of what or whom I shall leave unsaid. But it must have been an unconscious survival of something of the sort that prompted the butcher to adorn with gay ribbons the poor nag led to the slaughter in the wake of the town drummer. He designed it as an advertisement that there would be fresh horse-meat for sale that day. The horse took it as a compliment and walked in the procession with visible pride. And I found the church in which no collection was ever taken. It was the very Dom in my own old town. The velvet purses that used to be poked into the pews on Sundays on long sticks were missing, and I asked about them. They had not used them in a long time, said the beadle, and added, " It was a kind of Catholic fashion anyway, and no good." The pews had apparently suspected as much, and had held

"Horse-meat to-day!"

haughtily aloof from the purses. That may have been another reason for their going.

The old town ever had its own ways. They were mostly good ways, though sometimes odd. Who but a Ribe citizen would have thought of Knud Clausen's way of doing my wife honor on the Sunday morning when, as a young girl, she went to church to be confirmed? Her father and Knud were neighbors and Knud's barn-yard was a sore subject between them, being right under the other's dining-room window. He sometimes protested and oftener offered to buy, but Knud would neither listen nor sell. But he loved the ground his neighbor's pretty daughter walked upon, as did, indeed, every poor man in the town, and on her Sunday he showed it by strewing the offensive pile with fresh cut grass and leaves, and sticking it full of flowers. It was well meant, and it was Danish all over. Stick up for your rights at any cost. These secure, go any length to oblige a neighbor.

Journeying so, I came from the home of dead kings at last to that of the living, — old King Christian, beloved of his people, — where once my children horrified the keeper of Rosenborg Palace by playing "the Wild Man of Borneo" with the official silver lions in the great knights' hall. And I saw the old town no more. But in my dreams I walk its peaceful streets, listen to the whisper of the reeds in the dry moats about the green castle hill, and hear my mother call me once more her boy. And I know that I shall find them, with my lost childhood, when we all reach home at last.

CHAPTER XVI

THE AMERICAN MADE

LONG ago, when I found my work beginning to master me, I put up a nest of fifty pigeonholes in my office so that with system I might get the upper hand of it; only to find, as the years passed, that I had got fifty tyrants for one. The other day I had to call in a Hessian to help me tame the pigeonholes.

The Cross of Dannebrog.

He was a serious library person, and he could not quite make out what it meant when among such heads as "Slum Tenements," "The

Bend," and "Rum's Curse," he came upon this one over one of the pigeonholes: —

> Him all that goodly company
> Did as deliverer hail.
> They tied a ribbon round his neck,
> Another round his tail.

With all his learning, his education was not finished, for he had missed the "delectable ballad of the Waller lot" and Eugene Field's account of the dignities that were "heaped upon Clow's noble yellow pup," else he would have understood. The pigeonhole contained most of the "honors" that have come to me of late years, — the nominations to membership in societies, guilds, and committees, in conventions at home and abroad, — most of them declined, as I declined Governor Roosevelt's request that I should serve on the last Tenement-House Commission, for the reason which I have given heretofore, that to represent is not my business. To write is; I can do it much better and back up the other; so we are two for one. Not that I would be understood as being insensible of the real honor intended to be conferred by such tokens. I do not hold them lightly. I value the good opinion of my fellow-men, for with it comes increased power to do things. But I would reserve the honors for those who have fairly earned them, and on whom they sit easy. They don't on me. I am not ornamental by nature. Now that I have told all there is to tell, the reader is at liberty to agree with my little boy concerning the upshot of it. He was having a heart-to-heart talk with his mother the other day, in the course of which she told him that we must be patient; no one in the world was all good except God.

"And you," said he, admiringly. He is his father's son.

She demurred, but he stoutly maintained his own.

"I'll bet you," he said, "if you were to ask lots of people around here they would say you were fine. But" — he struggled reflectively with a button — "Gee! I can't understand why they make such a fuss about papa."

Out of the mouth of babes, etc. The boy is right. I cannot either, and it makes me feel small. I did my work and tried to put into it what I thought citizenship ought to be, when I made it out. I wish I had made it out earlier for my own peace of mind. And that is all there is to it.

For hating the slum what credit belongs to me? Who could love it? When it comes to that, perhaps it was the open, the woods, the freedom of my Danish fields I loved, the contrast that was hateful. I hate darkness and dirt anywhere, and naturally want to let in the light. I will have no dark corners in my own cellar; it must be whitewashed clean. Nature, I think, intended me for a cobbler, or a patch-tailor. I love to mend and make crooked things straight. When I was a carpenter I preferred to make an old house over to building a new. Just now I am trying to help a young couple set up in the laundry business. It is along the same line; that is the reason I picked it out for them. If any of my readers know of a good place for them to start I wish they would tell me of it. They are just two — young people with the world before them. My office years ago became notorious as a sort of misfit shop where things were matched that had got mislaid in the hurry and bustle of life, in which some of us always get shoved aside. Some one has got to do that, and I like the job; which is fortunate, for I have no head for creative work of any kind. The publishers bother me to write a novel; editors want me on their staffs. I shall do neither, for the good reason that I am neither poet, philosopher, nor, I was going to say, philanthropist; but leave me that. I would love my fellow-man. For the rest I am a reporter of facts. And that I would remain. So, I know what I can do and how to do it best.

We all love power — to be on the winning side. You cannot help being there when you are fighting the slum, for it is the cause of justice and right. How then can you lose? And what matters it how you fare, your cause is bound to win. I said it before,

After Twenty-five Years.

but it will bear to be said again, not once but many
times: every defeat in such a fight is a step toward
victory, taken in the right spirit. In the end you will
come out ahead. The power of the biggest boss is
like chaff in your hands. You can see his finish.
And he knows it. Hence, even he will treat you
with respect. However he try to bluff you, he is
the one who is afraid. The ink was not dry upon
Bishop Potter's arraignment of Tammany bestial-
ity before Richard Croker was offering to sacrifice
his most faithful henchmen as the price of peace;
and he would have done it had the Bishop but
crooked his little finger in the direction of any one
of them. The boss has the courage of the brute,
or he would not be boss; but when it comes to a
moral issue he is the biggest coward in the lot.
The bigger the brute the more abject its terror at
what it does not understand.

Some of the honors I refused; there were some
my heart craved, and I could not let them go.
There hangs on my wall the passport Governor
Roosevelt gave me when I went abroad, dearer to
me than sheepskin or degree, for the heart of a
friend is in it. What would I not give to be
worthy of its faithful affection! Sometimes when I
go abroad I wear upon my breast a golden cross
which King Christian gave me. It is the old Cru-
saders' cross, in the sign of which my stern fore-

fathers conquered the heathen and themselves on
many a hard-fought field. My father wore it for
long and faithful service to the State. I rendered
none. I can think of but one chance I had to
strike a blow for the old flag. That was when in a
typhus epidemic I found the health officers using it
as a fever flag to warn boats away from the emergency hospital pier at East Sixteenth Street. They
had no idea of what flag it was: they just happened to have it on hand. But they found out
quickly. I gave them half an hour in which to find
another. The hospital was full of very sick patients,
or I should have made them fire a salute to old
Dannebrog by way of reparation. As it was, I
think they had visions of ironclads in the East
River. They had one of a very angry reporter,
anyhow. But though I did nothing to deserve it,
I wear the cross proudly for the love I bear the
flag under which I was born and the good old
King who gave it to me. I saw him often when I
was a young lad. In that which makes the man he
had not changed when last I met him in Copenhagen. They told there how beggars used to waylay
him on his daily walks until the police threatened
them with arrest. Then they stood at a distance
making sorrowful gestures; and the King, who
understood, laid a silver coin upon the palace window shelf and went his way. The King must obey

the law, but he can forget the principles of alms-giving, as may the rest of us at Christmas, and be blameless.

Of that last meeting with King Christian I mean to let my American fellow-citizens know so that they may understand what manner of man is he whom they call in Europe its "first gentleman" and in Denmark "the good King." But first I shall have to tell how my father came to wear the cross of Dannebrog. He was very old at the time; retired long since from his post which he had filled faithfully forty years and more. In some way, I never knew quite how, they passed him by with the cross at the time of the retirement. Perhaps he had given offence by refusing a title. He was an independent old man, and cared nothing for such things; but I knew that the cross he would gladly have worn for the King he had served so well. And when he sat in the shadow, with the darkness closing in, I planned to get it for him as the one thing I knew would give him pleasure.

But the official red tape was stronger than I; until one day, roused to anger by it all, I wrote direct to the King and told him about it. I showed him the wrong that had been done, and told him that I was sure he would set it right as soon as he knew of it. And I was not mistaken. The old town was put into a great state of excitement and mystification when one day there arrived in a large official envelope, straight from the King, the cross long since given up; for, indeed, the Minister had told me that, my father having been retired, the case was closed. The injustice that had been done was itself a bar to its being undone; there was no precedent for such action. That was what I told the King, and also that it was his business to set precedents, and he did. Four years later,

King Christian as I saw him last.

when I took my children home to let my father bless them, — they were his only grandchildren and he had never seen any of them, — he sat in his easy chair and wondered yet at the queer way in which that cross came. And I marvelled with him. He died without knowing how I had interfered. It was better so.

It was when I went home to mother that I met King Christian last. They had told me the right way to approach the King, the proper number of bows and all that, and I meant to faithfully observe it all.   I saw a tired and lonely old man, to whom my heart went out on the instant, and I went right up and shook hands, and told him how much I thought of him and how sorry I was for his losing his wife, the Queen Louise, whom everybody loved.   He looked surprised a moment; then such a friendly look came into his face, and I thought him the handsomest King that ever was.   He asked about the Danes in America, and I told him they were good citizens, better for not forgetting their motherland and him in his age and loss. He patted my hand with a glad little laugh, and bade me tell them how much he appreciated it, and how kindly his thoughts were of them all. As I made to go, after a long talk, he stopped me and, touching the little silver cross on my coat lapel, asked what it was.

I told him; told him of the motto, " In His Name," and of the labor of devoted women in our great country to make it mean what it said.   As I spoke I remembered my father, and I took it off and gave it to him, bidding him keep it, for surely few men could wear it so worthily.   But he put it back into my hand, thanking me with a faithful grasp of his own; he could not take it from me, he said.   And so we parted.   I thought with a pang of remorse, as I stood in the doorway, of the parting bow I had forgotten, and turned around to make good the omission. There stood the King in his blue uniform, nodding so mildly to me, with a smile so full of kindness, that I — why, I just nodded back and waved my hand. It was very improper, I dare say; perfectly shocking; but never was heartier greeting to king. I meant every bit of it.

The next year he sent me his cross of gold for the one of silver I offered him. I wear it gladly, for the knighthood it confers pledges to the defence of womanhood and of little children, and if I cannot wield lance and sword as the king's men of old, I can wield the pen. It may be that in the providence of God the shedding of ink in the cause of right shall set the world farther ahead in our day than the blood-letting of all the ages past.

These I could not forego. Neither, when friends gathered in the King's Daughters' Settlement on our silver wedding day, and with loving words gave to the new house my name, could I say them nay. It stands, that house, within a stone's throw of many a door in which I sat friendless and forlorn, trying to hide from the policeman who would not let me sleep; within hail of the Bend of the wicked past, atoned for at last; of the Bowery boarding-house where I lay senseless on the stairs after my first day's work in the newspaper office, starved well-

The Jacob A. Riis House.
No. 50 Henry Street, New York.

nigh to death. But the memory of the old days has no sting. Its message is one of hope; the house itself is the key-note. It is the pledge of a better day, of the defeat of the slum with its helpless heredity of despair. That shall damn no longer lives yet unborn. Children of God are we! that is our challenge to the slum, and on earth we shall claim yet our heritage of light.

Of home and neighborliness restored it is the pledge. The want of them makes the great gap in the city life that is to be our modern civic life. With the home preserved we may look forward without fear; there is no question that can be asked of the Republic to which we shall not find the answer. We may not always agree as to what is right; but, starting there, we shall be seeking the right, and seeking we shall find it. Ruin and disaster are at the end of the road that starts from the slum.

Perhaps it is easy for me to preach contentment. With a mother who prays, a wife who fills the house with song, and the laughter of happy children about me, all my dreams come true or coming true, why should I not be content? In fact, I know of no better equipment for making them come true: faith in God to make all things possible that are right; faith in man to get them done; fun enough in between to keep them from spoiling or running off the track into useless crankery.   An extra good sprinkling of that!   The longer I live the more I think of humor as in truth the saving sense.   A civil-service examination to hit home might well be one to make sure the man could appreciate a good story.   For all editors I would have that kind made compulsory.   Here is one chiding me in his paper, — oh! a serious paper that calls upon parents to " insist that children's play shall be play and not loafing " and not be allowed to obscure " their more serious responsibilities," — chiding me for encouraging truancy!   " We are quite sure," he writes, " that no really well-brought up and well-disposed boy ever thinks of such a thing."   Perish the thought!   And yet, if he *should* take the notion, — you never can tell with the devil so busy all the time, — there's the barrel they kept us in at school when we were bad; I told of it before.   Putting the lid on was a sure preventive; with our little short legs we couldn't climb out.   Don't think I recommend it.   It just comes to me, the way things will.   It was held to be a powerful means of bringing children up " well disposed " in those days.

Looking back over thirty years it seems to me that never had man better a time than I.   Enough of the editor chaps there were always to keep up the spirits.   The hardships people write to me about were not worth while mentioning; and anyway they had to be, to get some of the crankery out of me, I guess. But the friendships endure. For all the rebuffs of my life they have more than made up. When I think of them, of the good men and women who have called me friend, I am filled with

Christmas Eve with the King's Daughters.

wonder and gratitude. I know the editor of the heavy responsibilities would not have approved of all of them. Even the police might not have done it. But, then, police approval is not a certificate of character to one who has lived the best part of his life in Mulberry Street. They drove Harry Hill out

2 F

of the business after milking him dry. Harry Hill kept a dive, but he was a square man; his word was as good as his bond. He was hardly a model citizen, but in a hard winter he kept half the ward from starving; his latch-string hung out always to those in need. Harry was no particular friend of mine; I mention him as a type of some to whom objection might be made.

But then the police would certainly disapprove of Dr. Parkhurst, whom I am glad to call by the name of friend. They might even object to Bishop Potter, whose friendship I return with a warmth that is nowise dampened by his disapproval of reporters as a class. There is where the Bishop is mistaken; we are none of us infallible, and what a good thing it is that we are not. Think of having an infallible friend to live alongside of always! How long could you stand it? We were not infallible, James Tanner! — called Corporal by the world, Jim by us — when we sat together in the front seats of the Old Eighteenth Street Church under Brother Simmons's teaching. Far from it; but we were willing to learn the ways of grace, and that was something. Had he only stayed! Your wife mothered my Elisabeth when she was homesick in a strange land. I have never forgotten it. And you could pass civil service, Jim, on the story I spoke of. I would be willing to let the rest go, if you will promise to forget about that bottle of champagne. It was your doings, anyhow, you know.

Amos Ensign, I did not give you the credit you should have had for our success in Mulberry Street in the early days, but I give it to you now. You were loyal and good, and you have stayed a reporter, a living denial of the charge that our profession is not as good as the best. Dr. Jane Elizabeth Robbins, you told me, when I was

James Tanner.

hesitating over the first chapters of these reminiscences, to take the short cut and put it all in, and I did, because you are as wise as you are good. I have told it all, and now, manlike, I will serve you as your sex has been served from the dawn of time: the woman did it! yours be the blame. Anthony Ronne, dear old chum in the days of adversity; Max Fischel, trusty friend of the years in Mulberry Street, who never said "can't" once — you always knew a way; Brother W. W. J. Warren, faithful in good and in evil report; General C. T. Christensen, whose compassion passeth understanding, for, though a banker, you bore with and befriended me, who cannot count; Mrs. Josephine Shaw Lowell, my civic conscience ever; John H. Mulchahey, without whose wise counsels in the days of good government and reform the battle with the slum would surely have gone against us; Jane Addams and Mrs. Emmons Blaine, leaven that shall yet leaven the whole unsightly lump out yonder by the western lake and let in the light; A. S. Solomons, Silas McBee, Mrs. Roland C. Lincoln, Lilian D. Wald, Felix Adler, Endicott Peabody, Lyman Abbott, Louise Seymour Houghton, Jacob H. Schiff, John Finley, — Jew and Gentile who taught me why in this world personal conduct and personal character count ever for most, — my love to you all! It is time I am off and away. William McCloy, the next time I step into your canoe and upset it, and you turn that smiling countenance upon me, up to your neck in the lake, I will surely drown you. You are too good for this world. J. Evarts Tracy, host of my happy days on restful Wahwaskesh! I know of a certain hole in under a shelving rock upon which the partridge is wont to hatch her young, where lies a bigger bass than ever you tired out according to the rules of your beloved sport, and I will have him if I have to charm him with honeyed words and a bean-pole. And Ainslie shall cook him to a turn. Make haste then to the feast!

Ahead there is light.   Even as I write the little
ones from Cherry Street are playing on the grass
under my trees.   The time is at hand when we
shall bring to them in their slum the things which
we must now bring them to see, and then the slum

"The little ones from Cherry Street."

will be no more.   How little we grasp the meaning of it all.   In a report of the Commissioner of
Education I read the other day that of kindergarten children in an Eastern city who were questioned
63 per cent did not know a robin, and more than
half had not seen a dandelion in its yellow glory.

And yet we complain that our cities are mis
erned! You who think that the teaching of
ics " in the school covers it all, I am not speal
to you. You will never understand. But the
of you who are willing to sit with me at the f(
little Molly and learn from her, listen: She
poor and ragged and starved. Her home ʋ
hovel. We were debating, some good wome;
knew her and I, how best to make a merry (
mas for her, and my material mind hung
clothes and boots and rubbers, for it was in
cago. But the vision of her soul was a pair c
shoes! Her heart craved them; aye, brethren
she got them. Not for all the gold in the Trea
would I have trodden it under in pork and be;
smothered it in — no, not in rubber boots, thou;
the mud in the city by the lake be both deep and
black. They were the window, those red shoes,
through which her little captive soul looked out
and yearned for the beauty of God's great world.
Could I forget the blue boots with the tassels which
I worshipped in my boyhood? Nay, friends, the
robin and the dandelion we must put back into
those barren lives if we would have good citizenship. They and the citizenship are first cousins.
We robbed the children of them, or stood by and
saw it done, and it is for us to restore them. That
is my answer to the missionary who writes to ask

the heart of our block. The old days are gone. I myself am gone. A year ago I had warning that "the night cometh when no man can work," and Mulberry Street knew me no more. I am still a young man, not far past fifty, and I have much I would do yet. But what if it were ordered otherwise? I have been very happy. No man ever had so good a time. Should I not be content?

I dreamed a beautiful dream in my youth, and I awoke and found it true. My silver bride they called her just now. The frost is upon my head, indeed; hers winter has not touched with its softest breath.

Here comes the Baby!

Her footfall is the lightest, her laugh the merriest in the house. The boys are all in love with their mother; the girls tyrannize and worship her together. The cadet corps elects her an honorary member, for no stouter champion of the flag is in the land. Sometimes when she sings with the children I sit and listen, and with her voice there comes to me as an echo of the long past the words in her letter, that blessed first letter in which she wrote down the text of all my after-life: "We will strive together for all that is noble and good." So she saw her duty as a true American, and aye! she has kept the pledge.

But here comes our daughter with little Virginia to visit her grandpapa. Oh, the little vixen! Then where is his peace? God bless the child!

I have told the story of the making of an American. There remains to tell how I found out that he was made and finished at last. It was when I went back to see my mother once more and, wandering about the country of my childhood's memories, had come to the city of Elsinore. There I fell ill of a fever and lay many weeks in the house of a friend upon the shore of the beautiful Oeresund. One day when the fever had left me they rolled my bed into a room overlooking the sea. The sunlight danced upon the waves, and the distant mountains of Sweden were blue against the horizon. Ships passed under full sail up and down the great waterway of the nations. But the sunshine and the peaceful day bore no message to me. I lay moodily picking at the coverlet, sick and dis-

"That minute I knew."

couraged and sore — I hardly knew why myself.
Until all at once there sailed past, close inshore, a
ship flying at the top the flag of freedom, blown out
on the breeze till every star in it shone bright and
clear. That moment I knew. Gone were illness,
discouragement, and gloom! Forgotten weakness
and suffering, the cautions of doctor and nurse. I
sat up in bed and shouted, laughed and cried by
turns, waving my handkerchief to the flag out
there. They thought I had lost my head, but I
told them no, thank God! I had found it, and my
heart, too, at last. I knew then that it was my flag;
that my children's home was mine, indeed; that I
also had become an American in truth. And I
thanked God, and, like unto the man sick of the
palsy, arose from my bed and went home, healed.